CONSTRAINTS ON THE SUCCESS OF STRUCTURAL ADJUSTMENT PROGRAMMES IN AFRICA

Also by Charles Harvey

AGRICULTURAL PRICING POLICY IN AFRICA: Four Country Case Studies (*editor*)

ANALYSIS OF PROJECT FINANCE IN DEVELOPING COUNTRIES

ECONOMIC INDEPENDENCE AND ZAMBIAN COPPER: A Case Study of Foreign Investment (*co-editor with Mark Bostock*)

ESSAYS ON THE BOTSWANA ECONOMY (*editor*)

EXPORTS AND THE PRESSURE OF DEMAND: A Study of Firms (*with R. A. Cooper and K. Hartley*)

MACROECONOMICS FOR AFRICA

MACROECONOMICS IN AFRICA

POLICY CHOICE AND DEVELOPMENT PERFORMANCE IN BOTSWANA (*with Stephen R. Lewis, Jr*)

RURAL EMPLOYMENT AND ADMINISTRATION IN THE THIRD WORLD: Development Methods and Alternative Strategies (*with B. L. Jacobs, G. B. Lamb and B. B. Schaffer*)

WORLD PRICES AND DEVELOPMENT: The Impact on Developing Countries of Imported Inflation (*co-editor with Stephany Griffith-Jones*)

Constraints on the Success of Structural Adjustment Programmes in Africa

Edited by

Charles Harvey
Professorial Fellow
Institute of Development Studies
University of Sussex, Brighton

First published in Great Britain 1996 by
MACMILLAN PRESS LTD
Houndmills, Basingstoke, Hampshire RG21 6XS
and London
Companies and representatives
throughout the world

A catalogue record for this book is available
from the British Library.

ISBN 0–333–64292–9 hardcover
ISBN 0–333–64293–7 paperback

First published in the United States of America 1996 by
ST. MARTIN'S PRESS, INC.,
Scholarly and Reference Division,
175 Fifth Avenue,
New York, N.Y. 10010

ISBN 0–312–12665–4

Library of Congress Cataloging-in-Publication Data
Harvey, Charles, M. A.
Constraints on the success of structural adjustment programmes in
Africa / Charles Harvey.
p.   cm.
Includes bibliographical references and index.
ISBN 0–312–12665–4 (cloth)
1. Structural adjustment (Economic policy)—Africa, Sub-Saharan–
–Case Studies.   2. Africa, Sub-Saharan—Economic conditions—1960– –
–Case Studies.   I. Title.
HC800.H378   1996
338.96—dc20   95–19961
                                                              CIP

10   9   8   7   6   5   4   3   2   1
05   04   03   02   01   00   99   98   97   96

Printed and bound in Great Britain by
Antony Rowe Ltd, Chippenham, Wiltshire

Contents

List of Tables   vii

List of Figures   ix

Preface   x

Notes on the Contributors   xi

1   Introduction   1
    Charles Harvey

2   Interest Rate Liberalisation and the Allocative Efficiency of
    Credit: Some Evidence from Small and Medium Scale Industry
    in Kenya   7
    Peninah Kariuki

3   The Structural Adjustment Implications of Real Exchange Rate
    Depreciation on the Manufacturing Sector in Zimbabwe   29
    Joseph Muzulu

4   The Impact of Economic Stabilisation on the Wage Structure in
    Zimbabwe: 1980–90   52
    Godfrey Kanyenze

5   Liberalisation of Maize Marketing in the Arusha Region in
    Tanzania   76
    Willy Parsalaw

6   Structural Adjustment, Labour Markets and Employment Policy   100
    John Toye

7   Constraints on Sustained Recovery from Economic Disaster in Africa   130
    Charles Harvey

8   Constraints on the Effectiveness of Structural Adjustment
    Packages in the Production and Availability of Pharmaceutical
    Products in Kenya   152
    Pius Owino

v

9   What Role for Stock Exchanges, Venture Capital and Leasing
    Companies in Developing the Private Sector in Africa?   174
    Mike Faber

10 Economic Crisis, Adjustment and the Effectiveness of the
    Public Sector in Zambia   192
    Dennis Chiwele and Christopher Colclough

11 Economic Adjustment, the Mining Sector and the Real Wage
    in Zambia   210
    Dennis Chiwele

Index   235

List of Tables

2.1	Major real interest rates (%): 1968–1980	8
2.2	Major real interest rates (%): 1982–1990	9
2.3	Proportion of SMEs with annual increases in commercial bank credit	15
2.4	Perceptions of major problems by borrowing and non-borrowing proprietors	19
3.1	Average sectoral shares of employment (%)	32
3.2	Average sectoral proportions to total GDP (%)	33
3.3	Proportion of output by activity and by firm (%)	34
3.4	Additional reasons for not shifting from capital to labour in production	37
3.5	Summary of reasons for not shifting	39
3.6	Export versus domestic prices of manufactured goods	41
3.7	Reasons for low exports	42
3.8	ICORs for the manufacturing sector	44
3.9	Main reasons for investing	46
3.10	Reasons for not investing	47
4.1	Real 1990 average annual earnings as a percentage of 1980 and peak 1982 levels	56
4.2	Difference between actual and predicted average annual real consumption earnings (%)	61
4.3	Quantity responses in the tradable and non-tradable goods sectors, annual average growth rates (%): 1981–90	63
4.4	Estimated labour demand functions by sector: 1970–90	67
5.1	Main economic indicators	77
5.2	Intra-regional transfers pattern of maize in Arusha region in the 1980s	83
5.3	Estimates of intra- and inter-regional maize trade in Arusha region in the 1980s	83
5.4	Classification of maize traders on the basis of date of entry in Arusha region	83
5.5	Estimates of the amount of maize marketed through different channels in Arusha region in the 1980s	84
5.6	Classification of maize traders on the basis of mode of transport used in Arusha in 1991	84
5.7	Private traders' storage capacity in Arusha	86
5.8	Maize marketing margin for private traders in Arusha	88
5.9	Maize marketing margin for official channels in Arusha	89
5.10	Regression coefficients for six markets in Arusha (1986–88)	91

5.11 Regression coefficients for six markets in Arusha (1989–91) 92
5.12 Co-operative profits and losses (1986–91) 94
5.13 Co-operative losses from non-marketing operations 95
5.14 National Milling Corporation profit and losses by 31 July of
      each year 95
6.1   Employment and unemployment in Chile, 1970–1990 117
6.2   Indices of real wages in Chile, 1970–1990 118
6.3   Unemployment in Indonesia, 1982–1990 119
6.4   Wage employment by sector in Indonesia, 1986 and 1990 119
6.5   Real wages indices in Indonesia, 1983–1991 120
7.1   Net ODA as a proportion of imports, 1991 133
7.2   Real interest rates, 1980–92 143
7.3   Real interest rates, 1980–92 144
7.4   Market share and bad debts of government-owned commercial
      banks in Ghana, Mozambique, Tanzania, Uganda and
      Zambia prior to restructuring 145
8.1   Health expenditure indicators, 1980–90 163
8.2   Actual distribution of drug kits as a percentage of requirements 165
9.1   Main features of some African emerging stock markets 181
10.1 Educational qualifications held by Zambian employees,
      1965 and 1983 194
10.2 Sample of employees by major occupational group and
      nationality, 1983 195
10.3 Index of real wages/salaries in the civil service, 1966/7–1991/2 199
10.4 Index of public sector compensation: basic salary plus
      housing benefits 202
10.5 Sex and age profiles of the informal sector 205
11.1 Economic indicators for Zambia: period averages 213
11.2 The financial performance of ZCCM 217
11.3 Classification of industries by tradables and non-tradables sectors 220
11.4 Capital–labour ratio by industry, 1980 220
11.5 Regression results for the SSR model 222
11.6 GFCF as a ratio of GDP and GFCF real index 225
11.7 Share of operating surplus and labour cost in GDP, 1979–89 226

List of Figures

2.1	Commercial bank real deposit rates	11
2.2	SMEs: some costs of borrowing	17
2.3	Real maximum lending rates	18
2.4	Share of bank credit to small farmers	24
3.1	Exchange rate indices	31
3.2	Relative prices	31
3.3	Relative factor prices	35
3.4	Capital–labour ratios	35
4.1	Trends in actual and predicted real average consumption wages: 1980–90	62
8.1	Price changes and contributions to GDP	153
8.2	Price changes and pharmaceutical exports supply	155
8.3	Liberalisation of pharmaceutical imports	160
10.1	Average government real wage	198
10.2	Ratio of director's to lowest paid civil servant's starting salary	200
10.3	Share of personal emoluments in total budgeted expenditure	201
10.4	Cost of a food basket to average government earnings (1975–89)	204
11.1	London metal exchange copper prices: 1962 to 1991	212
11.2	Annual average real wage	214
11.3	Tradables to non-tradables relative price movements (1965–1990)	221
11.4	The capital–labour ratio	222
11.5	The real wage with labour costs at constant share in value added	227

Preface

This book is the product of a research and training project for six (originally seven) doctoral students from Africa and their four supervisors at the Institute of Development Studies at the University of Sussex. The programme was funded by the Swedish International Development Agency (SIDA). The programme's budget included provision for recruitment so that the programme director (Charles Harvey) was able to interview applicants in Africa having read their masters' theses, provision for supervisors to visit the students while they were doing fieldwork in Africa, and provision for the supervisors to do related research. The students were allowed to choose their own research topic within the general framework of structural adjustment. This book reports on some of the resulting research. The students were encouraged to write up other parts of their research for publication, and most of them were given visiting fellowships at the Institute to enable them to do this. The programme budget also included a provision to enable the book to be more widely available in Africa; the subsidy has been used partly to reduce the cover price of the paperback edition and partly to enable a limited number of paperback copies to be distributed in Africa free, on application to IDS.

CHARLES HARVEY

Notes on the Contributors

Dennis Chiwele received his DPhil in development studies from the University of Sussex in 1994. Previously he worked for the Prices and Incomes Commission in Zambia and currently works for the Institute of African Studies in Lusaka.

Christopher Colclough is Professorial Fellow of the Institute of Development Studies at the University of Sussex. He has worked extensively in Africa, particularly on human resources issues. His recent books include *Educating All the Children: Strategies for Primary Schooling in the South* (with Keith Lewin) and *Public Sector Pay and Adjustment: Lessons from Five Countries* (editor).

Mike Faber was previously Director of the Institute of Development Studies (University of Sussex) and subsequently a Fellow. He is currently working as economic consultant at the Ministry of Finance and Development Planning in Botswana.

Charles Harvey is Professorial Fellow, Institute of Development Studies, at the University of Sussex; previously he held positions with the Bank of England, the Bank of Botswana, the University of Zambia, the University of Botswana and Williams College. His current research is on banking in Africa.

Godfrey Kanyenze completed his DPhil in development studies at the University of Sussex in 1993. He is currently working on consultancy projects with trade unions in the southern Africa region.

Peninah Kariuki received her DPhil in development studies from the University of Sussex in 1994. Before then, she worked at the Research Department in the Central Bank of Kenya. Upon completion of her doctorate, the Bank seconded her to work as an economist in the office of the IMF's Resident Representative in Nairobi.

Joseph Muzulu received his DPhil in development studies from the University of Sussex in 1993. He is currently working as Chief Economist of Zimbabwe Holdings Ltd in Harare.

Pius Owino received his DPhil in development studies from the University of Sussex in 1994. He is currently Lecturer in Economics at Kenyatta University in Nairobi.

Willy Parsalaw received his DPhil in development studies from the University of Sussex in 1994. He is currently working at the Cooperative College in Tanzania as Lecturer in Agricultural Economics.

John Toye is Director of the Institute of Development Studies, and a Professorial Fellow, of the University of Sussex. His recent research has focused on the evaluation of overseas aid. He has co-authored, with Michael Lipton, *Does Aid Work in India?* and, with Paul Mosley and Jane Harrigan, *Aid and Power*.

1 Introduction

Charles Harvey

As noted in the Preface, this book originated in the selection of seven doctoral students from Africa (from those countries where Sweden had an aid programme) to work, together with their supervisors, on topics related to structural adjustment. Although their detailed fieldwork could be, and was in several cases, microeconomic or sectoral, it was considered unproductive to research such issues without also understanding macroeconomic conditions. The point is that when macroeconomic conditions and policy are satisfactory, they can safely be ignored if the researcher wishes to concentrate on sectoral or microeconomic detail.

However, in most countries in Sub-Saharan Africa, macroeconomic conditions were and still are deeply unsatisfactory and they therefore affected, in ways that could not be ignored, every aspect of economic conditions and economic policy. For example, there is little point in doing research on industrialisation if an economy is in fact deindustrialising, and the reason is that gross macroeconomic imbalance is leading to extreme shortages of foreign exchange and credit, rather than that there is a problem with the details of industrial policy such as tax incentives or levels of protection.

As a consequence, these countries are in the process of trying to implement stabilisation and structural adjustment programmes. During the 1980s, there were various experiments with such programmes being devised and implemented by governments, without the IMF and the World Bank (the International Financial Institutions – IFIs) being involved. Increasingly, however, governments have been forced to reach agreements with the IFIs because of the failure of most of these home-grown programmes, the overwhelming need for aid and debt rescheduling, and the refusal of donors to provide support without IFI agreements.

The starting point for student research was, therefore, the reasons for and progress with the macroeconomic objectives of structural adjustment programmes, and secondly the success of structural adjustment programmes in achieving particular objectives such as increased lending to small and medium scale enterprises, more flexible wages, or increased manufactured exports, for which lengthy fieldwork was necessary.

The theme of much of this research is that the orthodox policies of the World Bank and the IMF may be necessary in order to achieve the objectives of stabilisation and structural adjustment, but they are not sufficient, or only partially sufficient, for a whole series of detailed reasons.

Thus financial liberalisation in Kenya (Chapter 2) did, from 1983 onwards, result in nominal interest rates higher than the rate of inflation. The stated objective was to increase the flow of lending to small and medium scale enterprises (SMEs) in particular, and to improve the allocation of finance in general. There was not a significant impact on the ratio of M2 to GDP. Partly this was because the taxation of interest on savings reduced the return significantly, and partly it was because other factors were more important. The latter included exchange rate expectations which were generally negative. Moreover, lending margins never rose above their 1980 level, and they would have needed to be much higher to cover the transaction costs of lending to SMEs, arguably above any level that would have been politically acceptable to the government, while higher nominal interest costs would have sharply increased the risk of borrowing. The transaction costs of small scale lending in the late 1980s were almost as high as interest costs, even if the transaction costs of the borrower were excluded.

Firm-level evidence shows that a declining proportion of those firms with access to commercial bank credit increased their borrowing. Among this category of firms, finance was said not to be the most important constraint. Non-borrowers complained of lack of finance, but were probably not creditworthy; some did not even have bank accounts despite the sample being taken from firms on industrial estates developed by a financial institution. At a more general level, higher real interest rates did not improve allocation efficiency significantly. The commercial banks lent very little to SMEs, while the specialised banks were mostly ineffective. The conclusion of Chapter 2 is that the market incentives created by positive real interest rates were not sufficient (even if necessary) for achieving their stated objectives. However, that does not make a case for government intervention in lending. It would be preferable to seek ways of improving the creditworthiness of borrowers.

There was a clear decline in the real exchange rate in Zimbabwe after 1985 (Chapter 3). This did have some of the intended effects: for example, there was an improvement in the rate of growth of employment in the tradable goods sector, although this occurred without a decline in the growth of employment in the rest of the economy because of there being spare capacity. In addition, the tradable goods sector slightly increased its share of output; and the capital labour ratio fell, but because firms did not replace capital rather than because of an increase in employment. However, the main reason for this last result was the absolute shortage of foreign exchange, and the Labour Relations Act which made it almost impossible to sack workers. Overall, a great deal of the adjustment intended to result from devaluation had already occurred because firms economised on imported capital and intermediate goods when foreign exchange was scarce, and therefore did not economise further when it became expensive (in any case, price controls allowed firms to pass on higher import prices). The exceptions were multinational and parastatal firms which had privileged access to foreign exchange during the period of scarcity and did therefore respond to devaluation by shifting to local inputs where possible. The impact of real devaluation on investment and exports was disappointing: firms exported more in response to the need to acquire foreign exchange than because of higher prices for exports; and investment continued to be constrained by absolute shortages of foreign exchange and unwillingness to hire labour while it remained so difficult to sack workers.

Chapter 4 establishes that real consumption wages in Zimbabwe were flexible, but that the burden of wage restraint fell disproportionately on the public sector. Moreover, the structure of wages within the public sector was seriously compressed. This caused an exodus of skilled workers from the public to the private sector, and a serious decline in the performance and morale of the civil service. Over the whole period after 1980, wages were above trend at first, as the new government pushed up the wages of unskilled workers in particular, but by the end of the decade they were below trend. Real product earnings responded to the decline in the real rate of exchange as expected, but the response of employment was disappointingly inelastic. In the long run, therefore, the impact of minimum wage legislation was relatively small, while the slow growth of the economy and the inelastic employment response to output growth (partly because of the laws on security of employment) were more important.

The study of agricultural marketing in Tanzania (Chapter 5) shows that liberalisation had many of the expected effects. The number of private traders increased sharply, even though there had been some private trading while it was still illegal: 65 per cent of the sample traders started in business in 1988 or later. Their share of trade increased from 29 per cent in 1986 to 93 per cent in 1991. The majority of farmers preferred to sell to private traders, not only because of price, but also because of prompt payment in cash, purchase at the farm, and the provision of gunny bags. The margins of private traders decreased each year except in 1991 when there were severe shortages, and there was a marked improvement in market integration, with smaller variations in price differences among markets despite poor roads and lack of access to transport and storage among the mainly small private traders.

On the other hand, local authorities and co-operatives continued to collect levies from private traders even though this was supposed to be illegal, and were able to get help from the Police in doing this. Furthermore, marketing margins increased rather than decreased in the official marketing agencies, but this was not enough to make them profitable. This appears to be a clear example of the reaction of public sector agencies to competition from the private sector: the former are more likely to try and use their government connections to protect themselves from competition than to react by becoming more efficient. Co-operatives even continued with other loss-making activities. The National Milling Corporation's losses did not increase, but that was only because reduced turnover reduced the loss it made on each transaction.

The transition to private marketing did not solve all the outstanding problems. For example, most traders were too small to have access to bank credit, and have invested very little in transport and storage. Investment may have been inhibited by uncertainty as to whether economic reforms would be sustained, as well as continued official harassment. The private sector was also unwilling to finance buying of surplus output in years of bumper harvests. This suggests a continuing role for government in agricultural marketing, but the past record of government intervention is so bad in Tanzania that it is difficult to recommend any new initiative.

The study of the supply of pharmaceutical products (Chapter 8), and their availability in rural clinics, again shows how structural constraints prevented some of the intended effects of structural adjustment. For example, pharmaceutical exports responded to a lower real exchange rate in only a few firms. Multinational firms did not increase their exports in order to avoid competing with their associate companies in other countries; small producers did not export at all because of the high overhead cost; so only a few locally owned medium-scale firms responded to the increased profitability of exporting, but they were probably more influenced by the difficulty of dealing with the government as a customer. The government paid late, and failed to compensate for devaluations which occurred between supply and payment even though compensation had been promised. Moreover, official export incentives were so badly managed that they had little impact on willingness to export.

Meanwhile, the supply of essential drugs to rural health facilities was constrained by cuts in government spending, bad administration and widespread corruption. It was only sustained at all by donor support which continued in spite of the government repeatedly failing to deliver its agreed share of the necessary finance.

The two chapters on wages and employment in Zambia show that the way in which the government managed the reduction in finance available for government services was very inefficient (Chapter 10), but that trades unions were less of a constraint on wage flexibility than had been believed (Chapter 11). There was a general and severe decline in the quality of government services: differentials were greatly reduced making it difficult to keep skilled workers, and this was exacerbated by the inefficient way in which expatriate workers were replaced; support spending was cut so severely that many employees were unable to do their jobs; real wages fell so far that people were forced to work in the informal sector to survive; corruption increased, and action against corruption shifted from investigating corruption caused by greed to corruption caused by necessity (although the amount needed to bribe an official got smaller over time). The obvious solution, to cut employment and the range of services provided while paying better wages to remaining employees, was on the agenda from 1983, but was not implemented except by a freeze on recruitment and accelerated retirement which was inefficient and worsened shortages of skilled labour.

It has always been argued in Zambia that the mining union was not only very influential in determining mining wages, but was also a major influence on wages in the rest of the economy. Econometric analysis (in Chapter 11) shows that the decline in the real wage was mainly caused by the fall in the price of copper and by adjustment policies. In other words, incomes policy was only effective when government was restraining expenditure. Even in the early days, mining wages rose because higher wages increased productivity and therefore suited the mining companies. What power the mining union had was further reduced when the government stopped supporting it. Nevertheless, the trades unions influenced government policy in other ways, for example by supporting government spending on subsidies. The unions also led the movement for multi-party democracy which led eventually to a change of government.

A wider analysis of the impact on wages and employment, in Chile, Indonesia and Tanzania, supports the view that real wages are flexible in developing country economies (Chapter 6). It argues that employment policy should not be isolated in a ministry of labour, but must be compatible with macroeconomic policy. Indeed, the most effective way of achieving employment objectives is to improve macroeconomic policies. The economy was sufficiently well managed in Indonesia for real wages to remain roughly constant while there were persistent increases in employment, in sharp contrast to Chile where real wages and employment fell over a long period although there was an eventual shift to policies that were positive for employment. The problem in Tanzania is rather different, having more in common with Zambia. Sustained progress requires large scale retrenchment in the civil service and the parastatals. This has proved very difficult politically to the point where there has been little progress, yet without it public sector wages cannot be increased as is essential.

Chapter 7 is a more general review of the difficulties of recovering from severe economic decline in a number of African economies. It has proved difficult even to stabilise these economies; where this has been achieved, it has taken several years. Progress has been even slower with the structural reforms necessary before private investment, whether foreign or local, can be expected to recover and grow in a sustained way. Some public sector investment has occurred, financed mainly by aid, but aid almost never flows directly into private sector investment. There has also been only a limited amount of foreign investment, mainly in enclaves such as gold mining in Ghana. Where progress has been made, with civil service retrenchment, reform and recapitalisation of decayed banks, and reform and privatisation of parastatals, it can be argued to be insufficient. For example, after a near halving of the civil service in Uganda and a doubling of the wage bill, the government is still unable to pay a minimum living wage; and the reform of banks is not certain to avoid further large scale accumulation of bad debts. It is suggested, therefore, that it may be necessary to consider more radical policies, such as closing decayed banks instead of trying for the uncertain gains of institutional reform.

Chapter 9 takes up in greater detail one of the issues in financial sector reform, namely the development of stock exchanges and venture capital companies, and ways of reducing the need for equity finance such as leasing companies. Despite the attention and resources devoted to stock exchanges and, to a lesser extent, venture capital companies, it seems unlikely that they will make a significant contribution at the macro level in the medium term, whereas leasing arrangements may be able to reach a much wider range of businesses, more quickly. In the long run, stock exchanges do have a range of advantages: among other things, they provide an additional method of privatisation, an alternative to nationalisation for gradually reducing foreign ownership, and an investment incentive in that eventual public sale can be a way for investors to realise part or all of a successful investment. For the time being, though, stock exchanges in Sub-Saharan Africa (with the exception of South Africa) are too small, and often too volatile, to play a significant role.

2 Interest Rate Liberalisation and the Allocative Efficiency of Credit: Some Evidence from Small and Medium Scale Industry in Kenya[1]

Peninah Kariuki

I INTRODUCTION

The maintenance of positive real interest rates is one of the main conditions attached to programmes with the International Monetary Fund (IMF) and the World Bank (Killick, 1984: 191; Kitchen, 1986: 87). Yet, although some countries in Africa have undertaken some interest rate and financial sector reforms, there '... has not been extensive research on these matters in a Sub-Saharan African context' (Helleiner, 1990: 42). In view of the doubts arising about the benefits of financial liberalisation, which have been expressed even by the World Bank itself (World Bank, 1989: 27), there is a strong case for empirical evidence from Sub-Saharan Africa.

The Kenyan experience provides an interesting case study. Various interest rate reforms were undertaken in the 1980s under stabilisation and structural adjustment programmes, culminating in a virtual decontrol in July 1991. These reforms resulted in positive real lending and savings rates from 1983.[2] One of the proclaimed goals of maintaining positive real rates has been to improve the access of small scale firms to formal credit. This derives from the theoretical propositions that positive real rates increase the volume of funds in financial institutions and that higher rates enable them to undertake more and riskier lending. These are the issues that are addressed in this chapter.

The chapter is organised as follows. Part II focuses on Kenya's interest rate reforms. The results of the study are reported in Parts III to VII while Part VIII offers concluding remarks.

II A REVIEW OF INTEREST RATE REFORMS IN KENYA

In the 1960s and 1970s, interest rate policy remained fairly inactive. The government administered interest rates through a regime of fixing minimum savings for

7

all deposit-taking institutions and minimum lending rates for commercial banks, non bank financial institutions (NBFIs) and building societies.[3] The first interest rate review in the post-independence era was not until June 1974 when the minimum savings and lending rates were raised by 2 and 1 percentage points respectively. Furthermore '... it had been official policy in Kenya since independence to follow a "low interest rate policy" in order to encourage investment and protect the small borrower' (Central Bank of Kenya, 1986: 54). Consequently, most interest rates were negative in real terms[4] in the 1970s (Table 2.1).

Although there were further reviews in June and September 1981, interest rates were still negative in real terms by the time the second structural adjustment loan (SAL) was negotiated in 1982 (Table 2.2). It is, therefore, not surprising that the maintenance of positive real interest rates was specified as a policy condition in the second SAL. A gradual liberalisation strategy was pursued until July 1991 when the rates were fully deregulated. From 1982, various reviews were made to the deposit and lending rates of commercial banks, NBFIs, and building societies. There were reviews in October 1982, June 1984, January 1988, April and November 1989 and in April 1990. Real interest rates became positive in 1983 (Table 2.2).

The liberalisation exercise was unmistakably justified along the theoretical expectations of the McKinnon–Shaw hypothesis.

Thus, its objectives were stated as '... to encourage mobilisation of savings and contribute to the maintenance of financial stability ... and to ensure that funds flow into those areas which are most productive, and that the biases which have existed against lending to small business ... are eliminated' (Central Bank of Kenya, 1988: 18). To what extent then have these objectives been achieved?

Table 2.1   Major real interest rates (%): 1968–1980
(annual average; selected years)

	1968	*1970*	*1972*	*1974*	*1976*	*1978*	*1980*
Deposit Rates							
Commercial Banks:							
Savings	4.0	1.6	–2.0	–11.8	–5.1	–9.7	–7.3
9 Month	3.5	1.1	–2.5	–11.3	–5.6	–10.1	–6.8
NBFIs	3.0	0.6	–3.0	–11.8	–5.7	–10.2	–6.4
Lending Rates							
Commercial Banks	7.0	4.5	0.8	–8.9	–1.2	–5.9	–2.5
NBFIs	12.0	9.4	5.5	–5.0	0.6	–4.2	–0.7

Note: These interest rates reflect the stipulated minimum rates.
Source: Calculated from Central Bank of Kenya, *Annual Report*, various issues.

Table 2.2   Major real interest rates (%): 1982–1990
(annual average; selected years)

	1982	1983	1984	1986	1988	1990
Deposit Rates						
Commercial Banks:						
Savings	–8.1	0.9	1.3	6.8	1.6	1.3
9 Month	–7.4	1.4	1.5	7.3	1.6	1.6
NBFIs	–6.7	2.2	2.9	8.8	1.6	1.0
Lending Rates						
Commercial Banks	–4.9	3.9	3.8	9.7	6.2	6.3
NBFIs	–4.9	4.6	8.4	14.5	8.9	6.3

Note: These are stipulated minimum deposit rates and maximum lending rates.
Source: Calculated from Central Bank of Kenya *Annual Report*, various issues.

This study set out to answer this question. In addition to secondary data, primary information was collected from a sample of five commercial banks and 89 small and medium scale enterprises (SMEs). For this purpose, the sample of SMEs was selected from firms with less than 50 employees operating on industrial premises provided by the Kenya Industrial Estates (KIE). In this respect, the firms were formal and could be expected to be big enough to use formal sector banks. In addition, the study focused on firms engaged in manufacturing and service industries. This definition allowed the inclusion of firms in the 'missing middle' which has been noted to be a characteristic of the country's industrial set-up (Kilby, 1988: 224; World Bank, 1987: 222). The results are reported in the following parts.

III   THE IMPACT OF REAL INTEREST RATES ON FINANCIAL SAVINGS

Empirical Evidence

The main theoretical bases for interest rate liberalisation and for financial liberalisation as a whole are those postulated by McKinnon (1973) and Shaw (1973). One of the major hypotheses of the Mckinnon–Shaw model is that, *ceteris paribus*, a relaxation of administrative controls on interest rates will increase the volume of funds in the deposit taking institutions. To test this hypothesis, the McKinnon–Shaw demand for real money balances was applied to Kenyan data.

This was done for real broad money (M2), defined as currency in circulation and demand deposits and for a broader definition which includes deposits with NBFIs (M3). The explanatory variables included real GDP, real deposit rate, the ratio of private investment to GDP and the lagged dependent variable.

The results show a negative although statistically insignificant relationship between the real deposit rate and M2. Indeed, the only variable which exerts a significant influence on M2 is real GDP. When M3 is considered, the real interest rate coefficient becomes positive but still remains insignificant. It is clear then that positive real interest rates may be necessary but are not sufficient to ensure increases in financial savings. It is important to consider the other factors which influence savings.

Other Factors that Influence Financial Savings

It has been noted that savings behaviour in developing countries is a function of macroeconomic policies (fiscal, monetary and external) as well as non-economic factors, such as size and structure of family, dependency ratios, life expectancy, etc. (Fry, 1988; Cho and Khatkhate, 1989; World Bank, 1989; Chandavarkar, 1990).

Fiscal Policy

Fiscal policy can influence the level of domestic savings through its influence on savings incentives. The conventional argument is that under most tax systems, savings tend to be taxed twice, first because total income is taxed and second when they generate taxable interest income (Blejer and Cheasty, 1986). This effectively lowers the real return to savers. In the 1980s, interest income on deposits held with commercial banks, NBFIs and building societies in Kenya remained liable to tax. There is a need, therefore, to adjust the real deposit rates by the personal income tax rates to reflect the true gain to savers, especially considering the fact that these institutions account for a very high proportion of total deposits. This is done using the minimum and maximum personal income tax rates.

Such an adjustment results in lower real rates (Figure 2.1). The real minimum savings rate unadjusted for tax became positive in 1983, and except in 1985, it remained positive in the 1980s. When adjusted for tax, the rate for savers taxed at the minimum rate has been marginally positive, except in 1986 and 1987. For those paying the maximum rate, the real rate was negative until 1987. Since then, it has remained marginally positive. These results suggest that fiscal policy has obstructed the benefits of the interest rate liberalisation process.

Exchange Rate Policy

Interest rate reforms are expected to induce capital inflows basically by altering the differentials between foreign and domestic rates. This, however, also depends on exchange rate expectations. To facilitate the analysis, only the major industri-

alised countries (UK, USA, Germany, France and Japan) were considered important for the purposes of determining possible capital outflows. The data used for
this exercise were the effective bilateral nominal rates[5] between Kenya and these
countries and the real deposit rate differentials.

In the second half of the 1980s, real deposit rates were higher in Kenya than in
the major OECD countries, with the exception of Germany. Assuming other
things remained equal, this would appear to imply that savers would be more
willing to hold assets locally. However, these differentials could only be expected
to be beneficial to savers if movements in the exchange rate did not erode the
interest rate advantage. The results show that the shilling depreciated against all
the five currencies under consideration. In the case of the pound sterling and the
French franc, the depreciations were high enough to wipe out the interest rate
advantage. On the whole, therefore, the increases in real deposit rates in Kenya
were apparently not enough to make it more profitable to save in the country, if
account is taken of the exchange rate changes. This may explain, in part, why
financial savings did not respond to the interest rate changes.

Other Factors

The other factors which have been noted to determine the amount and form of
savings in developing countries include the proximity of bank branches, the

Figure 2.1   Commercial bank real deposit rates (tax unadjusted and adjusted)

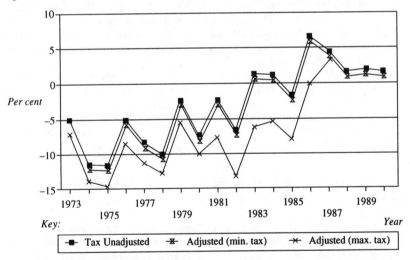

Source: Calculated from data in Central Bank Annual Report, various years, and
Budget Speeches, various years.

appropriateness of available financial instruments compared to other available alternatives, cultural values, etc. (Killick and Martin, 1990; Fry, 1989; Bhatt, 1986; Fernando, 1991). It is only possible to offer a broad overview here as an evaluation of the importance of all these factors would require a detailed empirical investigation.

As concerns the physical accessibility of banking services, information on the branch network of both commercial banks and NBFIs shows that there were substantial increases in the 1980s.[6] These increases in the branch network were larger than the increase in the population such that they resulted in higher branch catchment ratios. However, these branch catchment ratios are meaningful in a fairly distributed branch network. Information from the Central Bank indicates that there is a bias in the location of these branches to the big towns, especially Nairobi and Mombasa. This implies that the smaller towns and rural areas are less well served, and indicates that increases in branches do not necessarily guarantee proximity to banking services for the majority of the population.[7] Furthermore, geographical proximity in itself does not guarantee the appropriateness of banking services.

Turning to the semi-formal financial sector, savings and credit co-operative societies (SACCOs) have increasingly assumed importance in the economy. Mwandihi (1988) presents data which reveal substantial increases in the number of such societies, as well as in membership and in mobilised funds in the 1970s and 1980s.

In addition, the existence of an informal financial sector in Kenya has been noted (Killick and Mwega, 1990: 14–15). Although it is difficult to obtain indicators of its extent, anecdotal evidence suggests that rotating savings societies are popular and widespread. Such evidence also indicates that in some communities, the holding of commodity stocks is customary as a measure of social status and also for ceremonial purposes.

On the whole, it appears logical to conclude that there are non-interest factors which play an important role in the determination of the amount of savings and the form in which such savings are held. These factors could help to explain the rather inelastic response of financial savings to positive real deposit rates. Such rates are a necessary but not sufficient condition for increased mobilisation of savings by the formal financial sector.

IV   THE IMPACT OF REAL INTEREST RATES ON INTERMEDIATION MARGINS AND LENDING PRACTICES

Another hypothesis of the McKinnon–Shaw model is that controls on lending rates prevent financial intermediaries from charging rates that are commensurate with the risk and cost of lending, forcing them to concentrate on low risk, large scale borrowers. In this respect, it is expected that a relaxation of administrative controls on lending rates, *ceteris paribus,* will provide the intermediaries with incentives to diversify their lending activities by undertaking more risky lending, among which is lending to smaller scale borrowers.

Empirical Evidence

It is important to establish first whether the interest rate reforms in Kenya resulted in wider interest margins. Unfortunately, data on commercial banks' actual margins were not available. This necessitated the use of estimates using the various categories of deposits and loans, and official interest rates. The margins depicted a downward trend until 1984 and an upward trend since then such that by 1988, they were at the same level as in 1980. However, a fall was registered in 1990 and it is questionable if the upward trend can be sustained.

In any case, in order to test the possibility that higher margins encourage or allow more costly and riskier lending, there is a need to incorporate non-interest costs of lending (Bhatt and Roe, 1979; Saito and Villanueva, 1981; Roe, 1989). The next part focuses on this issue.

Transaction Costs of Lending

Transaction costs of lending comprise administrative costs of lending and default risk expenses. Administrative costs include all non-interest costs incurred in the process of mobilising deposits, running the payments mechanism, loan processing, disbursement, monitoring and recovery. Default risk expenses arise from lack of perfect information on the borrowers and, therefore, the inability to assess correctly their probability of default.

Ideally, it is the marginal cost which matters as it shows the cost associated with lending for new investment from an increase in available funds. Unfortunately, this is difficult to measure and the practice is to use the average cost as a proxy. Even for this, the lack of data necessitates the use of estimates. The results show that these costs squeeze the margins considerably. It can, therefore, be expected that banks would be less willing to undertake lending which entails high transaction costs. In the context of this study, it is important to consider whether such costs are higher for small scale than for large scale borrowers.

Due to data limitations, it is difficult to estimate the administrative costs of lending to SMEs (or to small scale borrowers as a whole) by commercial banks in Kenya. In view of the importance of this issue, it was considered necessary to evaluate the experiences of other financial institutions for which data were available to see whether these could offer useful insight. The logic of this was that if lending to small scale borrowers is more expensive, this could be expected to be reflected in significant differentials in the costs incurred by various institutions depending on the nature of their clients. The institutions chosen for this exercise were the Small Enterprise Finance Company (SEFCO) for lending to SMEs, and the Development Finance Corporation of Kenya (DFCK) for lending to large industries.

Administrative costs and default risk expenses incurred by these two DFIs were obtained from their published accounts. However, due to data limitations, it was only possible to obtain information for the period 1985 to 1990. The results show that the transaction costs incurred by SEFCO have been substantially higher than those incurred by DFCK, with the average annual difference for this period being 8.4 percentage points. Although there has been a downward trend since 1988, SEFCO's costs still remain high relative to those in DFCK. This may be taken to suggest that lending to small scale borrowers is more costly than lending to large scale borrowers. If these results are applied to commercial bank lending, then it is clear that lending to SMEs would require substantially higher lending rates if the higher costs are to be covered. This may be politically unacceptable, such that even with a relaxation in ceilings on lending rates, banks cannot raise their rates for such borrowers to the high levels implied by these costs. Although it can be argued that banks can circumvent this by concealing their true interest costs,[8] the important point to note is that relaxing controls on lending rates would not necessarily enable banks to charge rates which reflect the cost and risk of lending explicitly.

V THE IMPACT OF REAL INTEREST RATES ON INVESTMENT AND BORROWING DECISIONS

The McKinnon–Shaw hypothesis of financial repression posits a positive relationship between investment and real interest rates as it postulates that private investment is positively related to the accumulation of real money balances. Since borrowers are assumed to be constrained by the availability of funds, it follows that they stand to benefit from increases in funds stemming from increases in real deposit rates. This part, therefore, aims to assess the relationship between interest rates and investment in Kenya.

Empirical Evidence

Due to lack of data on SME's investment at a macro level, the econometric analysis was done for real investment in the manufacturing sector as a whole. In addition to real deposit rates, the other explanatory variables were capacity utilisation, real public sector infrastructure investment, real effective exchange rate, and capacity to import as a proxy for foreign exchange availability. It is, however, the results with regard to the real interest rate that are more important for this study.

The regression analysis was done using both the commercial bank deposit rate and the weighted average of banks' and NBFIs' rates. In both equations, there is a negative relationship between the real interest rate and investment. Furthermore, in the second equation which attempts to capture the importance of credit from NBFIs by incorporating their higher interest rate structure, the negative relationship is significant at the 1 per cent level. This implies that real interest rates were higher than their equilibrium levels and, consequently, discouraged rather than enabled investment. In this aspect, these results do not lend support to the positive relationship between investment and real interest rates postulated by the McKinnon–Shaw model. This outcome is not surprising given the negative relationship between real interest rates and financial savings that was observed above.

Firm-Level Evidence

At the firm level, differences were noted in the use of commercial bank facilities by the sample SMEs. At one extreme, there were four firms which did not even have bank accounts. The remaining 85 included 52 (58.4 per cent) who had used commercial bank credit and 33 who had not.

It was only possible to obtain data on the volume of credit from 34 firms. For these, the results do not portray a consistent trend in the annual changes in credit from commercial banks. Indeed for 30 SMEs (88.2 per cent), increases are noted in some years and decreases in others. Furthermore, whereas no single SME sustains increases in credit over the whole period, two firms record annual decreases from 1987 onwards. Another two initially experience both increases and decreases until 1986 when decreases set in and are not reversed. Table 2.3 shows the number and proportion of firms which increased their level of real borrowing from commercial banks on an annual basis from 1981 to 1990.

Table 2.3 Proportion of SMEs with annual increases in commercial bank credit

Year	Number of firms with increases	Number of firms which borrowed	Proportion (%)
1981	3	9	33.3
1982	6	9	66.7
1983	6	11	54.5
1984	8	12	66.7
1985	5	13	38.5
1986	8	18	44.4
1987	9	23	39.1
1988	10	25	40.0
1989	10	29	34.4
1990	6	31	19.4

Source: own survey.

The table shows that it was only in 1982–1984 that more than half of the SMEs who were already borrowing actually increased their credit. Such proportions have not been achieved since. In fact, in 1990, out of 31 SMEs which borrowed that year, only six (19.4 per cent) realised increases in commercial bank credit. These results support the finding at the macro level of a lack of a positive and significant relationship between real interest rates and the use of credit to finance investment. The next part offers some explanations for this outcome.

Other Factors That Influence Borrowing Decisions

In econometric studies that seek to explain the determinants of private invest-ment, the real interest rate is taken to represent the real cost of borrowing. It has been shown, however, that interest costs represent only one component of the overall costs (Nissanke, 1991; Ebrill, 1987; Faini, 1988). The other components which need to be considered are transaction costs incurred by the borrower and the price of capital goods. In addition, the absolute level of the nominal lending rate itself is important as it affects the risk of using borrowed funds. Finally, it is important to consider whether there are other non-financial operational constraints.

SMEs Transaction Costs of Borrowing

Just as financiers incur transaction costs in lending, borrowers also incur costs when borrowing. These include '... explicit cash costs that include expenditure on travel, entertainment, bribes and gratuities, forced purchase of other lender ser-vices and/or products, and other expenses connected with requirements by the lender;... and implicit or opportunity costs of time spent applying for and obtain-ing the loan, i.e., the opportunity cost of lost work time' (Ahmed, 1989: 362). In the case of small scale borrowers, such costs have been found to be surprisingly high and to act as deterrents to the use of formal credit (Adams and Lehman, 1979; Ahmed, 1989; Ladman, 1984).

Data from the sample SMEs only permit an estimation of part of their explicit transaction costs. This is because the firms could only furnish data pertaining to the total actual payments that they made to the banks without disaggregating them into interest costs and other charges. Figure 2.2 shows the average transac-tion and interest costs of borrowing for the SMEs with adequate data and their total costs of borrowing.[9]

The effect of transaction costs on the total costs of borrowing is clear. Indeed, the Figure shows that from 1985, transaction costs and total costs are almost per-fectly correlated. It is also worth noting that there was a sharp increase in these costs from 1987, such that by 1990, they were almost as high as interest costs. These results imply that the explicit transaction costs of borrowing for SMEs are high in relation to the interest costs. Analyses which do not take these costs into

Figure 2.2   SMEs: some costs of borrowing

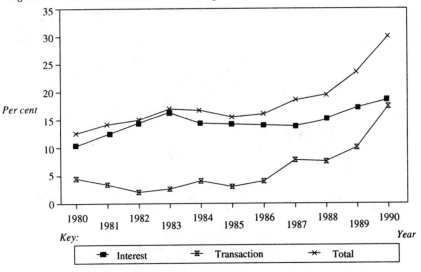

Key:

■ Interest   ☓ Transaction   ✕ Total

Source: own survey.

consideration are incomplete, especially considering that the opportunity costs of time spent in obtaining loans are not included.

The Cost of Capital

It is an established orthodoxy that interest costs reflect the costs of borrowed funds, and as such, represent only one element of the total cost of capital. It is equally important to consider the other determinants of the cost of capital of which the major ones are taxation and investment allowances.

It has been shown that tax deductibility of interest expenditure considerably reduces the interest costs of borrowing (Faini, 1988; Dailami and Walton, 1989; Ebrill, 1987). In Kenya, the Income Tax Act makes provisions for interest expenditure to be deductible provided the debt is contracted wholly and exclusively to produce taxable income. Figure 2.3 shows the effect of adjusting the real maximum lending rate for this provision using the nominal corporate income tax rate.

The Figure shows that this considerably lowers the real cost of borrowing. While the real rates unadjusted for tax have been positive since 1983, it is only in 1986 and 1987 that the rates adjusted for tax are positive in real terms. Even then, they are only marginally positive.

It is difficult to provide a firm level analysis due to unavailability of data regarding tax payments and deductibility. Available information, however, indi-

Figure 2.3   Real maximum lending rates (adjusted and unadjusted for tax)

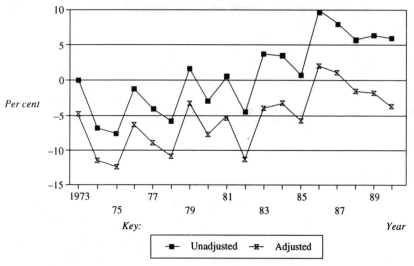

Source: Calculated from data in Central Bank Annual Report, various years, and Budget Speeches, various years.

cates that a majority of the firms were profitable and were, therefore, eligible for this provision. Anecdotal evidence, however, suggests that most entrepreneurs do not make use of this and of other investment allowances as a whole because they consider the procedures involved to be unduly laborious and costly.

Other Operational Constraints

In the McKinnon–Shaw model, lack of finance is depicted as the most binding constraint for investors in general and for small scale producers in particular. This implies that if the availability of funds is assured, SMEs would be willing and able to borrow from formal institutions. This amounts to an assumption that other operational constraints which would affect their willingness and ability to borrow are either absent, or can be solved by increased availability of finance.

To evaluate this proposition, the sample entrepreneurs were asked to enumerate their major problems. The results are summarised in Table 2.4. To capture the severity of the financial constraint, the perceptions of the entrepreneurs who had borrowed were separated from those who had not.

All the firms who had not borrowed felt that lack of working capital was a major constraint. By contrast, responses from borrowers imply that this was not the binding constraint. For these, demand constraints emerged as the most serious

Table 2.4   Perceptions of major problems by borrowing and non-borrowing
proprietors (% of respondents in each category)

	Borrowers	*Non-borrowers*
Raw Materials	48.1	45.9
Demand	73.1	83.8
Working Capital	50.0	100.0
Costs of Borrowing	53.8	–

Source: own survey.

problem while the second and third most important problems were lack of working capital and inadequate supplies of raw materials respectively. It is obvious that once availability of funds is assured, the other constraints become more apparent. Indeed, the complaint with regard to finance shifts to the limitations imposed by its cost.

The level of the nominal lending rates in the 1980s renders credibility to these complaints. There were increases in nominal rates from 1980 to 1983, and from 1987 to 1990. Trends in the rate of inflation generally reveal a decline between 1982 and 1986 and an increase since then. Consequently, borrowers faced higher nominal rates at higher inflation rates in the latter half of the 1980s. It can be expected that this increased the risk of using borrowed funds.[10] This is because under such circumstances, producers can expect their production costs to rise with the general price level. By contrast, a rise in their sales prices is less certain, thereby exposing them to a severe risk. Moreover, the greater variability of high inflation rates makes the risk even greater.

In addition to these external constraints, it is important to consider whether the firms faced internal constraints stemming from managerial and entrepreneurial deficiencies. These constraints do not emerge from interviews with the proprietors because it is usual for producers to enumerate only those problems which they perceive to be beyond their control and those which they think the researcher is in a position to help (Harper, 1984: 26). Yet, managerial and entrepreneurial capability affect the totality of firms' operations, including their access to formal credit.

The indicators of managerial and entrepreneurial capability used in this study were the entrepreneur's level of education, age of the firm and records maintained. All the proprietors had attained sufficient formal education to be functionally literate and numerate. As regards records, 66 (74.2 per cent) had well kept records. In addition, about a third of the firms have been in operation for at least ten years, and about a half for at least six years. Their survival in itself could be taken as a sign of success as the firms operate in competitive conditions. For a quarter of the firms, failure to maintain adequate records could prove to be an obstacle.

The overall conclusion from these findings is that credit availability by itself is not a sufficient condition to ensure increases in investment levels, especially by SMEs. The other factors which determine the use of finance are diverse and include the nominal level of the lending rate, transaction costs of borrowing, tax incentives and allowances and their effectiveness, and the nature of the other operational constraints.

VI THE IMPACT OF REAL INTEREST RATES ON ALLOCATIVE EFFICIENCY OF CREDIT

This part tests the McKinnon-Shaw hypothesis that interest rate liberalisation eventually leads to an improvement in the allocative efficiency of credit as a result of the incentive effects that it sets in motion. Financial markets can be said to be allocatively efficient if they direct resources to their most socially productive use. Allocative efficiency can, therefore, be measured across sectors (intersectoral) and across firms of different sizes (inter-firm). Although it is this latter measure which is more relevant for this study, available data only permit an intersectoral analysis.

Empirical Evidence

The method adopted is one used by Biggs (1991) whereby the efficiency of allocation is judged by relating the share of credit to a sector or firm to its return to capital. Efficient allocation can be said to occur if there is a positive correlation between these. An application of this method to Kenyan data produced negative correlation coefficients from 1980 to 1984 and positive coefficients thereafter. Although these positive coefficients from 1985 to 1990 suggest an improvement in allocative efficiency, they are not statistically significant even at the 10 per cent level. This suggests that allocative efficiency of commercial bank credit has not improved significantly in spite of the positive real rates achieved in the 1980s. This suggests that there were important non-interest factors which influenced allocative efficiency.

Non-Interest Determinants of Allocative Efficiency

The non-interest determinants of allocative efficiency include incomplete or shallow markets and imperfect information (Killick and Martin, 1990). It is accepted that imperfect information is a characteristic of all financial markets over which neither lenders nor borrowers have control. It would, therefore, be naive to expect the situation to be different for the Kenyan financial system.

Segmented, incomplete or shallow markets are the common types of market failures in developing countries. These market failures prevent efficient allocation of capital even if the banking system is liberalised along the McKinnon–Shaw framework. The Kenyan financial system is considered in this light.

The Nature of the Capital Market in Kenya

Kenya has a wide variety of financial institutions ranging from commercial banks, NBFIs, development finance institutions (DFIs), insurance companies, a stock exchange, a Post Office Savings Bank and several pension funds. This gives the impression of a fairly complete and deep financial system consisting of a banking sector and a capital market. The true position regarding the latter needs to be established as commercial banks only provide short term finance for working capital purposes.

There are nine DFIs which extend credit to major sectors of the economy. In spite of this impressive number, the extent to which they have filled gaps in the market and helped to improve the allocation of credit is questionable. The poor performance of most of them is well documented (Ikiara, 1987; Grosh, 1987a, 1987b; World Bank, 1987; Maynard, 1992). The problems include excessive political interference, inadequate monitoring systems and shortage of local investment resources. These problems have undermined their usefulness as sources of investment finance.

The importance of the Nairobi Stock Exchange as a source of finance for investors is also questionable. Business firms in Kenya rarely raise capital through public share issues. Market capitalisation has been low, the number of new issues infrequent and the amounts raised relatively small. However, there has been a resurgence in the market in the latter half of the 1980s which is a welcome development compared to its virtual dormancy in the 1970s. There has been an increase in the number of companies floating their shares. For example, between 1976 and 1985 there were only two new issues which raised shs 45.9 million, whereas between 1986 and 1989, there were four new issues from which shs 465.3 million was realised. This method of raising capital can only be used by well established firms, but is useful as an incentive by acting as a reward for success.

The same reservations apply to the insurance companies and pension funds as sources of long term investment finance. The insurance companies show a preference for holding a large proportion of their funds as bank deposits. For example, in 1988 (the latest year for which data are available) non-life insurance companies held 20.3 per cent of their funds in bank deposits while loans to the private sector accounted for only 2.1 per cent. The comparable figures for life insurance companies were 15 per cent and 13.3 per cent respectively. As regards the pension funds, investment by both private pension schemes and the government's National Social Security Fund face are governed by the Trustee Act which allows investment only in government or local authority securities, or in securities quoted on the Nairobi Stock Exchange with an unbroken five year record of dividend payments. They are also required to hold 50 per cent of their portfolio in fixed interest securities such as Treasury Bonds. These conservative provisions severely limit their scope as important sources of private sector finance.

The Capital Market for SMEs

In view of these considerations, the institutions that are relevant for SMEs are the three DFIs: the Kenya Industrial Estates (KIE), the Small Enterprise Finance Company (SEFCO) and the Industrial and Commercial Development Corporation (ICDC). One main feature of KIE's lending is that its lending rates are concessionary. They are below commercial rates and were below the rate of inflation until 1984. The loan repayment record has been poor mainly due to political interferences in the lending and recovery activities. Furthermore, the volume of funds at KIE's disposal has fallen over time. Given these circumstances, it is not surprising that its financial operations show a decrease in amount of loans approved and disbursed and in average loan sizes. Data on ICDC's financing operations also do not reveal appreciable increases in lending to SMEs. Indeed, the Corporation suspended its small scale lending programmes in the first half of the 1980s. SEFCO's experience is more encouraging. There have been increases in loans approved and disbursed and loan recovery has been high. The volume of funds at its disposal has also been increasing steadily over time. This supports the expectation that success in loan recovery influences the growth of DFIs by increasing total funds both from increases in recovered funds and from donor funds.

There are also alternative arrangements by way of special lending schemes operated by some of the commercial banks. The beneficiaries have been rather few and some operational problems have been experienced (Chege, 1988), but these schemes could be useful in forging links between bankers and small scale borrowers. In addition to the formal banking sector, there are NGOs, semi-formal and informal financial sectors. The volume of funds in most of these is limited (Aleke-Dondo, 1991) such that they can only be expected to be important for a small number of enterprises at the bottom end of the scale in terms of size.

Firm-Level Evidence: Borrower Survey

It is important to supplement this lender survey with experiences from the borrowers themselves. The borrower survey reveals that self-finance is by far the most important source of initial capital and of capital for further expansion. The DFIs rank second. This suggests that it is wrong to assume that all the institutions which are supposed to be providing finance to SMEs are effective and efficient. The implication is that unless these inefficiencies are rectified, an increase in the allocation of credit to SMEs cannot be realised.

The major finding here is that positive real interest rates are not sufficient to ensure allocative efficiency. Endogenous constraints, especially those arising from market failures, need to be addressed. Furthermore, interest rate ceilings are only part of the exogenous constraints. The next part considers the effect of the other types of government controls.

VII THE IMPACT OF OTHER (NON-INTEREST RATE) GOVERNMENT CONTROLS AND INTERVENTIONIST MEASURES IN THE FINANCIAL SYSTEM

In most developing countries, there is a high level of government intervention in the financial sector. In broad terms, government controls can be classified as macroeconomic, allocative and prudential. A liberalisation strategy which removes one distortion while others remain in place may make the situation worse rather than better, thereby impinging on realisation of the intended benefits.

Apart from interest rate ceilings, other controls in Kenya have included the setting of minimum cash and liquid assets ratios, overall credit ceilings and a minimum ratio of lending to agriculture. Prudential controls are also enforced through the licensing of banks and other financial institutions, the specification of minimum capital requirements and the restriction of certain types of lending. In addition, the government also controls two commercial banks and the institutions affiliated to them. How then have these controls affected the allocation of credit to SMEs?

In Part IV, it was argued that certain conditions are necessary if financial intermediaries can be expected to undertake more, and in the case of SMEs, more costly and riskier lending. Both the volume of funds at the disposal of the institutions, and the spread of intermediation are important. It can, therefore, be expected that those controls which reduce any of these effectively discourage lending to SMEs. Required reserves, selective and overall credit controls all exert such effects. While recognising that some capital and liquidity controls are absolutely necessary, it is worth noting that some controls could reduce the scope for banks to increase lending to SMEs.

The types of intervention which can be expected to be beneficial are government ownership of banks and indigenisation of the banking sector. However, the record of such banks suggests that this is not necessarily the case, and it is doubtful if they can correct the prejudicial treatment of some borrowers by expatriate banks and their resultant exclusion from credit (see for example Harvey, 1991).

The Kenyan experience is evaluated using the size distribution of credit among the commercial banks depending on ownership structure. Unfortunately, the only data that are available are those on lending to agriculture. Although this limits the extent to which the results can be generalised, the analysis provides useful insight.

The results are shown in Figure 2.4. Government-owned banks emerge as the leaders in financing small scale farmers. Surprisingly, foreign-controlled banks

Figure 2.4   Share of bank credit to small farmers (by ownership of banks)

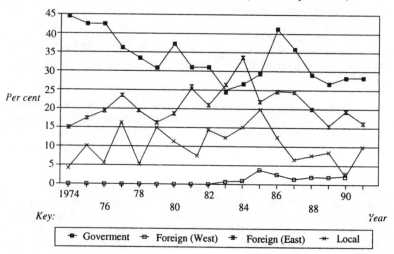

Source: Central Bank of Kenya, unpublished data, and Annual Report, various
          issues.

have also been more involved in such lending than the local private banks. It is
remarkable, however, that the proportion of this kind of lending in the portfolios
of local banks has increased considerably, if only from a low level and remaining
well below that in the other banks. This suggests that they have the potential to
undertake this kind of lending. On the other hand, it is suggested that imprudent
banking practices and constraints in administrative capacity (especially due to
limited branch network) in some of them could reduce the scope for increases in
lending to marginal borrowers. This implies that while the promotion of an
indigenous financial sector with a diversified branch network may be necessary, it
is not by itself sufficient to ensure increased small scale lending and would be
endangered if pursued too fast. It appears that indigenisation of the financial
sector needs to be accompanied by more and not less prudential regulation if it is
to be beneficial to small scale borrowers.

   This also emerges from a look at the bankers of the sample SMEs. The big four
banks (Kenya Commercial, National, Standard and Barclays) are the most
important in terms of banking relationships with the SMEs. The local private and
the other smaller foreign banks are involved to a much less extent. The preferred
banks have wider branch networks and are more established in terms of age.

   The conclusion to draw here is that in addition to interest rate liberalisation,
financial reforms need to consider other government controls and interventions.

This is because such controls could constrain financial intermediation and credit allocation decisions, although their prudential rationale may be justifiable. This implies that a liberalisation strategy which only removes controls on interest rates may not be sufficient to ameliorate the situation if other interventionist measures remain in place or are introduced.

VIII CONCLUSION

The findings in this study point to the inadequacy of the market in producing the magic which could correct imperfections in the financial system. The evidence fails to lend support to the McKinnon–Shaw hypotheses regarding the benefits of positive real interest rates. There are clear indications that while positive real interest rates may be necessary to correct imperfections in the financial sector, they are not by themselves sufficient to ensure such an outcome. There are important factors, distinct from the interest rate, which could pose considerable obstacles. Such factors could dampen the theorised positive impact of real interest rates on financial savings, on intermediation margins, on investment and on allocative efficiency.

This inadequacy of the market to correct imperfections in the financial system implies that there is a role for the government to play. The important thing is '... to identify which market failures can be ameliorated through non-market institutions (with perhaps the government taking an instrumental role in these non-market institutions) ....[and] ...to recognise both the limits and strengths of markets, as well as the strengths and limits of government interventions aimed at correcting market failures' (Stiglitz, 1989: 202).

As regards credit allocation, the question of how the government should intervene admits of no general answer. While government intervention may be necessary because market failures in financial markets in developing countries are endemic, it is difficult to ensure that this will not be perverted to corrupt use. The record of intervention in the allocation of credit is poor, and tends to lead to insolvent institutions. It may, therefore, be more efficient to try and improve the credit-worthiness of marginalised borrowers. This can be done by adopting measures which improve their productivity to enable them to meet the commercial criteria imposed by formal lenders. This underlines the need to complement a market-based interest rate policy with such measures in order to realise an improvement in the allocation of credit.

Notes

1. This chapter is a summary of the author's DPhil thesis (Kariuki, 1993). All the issues raised here are discussed in more detail in that study.

2. Real interest rates in this paper refer to interest rates adjusted for inflation but not for taxation.
3. It was not until April 1981 that the government switched to setting maximum rather than minimum lending rates.
4. Real interest rates are obtained by adjusting the nominal interest rates for inflation according to the formula: $100 \{[(1 + i)/(1 + p)] - 1\}$, where i is the nominal interest rate and p is the annual change in the consumer price index. Both rates are expressed as proportions rather than percentages. Although it is the ex ante real rate which is relevant, data on the expected rate of inflation are not available in Kenya, as is the case in many other developing countries.
5. The ideal depreciation rate is the ex ante rate, as it shows the expected exchange rate changes. However, such expectations are not known and the ex post rate is used as a proxy for the expected rate.
6. Commercial bank branches (full-time branches, agencies and mobile units) increased from 288 in 1980 to 518 in 1990, while the branch network of NBFIs increased from 29 to 95 over the same period.
7. Indeed, this was also observed in the towns that were visited during the fieldwork. While there were nine banks operating in Kisumu and seven in Nakuru, Karatina was only served by the big four. In Machakos and Kakamega, the number of banks represented was only three.
8. There are various ways of doing this. For example, charging monthly and cumulating interest rates such that 2 per cent a month appears to be 24 per cent a year, but cumulates to 27 per cent. Another alternative is to require borrowers to hold countervailing non-interest earning deposits. Banks can also resort to use of hidden fees and other charges.
9. The total costs of borrowing are calculated using the linearly additive method. The method suggested by Ahmed (1989) could not be used as there was no information on the term maturity of the loans.
10. See Harvey and Jenkins (1994) for a discussion of this aspect.

References

Adams, D.W. and G.I Lehman (1979) 'Borrowing Costs and the Demand for Rural Credit', *Journal of Development Studies*, 15 (2).

Ahmed, Z.U. (1989) 'Effective Costs of Rural Loans in Bangladesh', *World Development*, 17 (3).

Aleke-Dondo, C. (1991) 'Survey and Analysis of Credit Programmes for Small and Micro Enterprises in Kenya', *Kenya Rural Enterprise Research Programme Research Series*, 2.

Bhatt, V.V. (1986) 'Improving the Financial Structure in Developing Countries', *Finance and Development*, 23 (2).

Bhatt, V.V. and A.R. Roe (1979) 'Capital Market Imperfections and Economic Development', *World Bank Staff Working Paper*, 338.

Biggs, T.S. (1991) 'Heterogeneous Firms and Efficient Financial Intermediation in Taiwan', in M. Roemer and C. Jones (eds), *Markets in Developing Countries: Parallel, Segmented and Black* (San Francisco: International Center for Economic Growth).

Blejer, M.I. and A. Cheasty (1986) 'Using Fiscal Measures to Stimulate Savings in Developing Countries', *Finance and Development*, 23 (2).

Central Bank of Kenya (1986) *Central Bank of Kenya: Its Evolution, Responsibilities and Organisation* (Nairobi: Central Bank of Kenya).

Central Bank of Kenya (1988) *Economic Report for the year ended 30th June 1988* (Nairobi: Central Bank of Kenya).

Chandavarkar, A. (1990) 'Macroeconomic Aspects, Foreign Flows and Domestic savings Performance in Developing Countries: A "State of the Art" Report', *OECD Development Centre Technical Paper*, 11 (Paris: OECD).

Chege, J.D. (1988) 'Kenya Commercial Bank's Involvement in Financing Small Enterprise Development', mimeo, Kenya Commercial Bank.

Cho, Y.J. and D. Khathate (1989) 'Lessons of Financial Liberalisation in Asia', *World Bank Discussion Paper*, 50.

Dailami, M. and M. Walton (1989) 'Private Investment, Government Policy and Foreign Capital in Zimbabwe', *World Bank Policy, Planning and Research Working Paper*, 248.

Ebrill, L.P. (1987) 'Income Taxes and Investment: Some Empirical Relationships for Developing Countries', in V.P. Gandhi *et al.*, *Supply-Side Tax Policy: Its Relevance to Developing Countries* (Washington DC: IMF).

Faini, R. (1988) 'Export Supply, Capacity and Relative Prices', *World Bank Policy, Planning and Research Working Paper*, 123.

Fernando, N.A. (1991) 'Determinants of Rural Savings in Papua New Guinea', *Savings and Development*, 15 (4).

Fry, M.J. (1988) *Money, Interest and Banking in Economic Development* (Baltimore: Johns Hopkins University Press).

Fry, M.J. (1989) 'Financial Development: Theories and Recent Experience', *Oxford Review of Economic Policy*, 5 (4).

Grosh, B. (1987a) 'Performance of Development Finance Institutions in Kenya: 1964–89', *University of Nairobi, Institute for Development Studies Working Paper*, 450.

Grosh, B. (1987b) 'Performance of Financial Parastatals in Kenya: 1964–84', *University of Nairobi, Institute for Development Studies Working Paper*, 449.

Harper, M. (1984) *Small Business in the Third World* (Chichester: John Wiley and Sons).

Harvey, Charles (1991), 'On the Perverse Effects of Financial Sector Reform in Anglophone Africa', *South African Journal of Economics*, 59 (3).

Harvey, C. and C. Jenkins (1994) 'Taxation, Risk and Real Interest Rates', *IDS, Discussion Paper* No 336.

Helleiner, G.K. (1990) 'Structural Adjustment and Long Term Development in Sub-Saharan Africa', *Queen Elizabeth House Development Studies Working Paper*, 18.

Ikiara, G.K. (1987) 'The Role of Government Institutions in Kenya's Industrialisation', *University of Nairobi, Industrial Research Project Discussion Paper*.

Kariuki, P.W. (1993) 'Interest Rate Liberalisation and the Allocation of Credit: Some Evidence from the Small and Medium Scale Industry in Kenya', Unpublished DPhil Thesis, IDS, University of Sussex.

Kilby, P. (1988) 'Breaking the Entrepreneurial Bottle-neck in Late Developing Countries: Is there a useful Role for Government?', *Journal of Development Planning*, 18.

Killick, T. (1984) 'IMF Stabilisation Programmes', in T. Killick (ed.), *The Quest for Economic Stabilisation: The IMF and the Third World* (London: ODI and Heinemann Educational Books).

Killick, T. and M. Martin (1990) 'Financial Policies in the Adaptive Economy', *ODI Working Paper*, 35.

Killick, T. and F.M. Mwega (1990) 'Monetary Policy in Kenya: 1967–88', *ODI Working Paper*, 39.

Kitchen, R.L. (1986) *Finance for the Developing Countries* (Chichester and New York: John Wiley).

Ladman, J.R. (1984) 'Loan-Transaction Costs, Credit rationing and Market Structure: The Case of Bolivia', in D.W. Adams, D.H. Graham and J.D. von Pischke (eds), *Undermining Rural Development with Cheap Credit* (Boulder: Westview Press).

Maynard, J.E. (1992) 'The Influence of the Soft State on the Performance of Development Finance Institutions', Unpublished DPhil Thesis, Napier Polytechnic and IDS, Sussex.

McKinnon, R.I. (1973) *Money and Capital in Economic Development* (Washington DC: Brookings Institution).

Mwandihi, L.A. (1988) 'Co-operatives in National Development: Achievements, Constraints and Prospects', in J.E.O. Odada, H.A. Liyai and K.O. Litondo (eds), *Strategies for Improving Performance of the Co-operative Movement in Kenya* (Nairobi: Kenya Economic Association and Friedrich Ebert Foundation).

Nissanke, M. (1991) 'Theoretical Issues in Finance and Development: A Critical Literature Survey', *Queen Elizabeth House Development Studies Working Paper*, 36.

Roe, A.R. (1989) 'Interest Rate Policy, Employment and Income Distribution', in G.T. Renshaw (ed.), *Market Liberalisation, Equity and Development* (Geneva: ILO).

Saito, K.A. and D.P. Villanueva (1981) 'Transaction Costs of Credit to the Small Scale Sector in the Philippines', *Economic Development and Cultural Change*, 29 (3).

Shaw, E.S. (1973) *Financial Deepening in Economic Development* (New York: Oxford University Press).

Stiglitz, J.E. (1989) 'Markets, Market Failures and Development', *Papers and Proceedings in American Economic Review*, 79 (2).

World Bank (1987) *Kenya: Industrial Sector Policies for Investment and Export Growth*, Report No. 6711-KE, Volume 2 Main Report (Washington DC: World Bank).

World Bank (1989) *World Development Report* (Washington DC: World Bank).

3 The Structural Adjustment Implications of Real Exchange Rate Depreciation on the Manufacturing Sector in Zimbabwe[1]

Joseph Muzulu

INTRODUCTION

Real exchange rate depreciation lies at the heart of structural adjustment and stabilisation programmes, particularly those supported by the IMF and the World Bank. Notwithstanding this, there is still considerable controversy surrounding the efficacy of exchange rate depreciation in fostering export expansion and improving resource allocation.

This chapter examines the structural adjustment implications of exchange rate depreciation for the manufacturing sector in Zimbabwe. The chapter concentrates on the manufacturing sector for a number of reasons. Firstly, one of the main benefits claimed for real exchange rate depreciation is supposed to be the increased production of tradable goods of which the manufacturing sector is a significant part, especially in Zimbabwe where it accounts for 25 per cent of gross domestic product (GDP). Secondly, there is a general consensus that trade in manufactures grows faster than that in primary commodities (World Bank, 1981; Goldstein, 1986). Finally, manufacturing has been identified by government as a leading sector (GOZ, 1991c).

The rest of the chapter proceeds as follows. Part I outlines the theoretical benefits associated with a real exchange rate depreciation. The second part reviews Zimbabwe's exchange rate policy during the 1980s. It is shown that Zimbabwe achieved a real exchange rate depreciation after 1985. The third part analyses the extent to which this real exchange rate depreciation produced the predicted benefits. Finally, the fourth part concludes.

I REVIEW OF THEORY

A review of the literature suggests that currency depreciation generates price incentives that lead to a number of benefits:

(1) A shift in resources from the production of non-tradable goods to tradable goods (World Bank, 1990), and a faster growth in the tradable relative to the non-tradable goods sectors (Demery and Addison, 1988);

(2) A shift from production of goods that are heavy users of imported to those that depend on domestic inputs (Johnson, 1987);

(3) An increase in exports because of higher export prices in domestic currency or increased international competitiveness (Crockett, 1981; Thomas, 1989);

(4) An increase in investment in the tradable goods sectors because of the increase in prices of tradable relative to non-tradable goods (Serven and Solimano, 1991).

II ZIMBABWE'S EXCHANGE RATE POLICY IN THE 1980s

The Zimbabwe dollar appreciated against most currencies following expansionary fiscal and monetary policies that accompanied Zimbabwe's independence in 1980. Partly as a result of this and partly due to the liberalisation of factor payments and dividend remittances abroad as well as the increased demand for imports, the current account deficit widened from 4.6 per cent of GDP in 1980 to 10.3 per cent by 1983. In addition, growth in government revenues failed to keep pace with growth in expenditures resulting in a growing budget deficit that averaged 10 per cent of GDP throughout the 1980s.

To resolve these problems, government adopted a 'home-grown' stabilisation programme that included most of the elements contained in IMF supported programmes.[2] For our purposes, however, the Zimbabwe dollar was devalued by 20 per cent in December 1982. After this devaluation, the monetary authorities adopted a 'managed float' exchange rate system where discretionary changes were made to the nominal exchange rate depending on the inflation differential between Zimbabwe and its fourteen major trading partners as well as exchange rate movements taking place in major foreign markets of the world. Although government's initial intention was to maintain the real effective exchange rate at its 1983 level, the index first rose in 1984 before depreciating consistently from 1985 (Figure 3.1).[3] According to government, this was necessary in order to stimulate exports. Indeed, Figure 3.2 shows that following the 1982 devaluation of the Zimbabwe dollar and the subsequent removal of subsidies on most tradable consumer goods, the prices of tradable goods rose faster than those of non-tradable goods.[4]

Figure 3.1 Exchange rate indices (1985 = 100)

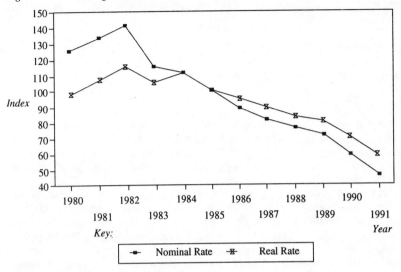

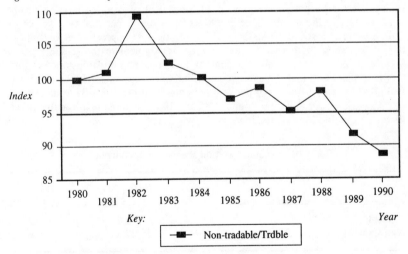

Source: Data from CSO, *Quarterly Digest of Statistics*.
Notes: Trdble = Tradable goods.

Given the price movements generated by exchange rate depreciation, to what extent did both employment and output respond in line with what theory predicts?

III   EMPIRICAL RESULTS

Employment and Output Responses[5]

Aggregate Level

Table 3.1 shows that the average contribution of the tradable goods sectors to total employment fell over time from 72.7 per cent when the real exchange rate was appreciating (1980–1984) to 70.2 per cent during the period of the sustained real depreciation of the Zimbabwe dollar (1985–1990), with that of the non-tradable goods sectors accounting for the remainder.

An analysis of the rate of growth in employment reveals that while the tradable goods sectors averaged a decline of 2.9 per cent per annum during the 1980–84 period, the private sector non-tradable goods activities recorded a positive growth rate of 3 per cent per annum over the same period. During the 1985–90 period, employment in the tradable goods sectors rose by an average of 1.5 per cent per annum while that in the non-tradable goods sectors grew by 4 per cent per annum. Although employment in the non-tradable goods sectors continued to grow faster than that in the tradable goods sectors, the improvement in the tradable goods sectors from –2.9 per cent a year to +1.5 per cent, was much larger than the improvement in the non-tradable goods sectors (from 3 per cent to 4 per cent). This was made possible by the fact that the economy was operating below capacity. In the event, there was no reason why employment in the tradable goods sectors should have grown at the expense of that in the non-tradable goods sectors.

Table 3.2 shows that the average contribution of the tradable goods sector to real GDP increased from 60.6 per cent per annum during 1980–84 to an average of 62.2 per cent per annum between 1985 and 1990, with the non-tradable goods sector accounting for the remainder.

Table 3.1   Average sectoral shares of employment (%)

	1980–1984	1985–1990
Tradable	72.7	70.2
Non-tradable less 'Gvt. & other services'	27.3	29.8

Notes: Gvt. = government.
Source: CSO, *Quarterly Digest of Statistics* (various).

Table 3.2   Average sectoral proportions to total GDP (%)

	1980–1984	1985–1990
Tradable	60.6	62.2
Non-tradable	39.4	37.8

Source: CSO, *Quarterly Digest of Statistics* (various).

On the basis of the evidence at the aggregate level, it can be argued that output and employment in both the tradable and non-tradable goods sectors responded to the real exchange rate depreciation in line with theoretical predictions.

Firm-level Evidence

Of the 38 firms surveyed, none produced purely non-tradable goods. However, six firms produced both tradable and non-tradable goods; the latter in the form of retailing, engineering and after sale services. Although it became difficult to test the hypothesis directly because of the absence of producers of purely non-tradable goods in the sample, evidence from the six firms provided some useful insights.

All the six firms argued that they did not experience a reduction in the profitability of their non-tradable activities following the depreciation of the Zimbabwe dollar. Table 3.3 shows the proportion of output by activity for firms that furnished numerical data over the period under consideration. It is clear that, except for firm 225, there appears to be no secular decline in the proportion of total output accounted for by the non-tradable goods activities. In fact, for firm 940, there appears to have been an increase in the proportion of output attributable to the non-tradable goods activities. Although there were some differences in the reasons given for such a phenomenon, they can be summarised into two main categories.

Firstly, five of the six firms contended that the tradable and non-tradable goods activities were provided as joint products. In fact, most of these firms owned chains of retail outlets where they sold their own products to consumers. In the event, any increase in demand that led to an increase in supply of tradable goods resulted in an increase in the retailing business. Under these circumstances, a real exchange rate depreciation need not necessarily lead to a fall in output of non-tradable goods.

Secondly, the sixth firm argued that it increased the proportion of output coming from the non-tradable goods activities because government controlled the prices of its tradable goods. Under such circumstances, there is a tendency for firms to alter their output mix in favour of non-tradable goods whose prices are not controlled.

Table 3.3   Proportion of output by activity and by firm (%)

Firm	50		225		940	
	Tr	*N-T*	*Tr*	*N-T*	*Tr*	*N-T*
1981	–	–	18.3	81.7	57.1*	42.9
1982	–	–	12.8	87.2	–	–
1983	–	–	12.7	87.3	–	–
1984	–	–	13.3	86.7	–	–
1985	–	–	15.6	84.4	–	–
1986	16.9	83.1	22.9	77.1	–	–
1987	14.9	85.1	23.0	77.0	–	–
1988	13.9	86.1	24.3	75.7	–	–
1989	15.6	84.4	25.2	74.8	48.0	52.0
1990	13.5	86.5	33.7	66.3	38.5	61.5
1991	15.0	85.0	20.0	80.0	35.2	64.8

Notes:
–	Data not available.
*	Refers to 1980.
Tr	Tradable goods activities.
N-T	non-tradable goods activities.

Source: Direct firm information.

Real Depreciation and Choice of Production Technique

Behaviour of Relative Prices of Capital and Labour

Figure 3.3 traces the movement in relative prices of capital and labour over time.[6] The graph shows that following independence in 1980 and the general increase in earnings during this period the price of labour rose faster than the price of capital. However, after the December 1982 devaluation and the implementation of a restrictive incomes policy, the real price of capital increased faster than the real price of labour.

Following the real depreciation of the Zimbabwe dollar from 1985, the relative price of capital and labour continued to rise reflecting a relative cost advantage in employing labour relative to capital. To what extent did the manufacturing sector adjust by employing more labour relative to capital?

Choice of Production Technique[7]

Figure 3.4 shows that generally, the capital–labour ratio has been falling since 1980. It is also clear that the rate of fall in the value of capital stock increases

Figure 3.3   Relative factor prices (1980 = 100)

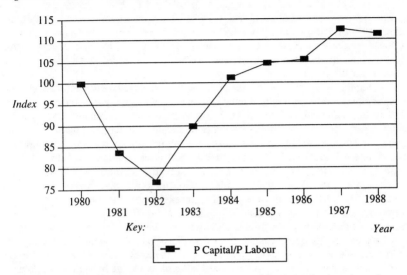

Source: Data derived from CSO, *Quarterly Digest of Statistics* (various issues).

Figure 3.4   Capital-labour ratios (1980 = 100)

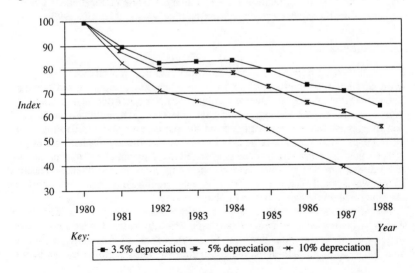

when higher rates of depreciation are used. The decline in the capital–labour ratio between 1980 and 1982 can largely be explained by the rapid growth in the economy after the end of sanctions in 1980. This period witnessed an increase in capacity utilisation from 60 per cent to about 98 per cent (Green and Kadhani, 1986). Due to this high level of economic activity, employment levels in the manufacturing sector rose in the face of declining capital stock leading to a significant fall in the capital–labour ratio.

During the post–1985 period, the capital-labour ratio fell consistently whichever rate of capital consumption is assumed. Such a fall was largely due to the continued fall in the real value of capital stock, rather than to any substantial increase in employment. Indeed, except in 1988 when employment in the manufacturing sector grew by 5.6 per cent, there was hardly any significant increase in employment between 1983 and 1988.[8] Although the fact that firms continued to extract output from old machinery may be taken as a form of substitution of labour for capital, most studies have shown that the main reason for postponing investment during much of the 1980s was the shortage of foreign exchange rather than the high cost of imported capital *per se* (UNIDO, 1986; Durevall, 1989). The latter did have the effect of exacerbating the problem, however. The fact that real capital stock declined during the period under review implies that investment levels were not sufficient to keep pace with the depreciation of existing machinery (Moyana, 1991).

From this discussion, it appears that the consistent fall in the capital–labour ratio was not a result of a conscious effort to substitute labour for capital following the real depreciation of the Zimbabwe dollar. The fact that employment levels in the manufacturing sector remained almost static during this period appears to lend credibility to this conclusion. Further analysis using factor productivity as a measure of factor intensity produced similar conclusions (Muzulu, 1993).

Firm-level Evidence

Of the 38 firms surveyed, four said that they had not imported new equipment while another four contended that the cost of capital equipment had not risen faster than that of labour. One of the latter firms argued that labour was more expensive than capital because, being a subsidiary of a UK multinational corporation, it gets its machinery as gifts from the parent company. According to the firm, the machinery will have been written off as technically obsolete in Europe.

The other three firms in this category stated that they could not shift production techniques from being capital-intensive to being more labour-intensive because labour was argued to be more expensive than capital equipment, even with the sustained real depreciation of the Zimbabwe dollar.

The views of these three firms regarding labour costs were, however, not shared by the majority of the firms surveyed who argued that they often increased wages and salaries by rates that were higher than those stipulated by government in its bid to control inflation, particularly before the introduction of free collective bargaining in 1990 (see Kanyenze, in this volume). The overwhelming evidence from most of the firms revealed that they did not want to increase employment substantially because of the security of employment regulations embodied in the Labour Relations Act (Fallon and Lucas, 1991). In fact, 20 per cent of the firms surveyed stated that they had resorted to employing 'quasi-permanent' contract workers in a bid to beat these regulations. All the firms welcomed the introduction of flexibility in the labour market during the 1990–95 SAP.

The firms that stated that the cost of imported capital rose faster than the cost of labour gave additional reasons for not substituting labour for capital in production, as shown in Table 3.4.

Just over 41 per cent argued that it was technically impossible to shift towards more labour-intensive techniques. However, all the firms in this category appear to have been referring to their central production processes. Tours of the firms' premises to inspect the level of mechanisation revealed that in most auxiliary jobs, such as moving inputs and outputs around the factory, cleaning, security, and so on, where there is a much wider choice of techniques, they were using labour-intensive techniques.

Of the remaining 17 firms, 11 stated that they were already labour-intensive. If all manufacturing were to be characterised by the five basic operations identified by Pack (1976): material receiving, processing, material handling among processes, packaging, and storage of finished products, then from the survey of the 11 firms in this category, it can be concluded that they all employed people to do most of the jobs except the processing stage.

Finally, six firms stated that even though the continued depreciation of the Zimbabwe dollar had led to a higher increase in the cost of imported capital than in the cost of labour, they did not shift production techniques because this would have led to a decline in the quality of their products. The firms went on to argue that the decline in the quality of their products would have resulted in a fall in their exports as they all stated that international competitiveness depended not only on price, but also on quality.

Table 3.4   Additional reasons for not shifting from capital to labour in production

Reason	Frequency	Percentage
Technically impossible	12	41.4
Already labour intensive	11	37.9
Fall in quality of products	6	20.7
Total	29	100.0

Source: Direct firm information.

Only one firm, a TV manufacturer, said that it had adjusted to using more labour-intensive techniques following the sustained real depreciation of the Zimbabwe dollar.

Given that some firms are naturally more capital-intensive than others and given also that such firms may find it difficult to increase employment levels even if the incentives exist to do so, it became necessary to check whether more labour-intensive firms increased employment faster than capital-intensive firms. Tests using Spearman's rank correlation coefficient before and during the period of the sustained real depreciation of the Zimbabwe dollar showed only a weak correlation between growth in employment and labour intensity.

The implication of these findings is that real exchange rate depreciation does not necessarily result in the adoption of labour-intensive techniques because the choice of production techniques is influenced by factors other than factor cost considerations. Most importantly, the fact that most firms did not increase employment levels because of strict labour regulations on dismissals implies that some liberalisation of the tight dismissal regulations was necessary for exchange rate depreciation to result in more employment.

Real Exchange Rate Depreciation and Sourcing of Inputs

Ideally, when the real exchange rate depreciates, the choice open to firms with regard to sourcing of consumable inputs, *ought to be* between tradable and non-tradable goods (Steel and Webster, 1991). This is because a real exchange rate depreciation results in an increase in the price of all tradable relative to non-tradable inputs. However, in practice, the main choice that has been emphasised in the literature has been that between imported and domestically sourced inputs (Bird, 1983; World Bank, 1989). To test this hypothesis, only firm-level evidence was used since, at the aggregate level, data on imports are not disaggregated by end use. Three methods were used to test the hypothesis.

Changes of Products within Firms

Of the 38 firms surveyed, only two did not directly import some of their inputs. The other 36 firms reported that the prices of imported inputs rose faster than those of domestically-sourced inputs following the sustained real depreciation of the Zimbabwe dollar. Of these firms, 11 stated that they changed their products during the period under consideration. However, only one large firm that produces a wide range of aluminium products stated that it introduced copper products in 1987 as a direct result of the depreciation of the Zimbabwe dollar. According to the firm, the declining purchasing power of the Zimbabwe dollar encouraged it to introduce copper products in order to '... offset the vulnerability of profit from the aluminium business to foreign exchange constraints'.[9] The other ten firms in this category, especially the textile firms, argued that they introduced new products to meet changing demand arising from changes in consumer tastes.[10]

The majority of the firms (69.4 per cent) did not report any changes in products (except in terms of improving quality) following the real depreciation of the Zimbabwe dollar.

Reduction of Imported Inputs within Firms

Of the 36 firms that directly imported some of their consumable inputs, the large majority (32) argued that they could not shift to domestically sourced inputs because there were no local substitutes for imported inputs (Table 3.5). They argued that the absolute shortage of foreign exchange during and after UDI had forced them to adjust to the minimal necessary imports for which there were no local substitutes so that when the real exchange rate depreciated, no further adjustments were made.

Two firms argued that they did not shift to sourcing inputs locally because this would have lowered the quality of their products leading to a fall in exports.

Only two large firms argued that they were forced to look for local substitutes mainly because of the depreciation of the Zimbabwe dollar. One of the firms, which is a large parastatal producing steel and steel products, realised a significant reduction in the proportion of the value of imported inputs to output ratio from 72.5 per cent in 1983 to 31.4 per cent by 1991. According to the firm, the items that are still being imported have no local substitutes, especially refractory bricks used to line the blast furnaces, and rollers for the mills. The other firm, which is also a parastatal producing industrial minerals, recorded a significant reduction in the proportion of the value of imported inputs to output ratio from 10.3 per cent in 1986 to 3.3 per cent by 1991. Both these firms which adjusted to real exchange rate depreciation by using more local inputs may not have adjusted earlier to the absolute shortage of foreign exchange, because, being parastatals, they might have had privileged access under the administration of exchange controls and import licensing.

Table 3.5 Summary of reasons for not shifting

Reason	Frequency	Percentage
Lower quality of products	2	6.3
No local substitutes	32	93.7
Total	34	100.0

Source: Direct firm information.

Import-intensive versus local content-intensive firms

In the short- to medium-term, one would expect more local content-intensive firms to do better than those that rely heavily on imported inputs, following a real exchange rate depreciation. This hypothesis was tested using Spearman's rank correlation coefficients to determine whether there was any negative association between import-intensity and profitability.

From the results, local content-intensive firms did not appear to have done better than import-intensive firms following the real depreciation of the Zimbabwe dollar. Not only were the signs inconsistent with *a priori* expectations, but the association was not statistically significant. The main reason for this was that firms were allowed to pass on any cost increases because price controls were largely administered on a cost-plus basis. The fact that imports of finished products were limited by extensive restrictions meant that consumers had little choice but to buy the goods at the higher domestic prices.

These results imply that real exchange rate depreciation does not necessarily result in a reorientation of production away from imported inputs, particularly in situations where foreign exchange has been rationed because of scarcity.

Responsiveness of Exports to Exchange Rate Depreciation

Aggregate Level

Using a simultaneous equation model of the demand for and supply of manufactured exports, this research established that the demand for Zimbabwe's manufactured exports was positively influenced by growth in the importing countries.[11] However, contrary to theoretical expectations, the volume of Zimbabwe's manufactured exports demanded was found to be positively associated with an increase in prices of Zimbabwe's manufactured exports relative to world prices of similar goods. Experiments with the real exchange rate in place of the relative price variable also yielded a positive association between exchange rate appreciation and increased demand for manufactured exports. Three main reasons can be advanced to explain this apparent paradox.

Firstly, it may reflect the fact that Zimbabwe's manufactured exports, especially to the regional markets, were price inelastic with regard to demand because of better quality and reliable after sales services (see also Riddell, 1990).

Secondly, the existence of various export incentives before and after independence may help to explain why real exports rose while export prices were also rising. Although export prices recorded in official statistics include incentives, the prices actually received by the firms from customers exclude these incentives (Davies, 1991), since they are paid retrospectively. In the event, even though 'official' export prices might have shown an upward trend, the actual prices paid by customers might have been falling relative to world prices, thereby boosting demand.

Finally, the existence of barter deals in the 1980s, mainly with socialist countries, may help to explain why real manufactured exports rose even though export prices were also rising relative to world prices. According to the then Minister of Trade and Commerce in 1987, about 25 per cent of Zimbabwe's trade was being conducted through barter deals (EIU No. 2 – 1987). Since it is difficult to compute the exact prices of such deals, the official price data exclude such prices, but include volume figures.

With regard to supply, it was established that real exchange rate depreciation resulted in an increase in the volume of goods supplied to the export market. Furthermore, it was found that an increase in manufacturing output resulted in more being supplied to the export market. Surprisingly, however, experiments with the dummy variable to take account of the structural changes after independence did not result in any significant improvement in the results.

Firm-level Evidence

Of the 38 firms surveyed, 29 exported a proportion of their output by 1991 with the remainder concentrating wholly on supplying the domestic market. In order to analyse the responsiveness of exports to exchange rate depreciation at the firm-level, the relationship between export and domestic prices of similar goods was analysed. Table 3.6 summarises the major findings.

Domestic prices greater than export prices   About 72 per cent of the exporting firms argued that despite the real exchange rate depreciation, domestic prices were always greater than export prices (Table 3.6). All the firms in this category stated that they exported mainly to get access to more foreign exchange through the different export incentive schemes which were directly linked to export earnings.

In addition to domestic prices being greater than export prices, the firms argued that there were other factors that constrained export growth. Table 3.7 summarises the major findings.

Table 3.6   Export versus domestic prices of manufactured goods

Description	Frequency	Percentage
Export < domestic prices	21	72.4
Export > domestic prices	5	17.2
Export = domestic prices	3	10.3
Total	29	100.0

Source: Direct firm information.

Table 3.7   Reasons for low exports

Reason	Cases	Percentage
Marketing problems	8	30.1
Low demand for goods	5	23.8
Poor support services	5	23.8
High transport costs	3	14.3
Total	21	100.0

Source: Direct firm information.

The existence of these other constraints to exporting implies that exchange rate depreciation is a necessary, but not sufficient condition for expanding exports.

Export prices greater than domestic prices   Five out of the 29 exporting firms argued that export prices were generally greater than domestic prices of similar goods. Notwithstanding this, a number of reasons were given for not increasing exports during the period under review. Two firms said they could not increase the supply of export products mainly because of foreign exchange shortages needed to purchase imported inputs. Although two of the remaining three firms argued that they could not expand exports because of high domestic demand as well as stiff competition in foreign markets, it is inconceivable that they failed to export more given higher export prices. Furthermore, they could have met competition by reducing their export prices.

Finally, the fifth firm, which mines coal and produces coke, argued that export prices were greater than domestic prices, not because of the depreciation of the Zimbabwe dollar, but because of government decree as per the Coal Price Agreement (CPA) of 1953, which has been renewed from time to time until 1995. According to the CPA, the company could not export its products at prices which were below domestic prices of similar goods. However, even domestic prices of coal and coke had to be approved by government.

In light of the price control constraint faced by the firm on the domestic market, one would expect it to have increased export volumes given that any profits arising from export sales, which did not exceed 5 per cent of the capital employed, could be retained without being included in the calculation of domestic prices. However, the firm pointed to a number of constraints. Firstly, the unreliability of the national railways of Zimbabwe (NRZ) in moving stocks of coal, particularly during the latter half of the 1980s (Kunaka, 1991), was argued to be a major constraint on the firm's exports. Secondly, the ability of potential customers to pay for the company's products was highlighted as a major problem limiting exports, especially to Zaire which was said to be the firm's main export customer for coke.

Domestic prices equal to export prices   Three firms stated that export prices were equal to domestic prices. Of these, one firm that manufactures ceramic products stated that it faced constraints in the form of high transport costs as well as poor packaging materials. Consequently, by 1991, it only exported 10 per cent of its total output, with the rest being sold on the local market. All the firms in this category argued that they exported their products because they wanted to get access to more foreign exchange through the export incentive schemes.

From the evidence assembled here, it would appear that the balance of trade incentives in Zimbabwe remained in favour of the domestic market, with manufactured exports increasing mainly because of the introduction of export incentives. However, more work still needs to be done to determine the extent to which the real depreciation of the Zimbabwe dollar reduced the 'anti-export bias' implicit in the ISI strategy pursued by Zimbabwe before and after independence.

Direction of Exports

One would expect more goods to be exported to those markets against which the domestic currency has depreciated most and less to markets against which it has appreciated. To test this hypothesis, a Spearman's rank correlation coefficient was computed to determine whether there existed a negative and significant association between depreciations in Zimbabwe's real bilateral exchange rates and growth in its real manufactured exports to these markets. Not only was the sign inconsistent with *a priori* expectations, but the association was also not significant at the conventional 5 per cent level. From this analysis, it can be concluded that the direction of Zimbabwe's manufactured exports was influenced by factors such as political relations, especially with the USA, trade agreements with South Africa and Botswana which are subject to frequent disruptions, and growth in importing countries, rather than movements in real bilateral exchange rates.[12]

The results discussed above show that the majority of firms realised higher returns on the domestic market than on export markets, implying that some liberalisation of imports so as to equate domestic prices with import prices of similar goods was necessary. However, as argued above, such a strategy needs to be implemented with care since it may lead to deindustrialisation and a dissipation of the accumulated base of past learning. What may be politically feasible is to encourage competition in the domestic market by encouraging investment in the production of goods that are already produced domestically as well as forcing the firms to export early by setting targets as was the case in South Korea (UNCTAD, 1992). Furthermore, the existence of other constraints to exporting implies that the government can help by setting up some support services in line with the experiences of South Korea (Lall, 1993).[13]

Real Exchange Rate Depreciation and Investment

Aggregate Level

Regression analysis showed that a real depreciation of the exchange rate had a negative effect on aggregate investment in Zimbabwe's manufacturing sector between 1970 and 1988. The results also showed that demand was a major determinant of investment.[14] Interestingly, both real domestic credit and real lending rates did not appear to have significantly influenced investment during the period under review. Such a finding is consistent with the fact that investment in Zimbabwe did not increase even though the financial market was characterised by excess liquidity, especially during the latter half of the 1980s.

The research then tested whether the real depreciation of the Zimbabwe dollar, by raising the price of imported capital equipment, resulted in an increase in the efficiency of use of capital in the manufacturing sector as a whole, using the incremental capital–output ratios (ICORs) (Reddaway, 1962; Drabu, 1992). From such analysis, a secular decline in the ICORs would, *ceteris paribus*, reflect a consistent improvement in the use of capital, while an increase would reflect an inefficient use of capital.

For the purposes of assessing the relationship between the growth of output and investment, the ideal form of capital–output ratio is a lagged ICOR (Drabu, 1992). In this study, therefore, ICORs were obtained by relating yearly real investment to the change in real manufacturing value added (MVA) with one year production lag.

Table 3.8 reports the ICORs for Zimbabwe's manufacturing sector between 1980 and 1988 (the latest date for which data are available). The ICORs have been extremely erratic. Indeed, they were negative in three of the eight years for

Table 3.8   ICORs for the manufacturing sector

Year	Change in real MVA (Z$ mn)	Real Investment (Z$ mn)	ICOR
1980	–	123	–
1981	37.5	179	3.28
1982	−92.9	135	−1.93
1983	118.9	121	1.14
1984	−52.7	88	−2.30
1985	58.7	74	1.50
1986	65.7	112	1.13
1987	−10.7	139	−10.47
1988	207.1	170	0.67

Source: Raw data from CSO, *Census of Production* (various).

which data are available, implying that, *ceteris paribus*, investment in the years preceding the negative ICORs yielded negative value added in the manufacturing sector. On closer analysis, however, there are two main reasons that can be advanced to explain this.

Firstly, the investment figures reported in the table are gross rather than net of replacements. Yet following the logic of the functional relationship underlying the ICOR as a measure of investment required to generate a unit increase in value added, it should be calculated on a net basis (Drabu, 1992). Thus, much of the investment went towards replacing obsolete equipment rather than to expanding capacity.

Secondly, during the period under review, other things did not remain constant. The periods of negative growth rates in MVA coincided with years of intense balance of payments crises which witnessed substantial cuts in foreign exchange allocations. Additionally, 1982–84 and 1987 were years of droughts which reduced manufacturing inputs.

Despite this, in periods when the ICORs were positive, they appear to be low, implying that capital was efficiently used in Zimbabwe's manufacturing sector. However, this efficient use of capital may have been necessitated by the absolute scarcity of foreign exchange during and after UDI rather than its cost during the 1980s. Nevertheless, the data are inadequate for deciding whether ICORs decreased after 1985.

Firm-level Evidence

Investing firms: reasons given   Of the 38 firms surveyed, 60.5 per cent undertook some investment projects between 1980 and 1991. All the investing firms stated that they imported the bulk of their capital equipment, mostly from OECD economies. All the firms said that they could have invested more had the Zimbabwe dollar not declined as it did during the period under consideration. However, the firms gave a number of reasons why they invested during this period.

As shown in Table 3.9, 47.8 per cent stated that they undertook expansion projects during the period under review. The overwhelming reason given for this was an increase in demand. Six of the firms in this category experienced increased demand from both the domestic and foreign markets. The increase in foreign demand may be attributed to the real depreciation of the Zimbabwe dollar. Of the remaining five firms, three, which produce tradable goods used in the construction industry, stated that the upturn in the construction industry during the second half of the 1980s led to an increase in domestic demand for their products. Since construction is conventionally classified as a non-tradable activity whose price should, by definition, fall following a real exchange rate depreciation, the increase in domestic demand for the firms' tradable goods can therefore be described as having been derived from the increase in demand from

Table 3.9   Main reasons for investing

Reason	Frequency	Percentage
Expansion	11	47.8
Replacing old equipment	12	52.2
Total	23	100.0

Source: Direct firm information.

construction whose relative price had fallen following the decline in the value of the Zimbabwe dollar.

The remaining two firms in this category gave other reasons for expanding capacity during the period under review. One of the firms argued that it expanded capacity because it had to cope with increased delivery of cotton especially from communal areas. Although the firm argued that there was no relationship between such investment and the real exchange rate depreciation, it is possible that the increase in the supply of raw cotton (which is a tradable good) may have arisen, in part, from the sustained real depreciation of the Zimbabwe dollar, particularly after 1985.

The other firm, which produces fabric, yarn and blankets, stated that its philosophy has always been to increase capacity. Although the firm tried to rationalise this by arguing that much of the investment went towards replacing old equipment, it is possible that in a situation where it is more difficult to obtain foreign exchange for spare parts and other imported inputs than it is to obtain foreign exchange to expand capacity, especially if the project saves foreign exchange, there is an incentive for the firms to expand capacity over and above ordinary requirements to ensure that output is maximised.

As shown in Table 3.9, the majority of the investing firms (52.4 per cent) stated that they invested in order to replace obsolete plant and equipment.

Non-investing firms: reasons quoted   As shown in Table 3.10, the majority of the non-investing firms (46.7 per cent) stated that they did not undertake investment because of a shortage of foreign exchange during the period under review. This is because 14 of the 15 firms depended on imported capital, with only one sourcing machinery locally. Additionally, all the 15 firms depended on some imported inputs either directly or indirectly via domestic suppliers. In the event, the absolute shortage of foreign exchange needed to import the necessary plant and equipment and other imported inputs, together with the depreciation of the Zimbabwe dollar during the 1980s forced the firms to postpone investment.

Table 3.10   Reasons for not investing

Reason	Frequency	Proportion (%)
Foreign exchange shortages	7	46.7
Labour regulations	4	26.6
Investment licensing	2	13.3
Price controls	1	6.7
Other	1	6.7
Total	15	100.

Source: Direct firm information.

Labour regulations introduced in 1980, particularly as they pertained to the firing of workers, came second as a major deterrent to investment. According to these measures, no firm could dismiss workers without obtaining permission from the Minister of Labour, Manpower Planning and Social Welfare (see Kanyenze, in this volume). Investment licensing came third as a major constraint to investment. Approvals often took a very long time because of the large number of committees involved in the approval of such investments.

Surprisingly, however, only one firm referred to price controls as the main constraint on investment. According to this firm, price controls often resulted in losses which discouraged it from investing. However, the views of this firm were not shared by the rest of the firms who blamed government bureaucratic delays in awarding price increases as the main constraint rather than price control *per se*. This may be because most price controls tended to be enforced on a cost-plus basis, thereby allowing firms to realise a return even in cases where costs were high due to inefficiencies. The existence of import controls ensured that consumers continued to purchase the goods at the higher prices compared to imports. Finally, one firm, established in 1986, stated that it did not invest because it was too new to undertake any further investment.

The implication of these findings is that real exchange rate depreciation does not necessarily result in an increase in investment, particularly if such a policy is not accompanied by reductions in regulations pertaining to factor and product markets.

IV   OVERALL CONCLUSION

From the above findings, it is clear that real exchange rate depreciation is a necessary but not sufficient component of an industrial strategy designed to enhance international competitiveness. This is because firstly, most firms had already adjusted to the absolute shortage of foreign exchange so that when the real exchange rate depreciated, there was little structural adjustment made.

Secondly, the theoretical benefits deriving from a real exchange rate depreciation are dependent on the existence of competitive factor and product markets. Once this assumption is relaxed, the predicted results may not hold. In the case of Zimbabwe, the existence of factor and product market distortions, investment licensing and the haphazard nature of protection arising from the foreign exchange allocation system meant that real exchange rate depreciation alone could not be relied on to increase industrial competitiveness. Given the pervasiveness of distortions in Zimbabwe, piecemeal attempts to address such distortions by depreciating the exchange rate were not sufficient to raise the competitiveness of the manufacturing sector.

Notes

1. For a fuller discussion of the issues raised here, refer to Muzulu (1993), on which this chapter is based.
2. There is considerable disagreement regarding the extent to which the programme was home-grown (see Stoneman, 1988). However, the fact that an IMF stand-by arrangement was agreed upon just three years after independence points to the view that the programme might have been influenced by the Bretton Woods institutions. The other elements of the stabilisation programme are not discussed here. For more details see Muzulu (1993) and Kanyenze (forthcoming). See also Davies, Sanders and Shaw (1992).
3. See *The Herald*, 6 May 1992.
4. Note that this can be true by definition especially if the real exchange rate is defined as a relative price of tradable to non-tradable goods (Edwards and Ng, 1985).
5. In view of the fact that government and other services sub-sectors do not necessarily respond to market signals, the analysis that follows relates to the private sector.
6. Refer to Muzulu (1993) for methodological details.
7. Due to limited resources, this study concentrated on evaluating actual technologies used by firms rather than potential techniques.
8. Additionally, the decline in the capital–labour ratio may also reflect problems in the measurement of capital stock since it consists of items of different vintages each of which need not be comprising homogeneous units, but which are depreciating in individual patterns. Although the PIM method used expresses all the past additions to the capital stock in terms of base year prices, the fact that the age structure of the assets for each year is not known can be a source of a degree of error in the estimates (Drabu, 1992). However, the non-marginal nature of the decline in capital stock clearly shows that it cannot be wholly attributed to a

statistical artefact. Kaplinsky and Posthuma (forthcoming) come to the same conclusion.

9. The statement was reported in the firm's 1986 Annual Report. Copper is produced locally while aluminium is imported.

10. Although changing consumer tastes may result from changing relative prices following an exchange rate depreciation, the fact that textiles are tradable goods implies that their prices rose with the depreciation of the exchange rate. Textiles are subject to frequent changes in fashion and tastes which have little to do with exchange rate changes.

11. See Muzulu (1993), particularly Chapter 8.

12. See also part on aggregate level above.

13. For an expansion on this point, see Muzulu (1993), especially Chapter 10.

14. Such a finding is consistent with previous studies (Hawkins *et al.*, 1988; Dailami and Walton, 1989).

References

Bird, G. (1983) 'Should Developing Countries use Currency depreciation as a Tool of Balance of Payments Adjustment? A Review of the Theory, Evidence and a guide for the Policy Maker', *Journal of Development Studies*, 19 (4).

Chhibber, A. and N. Shafik, (1990) 'Does Devaluation Hurt Private Investment? The Indonesian Case', *Policy, Research and External Affairs Working Paper*, WPS 418 (World Bank).

Crockett, A.D. (1981) 'Stabilisation Policies in Developing Countries: Some Policy Considerations', *IMF Staff Papers*, 28 (1).

Dailami, M. and M. Walton (1989) 'Private Investment, Government Policy, and Foreign Capital in Zimbabwe', *Policy, Research and External Affairs Working Paper*, WPS 248 (World Bank).

Davies, R. (1991) 'Trade, Trade Management and Development in Zimbabwe', in J.H. Frimpong-Ansah, S.M.R. Kanbur and P. Svedberg (eds), *Trade and Development in Sub-Saharan Africa* (Manchester: Manchester University Press).

Davies, R., D. Sanders and T. Shaw (1992) 'Liberalisation for Development: Zimbabwe's Adjustment without the Fund', in G.A. Cornia, R. van der Hoeven and T. Mkandawire (eds), *Africa's Recovery in the 1990s: From Stagnation and Adjustment to Human Development* (New York: St. Martin's Press).

Demery, L. and T. Addison (1988), 'Adjustment and Income Distribution: The Role of Labour Markets', *University of Warwick Development Economics Research Centre Discussion Paper*, 81.

Drabu, H.A., (1992) 'Capital to Output Ratios and Growth: Conceptual Issues and Empirical Evidence', in A. Ghosh, K.K. Subrahmanian, M. Eapen and H.A. Drabu (eds), *Indian Industrialisation: Structure and Policy Issues* (Delhi: Oxford University Press).

Durevall, D. (1989) 'Trade Policy, Employment and Equity in Zimbabwe', *SIDA Macroeconomic Studies*, 6, Stockholm.

Economist Intelligence Unit (EIU), *Zimbabwe, Malawi: Country Reports* (Various).

Edwards, S. and F. Ng (1985) 'Trends in Real Exchange Rate Behaviour in Selected Developing Countries', *World Bank Country Programs Department Discussion Paper*, 16.

Fallon, P.R. and R.E.B. Lucas (1991) 'The Impact of Changes in Job Security Regulation in India and Zimbabwe', *The World Bank Observer*, 5 (3).

Ffrench-Davis, R. and R. Madrid (1992) 'Trade Liberalisation in Chile: Experiences and Prospects', *UNCTAD Trade Policy Series*, 1

Goldstein, M. (1986) 'The Global Effects of Fund-Supported Adjustment Programs', *IMF Occasional Paper*, 42.

Government of Zimbabwe (1991a) *Zimbabwe: A Framework for Economic Reform (1991–95)* (Harare: Government Printer).

Government of Zimbabwe (1991b) *The Promotion Of Investment: Policy and Regulations* (Harare: Government Printer).

Government of Zimbabwe (1991c) *Second Five-year National Development Plan (1991–1995)* (Harare: Government Printer).

Green, R.H. and X. Kadhani (1986) 'Zimbabwe: Transition to Economic Crisis: Retrospect and Prospect', *World Development*, 14(8).

Hawkins, A.M, P.J. McBurney, M.A. Hadur and W. Clantanoff (1988) *Formal Sector Employment Demand Conditions in Zimbabwe* (Harare: University of Zimbabwe).

Johnson, O.E.G. (1987) 'Currency Depreciation and Export Expansion', *Finance and Development*, 24(1).

Kanyenze, G. (forthcoming) 'The Impact of Economic Stabilisation on the Wage Structure in Zimbabwe', DPhil Thesis (University of Sussex, Brighton: Unpublished).

Kaplinsky, R. and Posthuma, A. (forthcoming) *Organisational Change in Zimbabwean Manufacturing* (Maastricht: UN University).

Kunaka, C. (1991) 'The Railways and the Zimbabwe Coal Crisis of the late 1980s', *Geographical Journal of Zimbabwe*, 22.

Lall, S. (1993) 'Trade Policies for Development: A Policy Prescription for Africa', *Development Policy Review*, 11.

Moyana, K.J. (1991) 'Framework for Economic Reform in Zimbabwe (1991–1995)', Paper presented at the ICEG Conference, Nairobi, October 2–5.

Muzulu, J. (1993) 'Real Exchange Rate Depreciation and Structural Adjustment: The Case of the Manufacturing Sector in Zimbabwe (1980–1991)', DPhil Thesis (University of Sussex, Brighton: Unpublished).

Pack, H. (1976) 'The Substitution of Labour for Capital in Kenyan Manufacturing', *Economic Journal*, 86 (341).

Reddaway, W.B. (1962) *The Development of the Indian Economy* (London: George Allen & Unwin Ltd).

Riddell, R. (1990) 'Zimbabwe', in Riddell (ed.), *Manufacturing Africa* (London: James Currey).

Serven, L. and A. Solimano (1991) 'Adjustment Policies and Investment Performance in Developing Countries: Theory, Country Experiences, and Policy Implications', *Policy, Research, and External Affairs Working Papers*, WPS 606 (World Bank).

Steel, W.F. and L.M. Webster (1991) 'Small Enterprise under Adjustment in Ghana', *Industry and Finance Series*, World Bank Technical Paper, 138.

Stoneman, C. (1988) 'The Economy: Recognising the Reality', in Stoneman (ed.), *Zimbabwe's Prospects* (London: Macmillan)

Thomas, V. (1989) 'Developing Country Experience in Trade Reform', *Policy, Planning and Research Working Paper*, WPS 295 (World Bank).

UNCTAD (1992) *Trade and Development Report* (New York: UN).

UNIDO (1986) *The Manufacturing Sector in Zimbabwe* (Vienna: UNIDO).

Ward, M. (1976) *The Measurement of Capital: The Methodology of Capital Stock Estimates in OECD Countries* (Paris: OECD).

World Bank (1981) *Accelerated Development in Sub-Saharan Africa: An Agenda for Action* (Washington DC: World Bank).

World Bank (1989) *Sub-Saharan Africa: From Crisis to Sustained Growth* (Washington DC: World Bank).

World Bank (1990) *Making Adjustment Work for the Poor: A Framework for Policy Reform in Africa* (Washington DC: World Bank).

World Bank (1992) *World Bank Support for Industrialisation in Korea, India, and Indonesia* (Washington DC: Operations Department, World Bank).

4 The Impact of Economic Stabilisation on the Wage Structure in Zimbabwe: 1980–90

Godfrey Kanyenze

I   INTRODUCTION: THE ROLE OF LABOUR MARKETS DURING PERIODS OF ADJUSTMENT

In the introductory chapter, Harvey alluded to the pre-eminence of structural adjustment programmes in sub-Saharan Africa during the 1980s. In these ortho-dox adjustment programmes, the labour market is assigned a central role. This is so '...since the achievement of a real devaluation demands both real wage flex-ibility and intersectoral labour mobility' (Fallon and Riveros, 1989: 1).

What is important therefore is to examine what is being asked of labour markets during periods of adjustment.[1] At the heart of structural adjustment pro-grammes, is the desire to shift the composition of national output towards the production of tradable goods (both exportables and importables). To achieve this, such programmes usually include a policy of exchange rate depreciation as part of the overall package of reforms. A real depreciation of the exchange rate is expected to shift relative prices in favour of the tradable goods sector. Consequently, the real product wage in the tradable goods sector relative to that in the non-tradable goods sector is expected to fall, resulting in the former sector becoming more profitable than the latter.[2] Assuming other things remain con-stant, the change in the rate of growth of output and employment in the tradable goods sector is expected to be higher than that in the non-tradable goods sector. This shift to tradable goods requires labour mobility, as does expansion of labour-intensive production relative to import-intensive production, and these changes should favour employment of unskilled labour.

Within this theoretical framework, 'flexibility' or 'efficiency' of the labour market is measured in terms of the speed with which quantities (labour) adjust to changes in prices (real wages) [OECD, 1986; Horton *et al.*, 1991]. In this regard, the IMF laments the slow progress that has been made in dismantling labour market regulations, arguing that '...the persistence of high unemployment in a large number of countries remains a visible indication of the lack of progress in increasing the flexibility of labour markets' (1993: 39).

Some critics, however, associate flexibility with employment and income insecurity [Standing and Tokman (eds.), 1991]. In that sense, labour market flexibility may be judged to be a regrettable term '... because to be flexible is perceived as a virtue and it is not clear that many aspects of what is commonly meant by labour flexibility are desirable' (Standing, 1986: 1).

The efficiency of the labour market in Zimbabwe is examined in this chapter, namely, whether real wages fell following devaluation, whether labour shifted to the tradable goods sector, and the impact on security of employment and income.

II EXCHANGE RATE POLICY IN ZIMBABWE

The stabilisation measures adopted following the balance of payments crisis of the early 1980s were conventional. There was a 20 per cent devaluation of the Z\$ in December 1982 and subsequent depreciation of the exchange rate, which, after a delay, resulted in real depreciation.

Muzulu (in this book), has shown that following the 20 per cent devaluation of December 1982, the real exchange rate appreciated during the period 1983–4.[3] After 1985, a consistent real depreciation of the exchange rate was achieved. This contrasts with the Latin American experience, where 'distortions' are reported as having thwarted the effectiveness of devaluation (Lopez and Riveros, 1990).

However, the use of the exchange rate as an instrument for stabilisation or adjustment was not accompanied by a liberalisation of the trade regime and the removal of price controls in the period under review, as is often the case in orthodox programmes. The option of liberalising trade and foreign exchange allocation was rejected by the Zimbabwean government at that time.[4]

Despite government intervention, Zimbabwe's industrial sector has been found to be much more efficient than expected. The World Bank (1987, 1985) was surprised at the level of efficiency in the economy and praised government for its prudent and stable management of the economy (Lehman, 1990). Chhibber *et al.* observe that although widespread price controls, tight foreign exchange rationing and other controls exist in Zimbabwe '...these are only apparent, and empirical investigation reveals a quite well-behaved pattern of relationships' (1989: 6). This chapter examines the extent to which they were right, with reference to the labour market.

III THE WAGE STRUCTURE AND THE ROLE OF INSTITUTIONAL FORCES IN ITS DETERMINATION

Conventional stabilisation programmes, generally advocate a wage restraint policy. The underlying argument is that wages are already 'too high' and as such reductions can be sustained without necessarily compromising long-term stability and macroeconomic efficiency (Lindauer *et al.*, 1988). Thus, within this framework, the World Bank (1981: 92–3) argued that:

> African wages are high compared with those of Asia...Higher African wages reflect... government policy, which in many countries sets industrial wages above the level they would otherwise be. African labour productivity also tends to compare unfavourably with many other parts of the world.

This part examines the role of institutional forces in wage determination and links this analysis to the micro and macro economic implications of the stabilisation programme adopted at the end of 1982. Even though Zimbabwe's stabilisation programme was a heterodox one, its wage restraint aspect, which focused on reducing public and private sector expenditure, and containing inflation, had orthodox overtones. Of particular importance therefore, is to assess the extent to which government intervention, as is often alleged, pushed wages above their historical trend.

Government's Wages Policy After Independence

Following independence in 1980, the new government intervened extensively in the labour market. The basis of this intervention was that the trade unions were, at independence, weak, and hence collective bargaining would not be an effective mechanism for improving working conditions. The motives for government intervention were: i) to promote security of employment; ii) to raise the standard of living of the people and, in particular, the lowly paid; iii) to narrow income differentials and iv) to reduce inflationary pressures, especially after 1982 (GOZ, 1986: 90).

The central place accorded incomes policy is evident from the fact that a commission of inquiry, with broad terms of reference, was constituted in September 1980 to look into incomes, prices and conditions of service, with a view to correcting inherited anomalies. Earlier on, government had promulgated the Minimum Wages Act of 1980, and to forestall any unwarranted retrenchments, the Employment Act of 1980.[5] The latter Act effectively took away the right to fire from employers and vested it instead in the Minister of Labour who, on the basis of recommendations from the tripartite Retrenchment Committee, would grant or refuse to accede to a request to lay off workers. In order to discourage resort to employing casual labour as a way round the Employment Act provisions, the rate at which such employees were remunerated was set at double that for permanent workers. Maximum salary levels beyond which no pay increment was allowed were also determined by government as from 1981.

It was against the background of the findings of the Riddell Commission that government's wages policy was based. On the basis of the Poverty Datum Line

(PDL) for an average family of six, a father, mother and four children, the 'ideal' target income paths were plotted for urban and rural-based workers.[6] It was then recommended that the target for wage policy be to reach 90 per cent of the PDL by mid-1984, with a two-tier wage system.[7] The Commissioners appreciated the fact that the resulting wage increases were unsustainable and therefore suggested that top salaries be frozen until the minimum wage targets were achieved.

Informed by the general findings and recommendations of the Riddell Commission, government adopted a sliding scale mechanism, with those at the bottom of the earnings hierarchy receiving higher percentage increases and vice versa. Ceilings beyond which no increases were granted were also fixed by government.

Three broad periods can be observed in wage setting. The first period, from 1980 to 1985, was characterised by government unilaterally determining wage increases, which were then announced each year on May Day. The second period (covering the years 1986 to 1988), involved some level of consultations, albeit cosmetic, which preceded the announcement of wage reviews. This approach was, in the main, influenced by the promulgation of the Labour Relations Act of 1985 which provided for collective bargaining to take place at three levels, namely, at the national level (through a tripartite Wages and Salaries Advisory Board), at the industry level (through employment boards and employment councils)[8] and at the shop floor/firm level. Most negotiations occurred at the industry level, and it was on the basis of these that the Wages and Salaries Advisory Board would make recommendations to the Minister of Labour.

The third sub-period begins in 1989, and runs up to the time of writing. This sub-period coincides with the adoption of new investment guidelines (1989) marking the beginning of the economic structural adjustment programme. Collective bargaining increasingly became the mechanism through which wage reviews were conducted.

Government Wage Policy and the Wage Structure

The above account has outlined government's minimum wage policy. It is important to examine the trends in wages actually paid in order to explore the extent to which the overall labour costs (total earnings) were flexible. After all it is the overall employment cost with which the employers are concerned.[9] The level of real average annual consumption earnings by sector for selected periods are presented in Table 4.1.

For all sectors taken together, real average annual consumption earnings increased between 1980 and 1982, but declined significantly thereafter. Real average annual consumption earnings were above their 1980 levels in only three sectors namely, agriculture, mining and quarrying, and manufacturing. When the 1990 level is compared with the peak 1982 one, then real consumption earnings are substantially below that level in all sectors.

Table 4.1   Real 1990 average annual earnings as a percentage of
1980 and peak 1982 levels

Sector	% of 1980 level	% of peak 1982 level
Agriculture	130	81
Mining	117	92
Manufacturing	103	91
Electricity	95	91
Construction	77	66
Finance	95	92*
Distribution	84	75
Transport	91	85
Public Administration	61	69**
Domestic	82	73
Other	80	77
Total	103	86

Notes: * 1981 as the peak and ** 1980 as the peak.
Source: Calculated from CSO, *Quarterly Digest of Statistics*.

However, the collapse in real consumption wages experienced elsewhere in
sub-Saharan Africa is not reflected in the case of Zimbabwe (for Zambia, see
Chiwele and Colclough in this book). During the period of real wage expansion,
1980-82, most employers were critical of government's wage policy, arguing that
it discouraged employment creation (RAL Merchant Bank, 1982;[10] Chavunduka
Commission Report, 1982; Makings, 1988). Interestingly, this view changed dramatically during the period after 1982, to one generally sympathetic to the plight
of workers, a view reminiscent of the efficiency wage theory.[11]

RAL Merchant Bank, which had earlier argued that the expansionary wage
policy was 'pricing workers out of jobs', turned the argument around, expressing
concern that the prevailing low wages had created anxieties in the work force
and that '...these problems have been predicted by various commentators as cost
increases have outpaced wage increases and as the quality of life slipped back for
many in the high density areas of the larger towns' (1987: 1). Makings[12] concurs,
arguing further that '...in view of Government's precedent regarding the annual
award of increments, failure to award an increase in 1987 may lead to worker discontent, an increase in industrial relations problems and an associated loss of productivity which may not justify withholding an across-the-board increment'
(1988: 17).

These sentiments, symbolic of the efficiency wage theory, were also echoed by
the Confederation of Zimbabwe Industries (CZI), when Peter Harding of its

Manpower Committee conceded that '...simplistic focus on wages is misleading' arguing instead that '...moderation of nominal wage growth through the process of collective bargaining does not mean that policy should seek generally to hold down real wages' (CZI, 1989: 87).[13]

Indeed wage determination transcends economic issues. It involves questions of political economy. Kadhani and Green observed that '...wage employment policy selection appears to suffer from negative degrees of freedom. Reducing real wages – by holding increases below rises in cost of living – may be inevitable; but because for many workers they are already below [pre-independence] levels, this imposes great political strain and human hardship' (1985: 231).

A wage structure has to fulfil two potentially contradictory roles; it must be internally consistent on the grounds of equity, while at the same time being externally competitive. The official wage policy concentrated on the former, making it difficult for the public sector to retain technical, professional and managerial personnel. The burden of wage restraint fell disproportionately on the public sector (see Table 4.1). The lowest paid civil servants achieved real gains in wages, but those in skilled technical, professional and managerial grades witnessed a substantial erosion of real consumption wages. A marked compression of the wage structure was therefore observed. In the private sector, a different picture emerges. The application of flexible remuneration systems, reinforced by the circumvention of the wage controls, meant that the wage restraint policy was not as effective in the private sector as it was in the public sector (Chhibber *et al.*, 1989; World Bank, 1987). In this case, a dispersion of the wage structure occurred.

Within an environment of critical skill shortages, such a policy of compressing the wage structure can backfire, for it exacerbates the brain-drain to the private from the public sector, whose productivity and efficiency were adversely affected. Enforcing 'tight' wage policies tends to be effective only in the public sector, where the pay structure is based on basic pay. In the private sector, where a more flexible remuneration system applies, controlling one aspect of the earnings structure (in this case basic salaries) triggers adaptive reactions in other forms of remuneration, thus defeating the objective of wage restraint.

In view of government freezing wages at the top, employers responded by 'working around' the legislation. Exemptions from the controls imposed on salary adjustments could only be justified in cases of i) promotions into vacancies; ii) promotion or reward for attaining additional academic qualifications; iii) promotion within advancement schemes; iv) promotion or reward for undertaking the operation of new, specialised services; and v) increases in recognition of increased output and payment of normal annual increments. These exemptions made it possible to pay more to senior managerial employees. Although the penalty for contravening the regulations included a prison term not exceeding one year, this was not implemented.

In addition, private sector employers circumvented the 'tight' wage restraint measures adopted by government through increased recourse to non-salary perks and regrading of employees (World Bank, 1987). The non-salary benefits accruing to the position of permanent secretary in the civil service, amounted to only 13 per cent of those enjoyed by the equivalent private sector position of chief executive in 1991. Such a system imposes the burden of wage restraint disproportionately on civil servants.

Impact of Policy of Compressing Public Sector Wage Differentials

Public sector pay, especially in technical/professional and managerial grades suffered immensely, to the extent that the civil service could not recruit and retain competent staff. Lindauer *et al.* rightly observe that a major weakness of stabilisation-cum-structural adjustment programmes is that they '...have rarely considered the microeconomic implications of government wage and employment decisions on the actual provision of public goods and services' (1988: 2). Medium to longer-term development issues are thus sacrificed on the altar of short-term stabilisation.

The adverse effects of declining morale, work effort, chronic absenteeism, the appearance of 'ghost workers', unfilled vacancies, multiple jobbing or moonlighting, reduced incentives for human capital formation, paucity of complementary inputs required to produce public goods, and corruption are well documented from other countries.[14] The oft-quoted case in this respect is the extreme example from Uganda, where civil servants are reported as having spent only a third or half their normal working time on government duty (Lindauer *et al.*, 1988), the rest of the time being devoted to moonlighting. The Public Salaries Review Commission (1982 – Uganda) established that '...the civil servant had either to survive by lowering his standards of ethics, performance and dutifulness, or remain upright and perish. He chose to survive.'[15] Although the Zimbabwean situation has not necessarily reached the proportions of Uganda, many of the characteristics are already evident, as the findings of the Public Service Review Commission (1989) reveal.

Following independence in 1980, the civil service grew markedly from 45 000 in 1980 to 190 000 by June 1991 (Agere, 1992). The retirement *en masse* of experienced white cadres left behind a young and inexperienced civil service; as the Review Commission found, '...an inexperienced Public Service had to meet a challenge that would have tested a long-established system; there was an inevitable tendency to play safe and refer decisions upward' (Public Service Review Commission Report, *op. cit.*: 10). Add to that political interferences in the implementation of set goals, the extent of which was '...excessive and detrimental to efficiency' (*ibid.*, 11). Corruption and dishonesty were widely raised in the evidence to the Commission. What is particularly worrying is that it is the political echelons of the public service that festered first. The Willowvale scandal did expose the extent of corruption in government. In this respect, Agere[16] notes that '...the unethical behaviour of some leaders not only reduced the morale of many committed people but also negatively influenced others. The values and norms that had been widely respected disintegrated quickly particularly in a society that respects leaders and elders in their communities' (1992: 46). The familiar problems emerge as the Review Commission found:

> Many complaints concerned public servants' absences from their offices or other places of work. It was suggested that they arrive late, go early, take long lunch hours, and conduct private business instead of attending to the public. The complaints also include references to officials engaging in long private telephone calls or tea sessions, while the visitors are waiting, as if the public was an intrusion into the officials' 'private lives'. (*op. cit.*: 14)

Another area of concern was the paucity of complementary inputs required for the effective provision of public services. The Review Commission argued that the focus in resource allocation had been on staffing, such that '...a large proportion of the Public Service is immobilised for relatively long periods of the fiscal year due to the absence of travel funds, materials and equipment to carry out the tasks assigned to them' (*ibid.*: 45). In 1989/90, 41.4 per cent of recurrent expenditure went to salaries, wages and allowances, compared with 33 per cent in 1980/81.

The Commission was highly critical of the lack of proper personnel functionaries within the service, and complained that the absence of clearly defined career development paths tended to discourage the 'high fliers'. With the prevailing short career paths, it was noted one would reach the ceiling fairly early in his/her career, thus discouraging further human capital formation. The grading structure was found to be ad hoc to the extent that '...similar grades may be wide apart in salary terms' (*ibid.*: 80). The creeping in of favouritism and nepotism is said to have exacerbated an already disadvantaging environment, and as the report notes, '...public servants seem to have lost faith in the current performance appraisal system' (*ibid.*: 85) leading to '...very widespread dissatisfaction with current terms and conditions of service' (*ibid.*: 97). Within such an environment, it was extremely difficult for government to retain staff and motivate existing ones. Staff turnover has been extremely high in areas of critical skill shortage such as accounting, electronic data processing and industrial relations.

For instance, the Accountant General is reported to have recruited a third of the accountancy graduates in 1987, but only a year later, half had left. In the Comptroller and Auditor General's office, about 15–20 per cent of the professional staff resigned each year during the period 1987–9. In 1987, 41 per cent of all engineers, architects and geologists working in the public service were expatriates (Public Service Review Commission, *ibid.*). Agere argued that '...it is no longer attractive for the state to appeal to good ideals of commitment and loyalty of civil servants without adequate remuneration. This is more untenable in circumstances or an environment in which the political leadership appears to earn more and acquire better conditions of service for itself' (*op. cit.*: 52).

The Impact of Minimum Wage Policy on the Wage Structure: An Econometric Approach

The impact of government's minimum wage policy on the overall wage structure can also be estimated quantitatively. One such method, used by World Bank (1987) involves predicting real average annual consumption earnings for the period minimum wages were in operation, from their historic trend. The model specification takes the following form:

$$\log (w/p) = a_0 + a_1 t + a_2 t^2 + a_3 \, CYC \tag{1}$$

where: $\log (w/p)$ = real average annual consumption earnings in logarithmic form; t = the linear time trend; t^2 = quadratic time trend; CYC = the deviations of logarithm of real GDP about its quadratic trend.[17]

The deviations of logarithm of real GDP about its quadratic trend (the CYC variable) are derived by storing the residuals obtained from estimating a model of the form:

$$\log (GDP) = b_0 + b_1 t + b_3 t^2 \tag{2}$$

The stored residuals (variable CYC)[18] are then used as a regressor in equation 2. These models were run for all sectors and at aggregate level (except for public sectors) for the period 1955–79. Using this as the historic trend, average real annual consumption wages were forecast for the 1980–90 period using the Time Series Processor (TSP). The predicted values were estimated after correcting for auto correlation (using the Cochrane–Orcutt procedure), and the results, reported as the percentage differences between actual and predicted real annual average consumption wages, are presented in Table 4.2.[19]

As seen from the table, minimum wages had the effect of pushing the earnings structure beyond its historical trend during the period of expansionary minimum wage policy (1980–82). The impact is highest when real minimum wages peaked in 1982, with the differential between actual and predicted real average annual consumption earnings at its widest level in that year.

The table also shows that the influence of minimum wages on the wage structure tended to be much higher in sectors where the unskilled are dominant, and less pronounced where the skill levels are high.[20] For example, in a sector employing predominantly unskilled labour such as agriculture (and particularly so in domestic service), the impact of minimum wages is felt even during the period of wage restraint (from 1983), although the influence diminishes after 1982. On the other hand, in sectors employing predominantly skilled labour, such as the extreme cases of electricity and water, and finance, insurance and real estate, actual wages were lower than predicted wages for the whole period, although the gap narrows to its lowest level in 1982 before widening again thereafter.

Table 4.2   Difference between actual and predicted average annual
real consumption earnings (%)

Sector	1980	1982	1985	1988	1990
Agriculture	5.5	64.1	32.4	20.1	15.1
Mining	9.6	32.2	11.6	0.2	−1.5
Manufacturing	9.9	23.7	12.3	12.3	16.4
Electricity	−2.6	−2.4	−14.7	−18.8	−22.5
Construction	2.4	15.9	−5.7	−23.5	−31.6
Finance	−5.7	−12.9	−28.5	−31.8	−35.1
Distribution	10.5	25.0	11.3	4.2	2.4
Transport	10.3	19.7	−9.4	−2.1	14.6
Domestic	28.3	61.2	53.5	134.8	165.9
Other	4.9	6.3	−14.9	−25.2	−19.9
Total	12.6	29.9	4.3	−1.1	−2.5

Source: Calculated from CSO, *Quarterly Digest of Statistics*.

For all sectors, average annual real consumption earnings were 13 per cent above their predicted level in 1980, rising to a peak 30 per cent differential in 1982. The differential narrows with the inception of the wage restraint policy of 1983, the influence tapering off to a differential of 4 per cent in 1985. Thereafter, predicted real earnings exceeded the actual such that by 1990, the actual was 3 per cent below the predicted value (Figure 4.1).

IV   REAL EXCHANGE RATE DEPRECIATION AND STRUCTURAL SHIFTS IN EMPLOYMENT

In his chapter, Muzulu shows that a sustained depreciation of the Z$ was achieved since 1985. He further shows that following the period of real exchange rate depreciation (post 1985), prices of non-tradable goods relative to those of tradable goods generally moved in line with the real exchange rate, as predicted in theory.[21]

Given then that a favourable adjustment of tradable goods prices occurred following the real depreciation of the exchange rate, the next stage is to check whether this resulted in the predicted shift in resources in favour of the tradable goods sector. In particular, we are interested in checking whether there was a response in employment along the lines predicted by theory. The responsiveness of employment to real exchange rate induced changes in real product earnings, output and profits is discussed below.

Figure 4.1   Trends in actual and predicted real average consumption wages: 1980–90

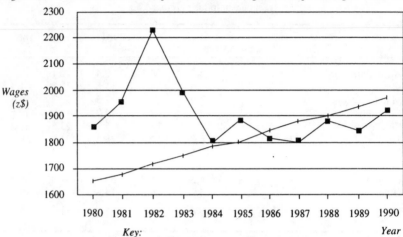

Source: Computed from data from *Quarterly Digest of Statistics*, Central Statistical Office (various issues).

Two approaches are used to examine the responsiveness of changes in employment following the real depreciation of the exchange rate. The first method employed below involves comparing the changes in the growth rate of real product earnings, profits and output and checking whether changes in the growth rate of employment are in the direction postulated in theory. This is essentially a static analysis.

However, given that the predictions of theory only hold when all other things remain constant, an empirical problem arises because in reality these change. In this case, the method used involves comparing the outcome in the tradable and non-tradable goods sectors following the period of sustained real depreciation of the exchange rate with the predictions of theory. Since both the tradable and non-tradable goods sectors operate in the same macroeconomic framework, such an approach minimises the effects of allowing other things to vary. This therefore presents a more reasonable basis for checking whether the potential resource switching process occurred in accordance with theoretical predictions.

More importantly, the response to changing relative prices (and indeed to other policy changes) is likely to be lagged. Such a static approach will not capture the delayed responses. Moreover, classifying sectors into tradable and non-tradable activities is too aggregative and crude. To take care of some of these weaknesses, a regression analysis is used (below) to reinforce the analysis of the following part. However, the problem of determining causality in the relationships remains.

Employment Response in the Tradable and Non-Tradable Goods Sectors: A Before and After Analysis

The overall quantity responses following the real depreciation of the exchange rate in the tradable and non-tradable goods sectors are shown in Table 4.3.[22] Real product earnings, profits and employment changed as predicted by theory; only output reacted perversely. The rate of growth of average real product earnings in the tradable goods sector declined markedly from an average annual rate of growth of 8.5 per cent during the period of real exchange rate appreciation, to a negative average rate of growth of 2.1 per cent during the period of real exchange rate depreciation.

The rate of growth of average real product earnings in the non-tradable goods sector decelerated only slightly, from an average annual growth rate of 1.1 per cent (1981–84) to 0.3 per cent (1985–90). The rate of decline in the growth of average real product earnings of 10.6 percentage points in the tradable goods sector, was very much steeper than that of 0.8 percentage points experienced by the non-tradable goods sector following the real depreciation of the exchange rate. Thus, as predicted in theory, the tradable goods sector experienced a comparative labour cost advantage compared to the non-tradable goods sector during the period of sustained real exchange rate depreciation.

Whereas real output grew at an annual average rate of 1.1 per cent during the before-period (1981–84), its rate of growth accelerated to an annual average rate of 3.8 per cent following the period of sustained real depreciation of the exchange rate. But real output growth in the non-tradable goods sector also increased, from

Table 4.3 Quantity responses in the tradable and non-tradable goods sectors, annual average growth rates (%), 1981–90

| Variable | Tradables | | Non-tradable | |
	1981–84	1985–90	1981–84	1985–90
ARPE	8.5	–2.1	1.1	0.3
Real Output	1.1	3.8	–0.6	4.1
Profits	11.6	16.8	22.4	16.2
Employment	–2.9	1.5	3.0	4.1

Notes: ARPE denotes average real product earnings. Growth rates of profit in the after-period refer to 1985–87.

Source: Calculated from CSO, *Quarterly Digest of Statistics* (various issues).

an annual average rate of -0.6 per cent to 4.1 per cent during the two respective periods, and this improvement was larger than in the tradable goods sector. This contradicts the predictions of theory. Where for instance tradable and non-tradable goods are complements, the responsiveness of production to a sustained real depreciation of the exchange rate may be higher in the latter.

Profits behaved as expected theoretically: the rate of growth of profits in the tradable goods sector improved by 5.2 percentage points, while declining by 6.2 percentage points in the non-tradable goods sector, following the real depreciation of the Z$.

Table 4.3 shows that whereas the rate of growth in tradable sector employment averaged a negative 2.9 per cent per annum over the period 1981–84, it improved markedly, to an average annual rate of growth of 1.5 per cent during the period 1985–90 (the period of real exchange rate depreciation). The growth of employment in the non-tradable goods sector also improved, but more slowly, from 3.0 per cent (1981–84) to 4.1 per cent (1985–90),[23] thus responding to real depreciation of the Z$ as predicted by theory.

Since the tradable goods sector is expected to carry the bulk of the burden of employment creation in structural adjustment programmes, it is useful to trace how responsive employment was to the relative price signals generated by the real depreciation of the exchange rate. A decline in the average rate of growth of average real product earnings of 10.6 percentage points is associated with a rise in the rate of growth of employment of 4.4 percentage points, in the tradable goods sector. Although changes in the growth rate of employment and changes in the rate of growth of average real product earnings have the predicted inverse relationship, it appears relatively inelastic.

The relationship between changes in the growth rate of employment, and changes in the growth rate of real output and profits in the tradable goods sector is, as expected, positive, but also appears to be inelastic (for the underlying reasons, see below).

Real Product Earnings, Real Output and Employment Response: A Regression Analysis

So far, the issue of whether employment responded to changes in average real product earnings, real output and profits involved tracing the movements in these variables for the period before and during the real depreciation of the exchange rate. However, no conclusive statements could be made relating to the direction and size of the relationships. Firstly, the results were based on average trends. The sub-sectoral trends differed, suggesting variations in the relationships. Secondly, the influence of other factors could not be isolated in such a qualitative analysis.

Thirdly, and perhaps most importantly, as suggested by Oi (1962), labour is a quasi-fixed factor of production and hence the employment response may be spread over a period of time. The treatment of labour as a variable factor is problematic in that firms incur costs in training workers and hence the degree of fixity of labour rises with the level of human capital embodied in the workers. The more sector or firm specific the human capital is, the greater the level of fixity. As Oi observed, '...it behoves a firm to initiate practices that tend to minimise the turnover of specifically trained workers' (*op. cit.*, 93). Where foreign exchange shortages exist and strict security of employment regulations apply, as is the case in Zimbabwe, employers may be hesitant to hire additional workers, at least in the short term. In this context of a lagged response in employment, examining the responsiveness of employment to changes in real product wages, real output and profit by analysing the annual changes might conceal the delayed responses.

In order to address the foregoing problems, the responsiveness of employment can be examined through regression models derived from production functions. Most regression models were developed for advanced economies, and even for developed countries, the derivation and estimation of such models has generated a lot of controversies. Empirical studies, even for the same country and covering the same periods have yielded divergent results.[24] The size and direction of the relationships depend on the assumptions underlying the models (Morawetz, 1976). For instance, in neo-classical theory, employment is expected to rise when real product wages fall and vice versa. However, within a Keynesian framework, falling real product wages may lead to a decline in aggregate demand, which feeds into a reduction in employment and vice versa (see for instance, Solow, 1986; Hahn and Solow, 1986).

The neo-classical prediction of an inverse relationship between employment and real wages derives from the assumption that the wage level is exogenously determined. However, the Keynesian position takes real wages as endogenous and hence as dependent on other determinants of the growth process (Solow, *op. cit.*; Malinvaud, 1982). Another source of difference between orthodox and Keynesian approaches is the manner in which they treat both output and input markets. The former takes these to be equilibrium markets, with factors earning their marginal products. The Keynesian approach, however, treats both markets as disequilibrium markets. Nevertheless, the empirical problem associated with Keynesian approaches relates to the complexity of the models derived from their framework. Most empirical studies have therefore been derived from the orthodox framework, in spite of the heroic assumptions underlying it.

The Model Specification

From the foregoing, it is clear that modelling labour market behaviour, and especially in developing economies, is difficult. The few models that have been estimated assume an infinite supply of labour, in which case wages in the modern sector are taken as exogenous. The simultaneity bias is, in this case, considered minimal and estimates of employment functions are based on the partial approach.

The few developing country studies reviewed in Bourguignon (1988) estimate models of the CES-type,[25] with the following log linear functional form:

$$\text{Log } L_t = a_0 + a_1 \text{ Log } Q_t + a_2 \text{ Log } (w/p)_t \qquad\qquad [4]$$

where L_t, Q_t, $(w/p)_t$ stand for employment, real output and the ratio of wages to output price (the real product wage) respectively. The coefficient a_2 measures the elasticity of substitution between labour and other factors of production. To get the real product wage elasticity of employment, the coefficient of real product earnings has to be multiplied by the non-labour share in value added (Bourguignon, 1988).

Interestingly, a World Bank study (1987) estimated employment functions for Zimbabwe covering the period 1969–86 and for all sectors which respond directly to market forces.[26] This study further explores the real product wage – employment and real output – employment relationship for the period 1970–90. As in the World Bank study, an additional variable, the lagged employment variable is included as a regressor (to capture delayed response).

Variables Used and Sources of Data

Fitting the models to empirical data is problematic. As noted in Bourguignon (ibid.) and Hamermesh and Rees (1988), hours of work appear to be the best measure of employment since they approximate the theoretical concept of labour input. Such data are not readily available and hence the number of employees engaged is used instead. The measurement of capital input is the most difficult and controversial. The ideal measures of costs of labour and capital are their unit costs, and these are not observable. However, real product earnings are often used to measure the cost of labour, while interest rate, implied investment deflator or import prices are used as surrogates for the cost of capital.

This study estimates equation 4 for all sectors which respond directly to market signals. Data on employment, earnings, and real output, required for the estimation of the model, were obtained from various issues of the *Quarterly Digest of Statistics*, published by the CSO.[27] Real output was taken as factor cost gross value added at constant 1980 prices. Average real product earnings were computed by deflating average earnings by the implied GDP deflator for each sector.

Model Estimation and the Results

The labour demand functions were estimated using the Time Series Processor (TSP) and the results were corrected for first order auto correlation using the Cochrane–Orcutt (AR1) procedure, for mining, manufacturing, construction, finance and distribution. As in the World Bank study (*ibid.*), the real wage and output variables for the agricultural sector were treated as endogenously determined and estimation was by two stage least squares.[28] The results are summarised in Table 4.4.

In all sectors, the model explains the variations in employment very well, as shown by the high adjusted coefficients of determination (R^2). The results suggest an inverse relationship between average real product earnings and employment. However, the coefficients of average real product earnings are significant at the 10 per cent level in only three of the nine sectors, namely agriculture, mining and finance. Even in these sectors, the estimated elasticities are low. The fact that the equations apply for both periods with and without minimum wage regulations suggest that minimum wages had no (or little) effect.

In a broad sense, the results are consistent with those in the World Bank study, where it was inferred that '...there seems to be little reason to believe that minimum wage legislation had much overall effect, either because there is no reason to believe that average wages were increased, or because, as in the case of manufacturing, the wage elasticity was near zero' (*op. cit.,* 16).

Table 4.4   Estimated labour demand functions by sector, 1970–90

Sector	Dependent variable = log (employment)				
	Constant	Log (w/p)	Log Q	Log L(−1)	R^2
Agriculture	7.97	−0.29	−0.32	0.28	0.83
	(1.20)	(−1.69)[c]	(−0.65)	(0.55)	
Mining	2.65	−0.07	−0.17	0.72	0.65
	(1.99)[b]	(−1.63)[c]	(−0.81)	(3.68)[a]	
Manufacturing	0.65	−0.06	0.48	0.33	0.99
	(1.67)[c]	(−0.81)	(7.47)[a]	(4.89)[a]	
Electricity	0.14	−0.00	0.1	0.73	0.82
	(0.27)	(−0.02)	(1.66)[c]	(7.52)[a]	
Construction	0.59	−0.03	0.23	0.66	0.80
	(0.46)	(−0.23)	(1.65)[c]	(3.49)[a]	
Finance	1.84	−0.36	0.40	0.68	0.97
	(2.47)[b]	(−2.66)[a]	(2.41)[b]	(5.34)[a]	
Distribution	0.17	−0.05	0.21	0.76	0.92
	(0.29)	(−0.59)	(2.67)[a]	(6.46)[a]	
Transport	−0.49	0.08	0.08	0.85	0.97
	(−1.10)	(1.48)[c]	(1.51)[c]	(12.62)[a]	
Other Services	−1.44	0.02	1.01	−0.04	0.99
	(−6.57)[a]	(0.79)	(14.98)[a]	(−0.64)	

Notes: The time trend was initially included as a regressor, however, it proved insignificant and was therefore dropped. Supercripts [a], [b] and [c] denote statistical significant at the 1 per cent, 5 per cent and 10 per cent levels respectively. T ratios in parentheses.

The real output coefficients carry the expected positive sign and are significant in all sectors, with the exception of agriculture and mining.[29] In agriculture and mining, the coefficients are negative, albeit insignificant at the 10 per cent level of significance. The two sectors have generally experienced a secular decline in employment, which was not necessarily associated with real output performance. However, the computed real output elasticities of employment are less than one in all sectors (except in other services where it is one), implying an inelastic response.

The underlying problem has been the inability of the economy to achieve output growth rapid enough to deliver adequate growth of employment.[30] The obsolete and worn out state of capital stock, worsened by the inability of new investment to cover depreciation inhibited production. Growth alone may not have been sufficient for employment expansion. As the early World Employment Missions to Colombia, Sri Lanka and Kenya found '...while the rate of growth might be satisfactory, the pattern of growth was such as to create or perpetuate under utilisation of labour' (Singer, 1992: 12). In the case of Zimbabwe, the capital intensity of new investment militated against substantial employment growth (Kanyenze, 1993).

The high level of significance for the lagged employment variable suggests the responsiveness of employment is spread over time.[31] This is particularly so in view of the absolute shortage of foreign exchange and the ad hoc foreign exchange allocation system which may have presented a risk of uncertainty. Employers would not commit themselves to more workers under such conditions. Furthermore, firms would exercise caution given the cumbersome process involving dismissals and retrenchments. The Employment Act of 1980 required that government permission be granted prior to any dismissals or retrenchments. These regulations were further tightened through statutory instruments in 1981, 1982 and 1985. Circumventing these regulations by substituting casual for permanent workers was made difficult by the requirement that such workers be paid double the rate applying to permanent employees. Some shift towards employing more contract workers (though on average not pronounced) occurred (Kanyenze, 1993).[32]

Although the job security regulations did not stop the adjustment of the size of the work force, they reduced the demand for labour (Fallon and Lucas, 1993; Kanyenze, 1993; Hawkins *et al.*, 1988). The fact that the equation applies to both the period before and during the application of the security of employment regulations suggests that other factors were at work besides the rising marginal costs of adjusting labour (see also Fallon and Lucas, 1993). The insignificant coefficient for agriculture suggests an instantaneous response. This might not be surprising considering the seasonal nature of agricultural activities and its susceptibility to weather conditions. In view of the security of employment regulations, employers in agriculture maintained a core of permanent employees, which accounted for on average 69.3 per cent of the work force between 1985 and 1991, leaving a flexible margin of temporary (contract) employees.

Overall, the results suggest the importance of aggregate demand in explaining variations in employment.

V   CONCLUSION

This chapter traced the role played by the labour market during the period of economic stabilisation in Zimbabwe. Part III examined whether real consumption wages are flexible. Central to the argument for real wage flexibility, is the assumption that wages are exogenously determined – in which case, inappropriate real wages, allegedly set above what they would otherwise have been by institutional forces, may result in unemployment. Using both qualitative and quantitative approaches, it is shown that real consumption wages were flexible.

The burden of wage restraint fell disproportionately on the public sector where a marked compression of the wage structure occurred. In the private sector, a different picture emerges. The application of flexible remuneration systems, reinforced by the circumvention of wage controls, suggests that the wage restraint policy was not as effective in the private sector as it was in the public sector. In this case, a dispersion of the wage structure occurred.

Part IV examined whether the expected benefits resulting from the real depreciation of the exchange rate occurred. Real product earnings, profits and employment changed as predicted by theory; only output reacted perversely. It is suggested that where for instance tradable and non-tradable goods are complements, the responsiveness of production to a sustained real depreciation of the exchange rate may be higher in the latter.

Regarding the real product earnings–employment relationship, although the expected negative association is suggested, the coefficients were either insignificant or very small. The results suggest the importance of real output growth in determining employment growth, as reflected in the positive and significant real output–employment relationship. However, the real output elasticity of employment is low, suggesting an inelastic employment response to variations in real output growth.

In the case of Zimbabwe, real wages (whether consumption or product), were found to be flexible and not to have adversely affected employment creation. Most studies on the real wage-employment relationship have come to the same conclusion. Notably, a World Bank staff working paper which summarised seven issue and 12 country studies examining the interaction between labour markets and the adjustment process concluded that '...the evidence of our case studies certainly does not favour the view that real wages were rigid and therefore led to unemployment. Even for Chile, where unemployment was highest and persisted the longest, real wages fell dramatically' (Horton *et al.*, 1991: 17).[33]

An important issue emerging from the discussion of part IV is that labour market constraints were not necessarily the main factor inhibiting output, and consequently employment growth. More important may have been the absolute shortage of foreign exchange, the rising cost of capital (both local and imported) and strict security of employment regulations. With low levels of investment, inadequate foreign exchange earning capacity and the ensuing fragile growth patterns, the unemployment-underemployment crisis will deteriorate further, notwithstanding the continued compression of real wages. It would seem right, therefore, that the main objective of the current structural adjustment programme is to resolve the balance of payments constraint through trade liberalisation and export promotion.

Notes

1. The role of the labour market in the adjustment process is often derived from the Australian dependent economy models. A detailed discussion of these models is in Kanyenze (1993). Suffice it here to summarise their main predictions.

2. Real product wage is defined as the nominal wage in a particular sector deflated by the corresponding output price. On the other hand, the real consumption wage is derived by dividing the nominal wage by the overall consumer price index.

3. In the case of Zimbabwe, the real effective exchange rate is the trade weighted index of nominal exchange rate adjusted for inflation differentials between Zimbabwe and its trading partners.

4. These are now being implemented under the current (1990–95) structural adjustment programme.

5. These two pieces of legislation were subsequently incorporated into the Labour Relations Act of 1985.

6. The concept of the Poverty Datum Line is problematic. It differs according to family size, regions, countries, and over time.

7. For urban areas, the PDL was fixed at Z$128 (at December 1980 prices) and the minimum wage was Z$85 in 1981. For commercial farms, the PDL was estimated at 60 per cent of the urban PDL (Z$77). Achieving 90 per cent of the PDL by mid-1984 was recommended as the target so that the remaining 10 per cent would be a flexible element to permit rewarding human capital investment.

8. These were successors to the colonial industrial boards and industrial councils where trade unions and their respective employers' associations negotiate agreements stating conditions of employment. Employment Boards meet at the behest of government and as at June 1992, there were 44 of these. Employment Councils exist independently and are only required to submit their agreements for government approval (they are in this respect more ideal structures for 'free' collective bargaining). By June 1992, they were only 26.

9. This is so because '…wages are most likely irrelevant indicators when examining the issue of rigidity versus flexibility, as compensating changes in non-wage labour costs can introduce substantial rigidity in total labour costs … the rel-

evant variable when analysing employment and production decisions' (Riveros and Bouton, 1991: 12).

10. It is now called the First Merchant Bank of Zimbabwe.

11. The efficiency wage theory is an amalgam of theories which share the conviction that paying a higher than market clearing wage provides benefits to the employer in the form of increased productivity, low labour turnover rates, the workers identify more with the company and above all, it leads to industrial peace and stability. For a detailed recent discussion of these, see for instance Riveros and Bouton, 1991.

12. The views of Makings are especially interesting in that he was the first executive director of the Employers Confederation of Zimbabwe (EMCOZ) at its formation in the early 1980s and also given his influence as an independent consultant to employers on labour matters.

13. At a meeting held in July 1991, the Governor of the Reserve Bank and the Minister of Labour failed to convince trade unions and employers that the wage settlements they had reached were inflationary and that the wage awards be implemented in two phases.

14. For interesting detailed discussions, see for instance ILO/JASPA, Chew, Robinson, Schiller (all 1990); ILO, 1989; Levy and Newman, 1989; Gaag *et al.* 1989; Lindauer *et al.*, 1988 and Chiwele and Colclough (in this book).

15. Quoted in Lindauer *et al.*, 1988: 21 and Schiller, 1990: 85.

16. The views of Agere are most interesting given that until December 1992, he was the permanent secretary in the Ministry of the Public Service. He now heads the government-owned Zimbabwe Institute of Public Administration and Management.

17. Such a functional form of the model is meant to capture the cyclicality of real consumption wages in relation to the time path followed by real GDP.

18. These are derived after correcting for serial correlation where it exists.

19. For the problems of using this method of estimating the counterfactual, see Kanyenze, 1993, Chapter 4.

20. In line with government's objective of narrowing income differentials.

21. Since the focus of this section is on responsiveness to market signals, non-tradable subsectors which do not respond directly to market signals are, unless stated otherwise, excluded. These are government, private domestic and other services.

22. Average real product earnings for each sector were obtained by deflating average earnings by the implied gross domestic product deflator. Real output is taken as factor cost gross value added for the sector at constant 1980 prices. The data were obtained from various issues of the *Quarterly Digest of Statistics*, CSO. Figures on profits by sector are provided in the *National Income and Expenditure Report*, 1990 and the latest figures are for 1987. Data on employment were extracted from the *Quarterly Digest of Statistics*, CSO, various issues.

23. When government, private domestic and other services are included in the definition of non-tradable goods, the rate of growth of employment actually

decelerates, from an average annual rate of 4.5 per cent (1981–84) to 3.1 per cent (1985–90).

24. The divergencies related not only to the size of the elasticities, but even to the nature of the relationship. Some studies reviewed in Bourguignon (1988) found, for instance, positive real product wage coefficients, while others found negative ones.

25. The constant elasticity of substitution (CES) framework is based on the restrictive assumptions of constant returns to scale, the existence of perfect competition in both product and factor markets and profit maximisation.

26. Public administration, education, health and private domestic service were excluded.

27. The sample period started in 1970 because data on sectoral value added deflators are available from that period.

28. Real wage exogeneity is based on the assumption that the modern sector faces an infinite supply of labour. However, for the traditional sector, which is assumed to be the source of surplus labour, the real wage is therefore assumed as endogenously determined (Bourguignon, 1988).

29. It is generally acknowledged in textbook theory that the demand for factor inputs is a derived one, depending on the demand for output.

30. In the Transitional National Development Plan covering the period 1982/83–84/85, real output was envisaged to grow at an annual rate of 8.1 per cent with employment growing at an annual average of over 3 per cent. In reality real output grew at only 2 per cent per annum and employment increased at 0.2 per cent per year over the plan period. The First Five Year National Development Plan revised the planned annual growth patterns downwards to 5.1 per cent for real output and 2.7 per cent for employment over the five year period 1986–90. The achieved annual growth rates amounted to 3.1 per cent per year for real output and 2.5 per cent for employment.

31. The coefficients of lagged employment are significant at the 1 per cent level of significance test, except for agriculture where the coefficient is insignificant.

32. Contract workers were covered by these regulations only for the duration of their contracts.

33. The country studies covered Argentina, Brazil, Bolivia, Chile, Costa Rica, Cote d'Ivoire, Egypt, Ghana, Kenya, South Korea, Malaysia and Thailand.

References

Agere, S. (1992) 'The Promotion of Good Ethical Standards and Behaviour in Public Services in Africa: the Case of Zimbabwe', *Africanus – Journal for Development Administration*, 22 (1 and 2).

Bourguignon, F. (1988) 'The Measurement of the Wage-Employment Relationship in Developed and Developing Countries: A Short Survey' (Geneva: International Labour Organisation).

Chavunduka Commission Report (1982) *Report of the Commission of Inquiry into the Agricultural Industry Under the Chairpersonship of Professor G.L. Chavunduka.*

Chew, D.C.E. (1990) 'Internal Adjustment to Falling Civil Service Salaries: Insights from Uganda', in *World Development*, 18 (7).

Chhibber, A., J. Cottani, R. Firuzabadi and M. Waltan (1989) 'Inflation, Price Control and Fiscal Adjustment in Zimbabwe', *World Bank PPR Working Paper*, No. 192.

Colclough, C. (1991) 'Wage Flexibility in Sub-Saharan Africa: Trends and Explanations', in G. Standing and V. Tokman (eds).

Confederation of Zimbabwe Industries (CZI) (1989) *Industrial Review*, August.

Fallon, P.R. (1987) 'The Labour Market in Zimbabwe: Historical Trends and An Evaluation of Recent Policy', *World Bank DRD*, 296.

Fallon, P.R. and Lucas, R.E.B. (1993) 'Job Security Regulations and the Dynamic Demand for Industrial Labour in India and Zimbabwe', in *Journal of Development Economics*, 40.

Fallon, P.R. and Riveros, L.A. (1989) 'Adjustment and the Labour Market', World Bank, *WPS* 214.

Gaag, K., M. Stelcner and W. Vijverberg (1989) 'Wage Differentials and Moonlighting by Civil Servants: Evidence from Cote d' Ivoire and Peru', in *The World Bank Economic Review*, 3 (1).

Government of Zimbabwe (1981) *Growth With Equity: An Economic Policy Statement* (Government Printer: Ministry of Finance, Economic Planning and Development).

Government of Zimbabwe (1982) *Transitional National Development Plan, 1982/83–1984/85*, 1, November.

Government of Zimbabwe (1986) *First Five-Year National Development Plan, 1986–1990*, 1, April.

Government of Zimbabwe (1986) *Socio-Economic Review of Zimbabwe, 1980–1985*, Ministry of Finance, Economic Planning and Development.

Government of Zimbabwe (1991) *Second Five-Year National Development Plan (1991–95)* (Harare: Government Printer).

Hahn, F.W. and R.M. Solow (1986) 'Is Wage Flexibility a Good Thing?', in W. Beckerman (ed.), *Wage Rigidity and Unemployment* (London: Gerald Duckworth and Company).

Hamermesh, D.S. and A. Rees (1988) *The Economics of Work and Pay* (New York: Harper and Row Publishers, Inc).

Hawkins, A.M., P.J. McBurney, M.A. Shadur and W. Clatanoff (1988) *Formal Sector Employment Demand Conditions in Zimbabwe* (Harare: University of Zimbabwe).

Horton, S., R. Kanbur and D. Mazumdar (1991) 'Labour Markets in an Era of Adjustment: An Overview', The World Bank, *PRE Working Paper Series WPS*, 694.

ILO (1989) 'The Callenge of Adjustment in Africa', Tripartite Symposium on Structural Adjustment and Employment in Africa, Nairobi, 16–19 October 1989, Geneva.

ILO/JASPA (1990) *African Employment Report*, World Employment Programme.

IMF (1993) *World Economic Outlook*, International Monetary Fund, Washington DC, May.

Kadhani, X. and R.H. Green (1985) 'Parameters as Warnings and Guide-Posts: The Case of Zimbabwe', *Journal of Development Planning*, 15.

Kanyenze, G. (1989) *The Structure of Wages in Zimbabwe's Manufacturing Industries: 1980–1985*, Unpublished MA Dissertation, University of Kent at Canterbury.

Kanyenze, G. (1993) *The Impact of Economic Stabilisation on the Wage Structure in Zimbabwe: 1980–90*, Unpublished DPhil Thesis, University of Sussex.

Kavran, D. (1989) *Report of the Public Service Review Commission of Zimbabwe, Under the Chairmanship of Professor D. Kavran*, 1, Harare (May).

Lehman, H.P. (1990) 'The Politics of Adjustment in Kenya and Zimbabwe: The State as Intermediary', *Studies in Comparative International Development*, 25 (3).

Levy, V. and J.L. Newman (1989) 'Wage Rigidity: Micro and Macro Evidence on Labour Market Adjustment in the Modern Sector', *World Bank Economic Review*, 3 (1).

Lindauer, D.L., O.A. Meesook and P. Suebsaeng (1988) 'Government Wage Policy in Africa: Some Findings and Policy Issues', *The World Bank Research Observer*, 3 (1).

Lopez, R. and Riveros, L. (1990) 'Do Labour Market Distortions Cause Overvaluation and Rigidity of the Real Exchange Rate?', *World Bank WPS*, 485.

Makings, G. (1988) 'A Guide To The Wages and Salaries Legislation in Zimbabwe', Institute of Personnel Management of Zimbabwe, Concorde Services (Pvt) Ltd.

Malinvaud, E. (1982) 'Wages and Unemployment', *The Economic Journal*, 92 (365).

Morawetz, D. (1976) 'Elasticities of Substitution in Industry: What Do We Learn From Econometric Estimates?', *World Development*, 4 (1).

Nurenberg, B. (1989) 'Public Sector Pay and Employment Reform: A Review of World Bank Experience', *World Bank Discussion Papers*, 68.

OECD (1986) *Flexibility in The Labour Market: The Current Debate* (Paris: OECD).

Oi, Y. (1962) 'Labour as a Quasi-Fixed Factor', in J.E. King (ed.), *Readings in Labour Economics* (Oxford: Oxford University Press, 1980).

RAL Merchant Bank (1982) *Executive Guide to the Economy*.

RAL Merchant Bank (1987) *Executive Guide to the Economy*.

Riddell Commission Report (1981) *Commission of Inquiry Into Incomes, Prices and Conditions of Service* (Harare, Zimbabwe: Government Printer).

Riveros, L.A. and L. Bouton (1991) 'Efficiency Wage Theory, Labour Markets and Adjustment', *World Bank Working Paper*, WPS 731.

Robinson, D. (1990) 'Civil Service Remuneration in Africa', *International Labour Review*, 129 (3).

Schiller, C. (1990) 'Government Pay Policies and Structural Adjustment', *African Development Review*, 2 (1), African Development Bank.

Singer, H. (1992) *Research of the World Employment Programme: Future Priorities and Selective Assessment*, World Employment Programme (Geneva: ILO).

Solow, R.M. (1986) 'Unemployment: Getting the Questions Right', in Bean *et al.* (eds) *The Rise in Unemployment* (Oxford: Basil Blackwell).

Standing, G. (1986) *Aspects of Labour Market Analysis: Labour Flexibility: Towards A Research Agenda*, World Employment Programme, April (Geneva: ILO).

Standing, G. (1991) 'Structural Adjustment and Labour Market Policies: Towards Social Adjustment', in G. Standing and V. Tokman (eds).

Standing, G. and V. Tokman (eds) (1991) *Towards Social Adjustment: Labour Market Issues in Structural Adjustment* (Geneva: International Labour Office (ILO)).

Stevenson, G. (1992) 'How Public Sector Pay and Employment Affect Labour Markets: Research Issues', *Policy Research Working Papers*, WPS 944.

Turnham, D. (1993) *Employment and Development: A New Review of Evidence*, Development Centre Studies (Paris: OECD).

van Ginneken, W. (1990) 'Labour Adjustment in the Public Sector: Policy Issues for Developing Countries', *International Labour Review*, 129 (4).

World Bank (1981) *Accelerated Development in Sub-Saharan Africa: An Agenda for Action* (Washington DC: The World Bank).

World Bank (1985) *Zimbabwe: Country Economic Memorandum, Performance, Policies and Prospects*, 3 Vols.

World Bank (1987) *Zimbabwe: A Strategy for Sustained Growth*, 2 Vols.

World Bank (1989) *Sub-Saharan Africa: From Crisis to Sustainable Growth*, Washington DC.

5 Liberalisation of Maize Marketing in the Arusha Region in Tanzania

Willy Parsalaw

I INTRODUCTION

Tanzania experienced economic problems beginning in the late 1970s which persisted through the 1980s. One of the factors that contributed to this poor economic performance was the inefficiency of the agricultural marketing system. It caused a decline in producer prices for both food and export crops. This provided a disincentive to produce export crops and a shift to food crops sold through the parallel market. Co-operatives and marketing boards made huge losses which were covered by the government, sometimes through bank borrowing and guaranteed credit.

The share of domestic credit to co-operatives and marketing boards increased sharply, crowding out other potential users and becoming a source of monetary expansion. This created inflationary pressures with adverse consequences on trade and balance of payments. One change advocated under economic reform measures which began in 1986 was to liberalise the grain marketing system in order to improve its performance.

This chapter reports on research into the effectiveness of this policy change in the Arusha region, for maize marketing. Part II briefly reviews Tanzania's economic performance and the factors responsible. Part III reviews maize market and pricing policies, their consequences, and Government's eventual decision to liberalise agricultural marketing. Part IV provides evidence on the impact of liberalisation measures on the structure and competitiveness of the maize marketing system. Part V provides evidence on the impact of liberalisation on economic performance of the maize marketing system. Part VI provides a concluding summary and recommendations.

II TANZANIA'S ECONOMIC PERFORMANCE

The Tanzanian economy performed well after independence in 1961: GDP grew at an annual rate of 5.3 per cent per annum between 1965 and 1976. During much of the 1960s the trade balance was in surplus as a result of expansion of smallholder export crops production particularly cotton, coffee and cashew nuts (Ndulu and Lipumba, 1991). Inflation was approximately 4 per cent and the balance of payments position was stable with the current account deficit about 3 per cent of GDP (Green *et al.*, 1980).

The decline in growth started in the second part of the 1970s and by the early 1980s the Tanzanian economy was characterised by deep macro-economic crisis: widening external imbalance, huge unsustainable budget deficits, high rates of monetary growth and inflation (Table 5.1).

Factors Responsible for Tanzania's Economic Decline

Several factors were responsible for Tanzania's economic decline. On the external front they include: the decline in terms of trade for the whole of the 1980s; the break-up of the East African Community in 1977 and the Idi Amin war in 1979 (Green *et al.*, 1980; Wagao, 1992).

Despite the adverse impact of these external shocks, the economic problems the country experienced resulted from inappropriate domestic policies and an inadequate response to external shocks (Hyden and Karlstrom, 1993). Beginning in 1967 the country adopted a development strategy based on socialism. This led to the creation of a large number of parastatals which increased from 40 in 1967

Table 5.1   Main economic indicators

Year	1970–75	1976–80	1981–85	1986	1987	1988	1989	1990
1 GDP (annual average % change)	5.1	2.1	0.8	5.3	4.1	5.3	4.4	4.1
2 Inflation (annual average)	12	15	30	32	30	31	26	20
3 Budget deficit as of % of GDP	7	12	11	12	12	11	11	14
4 Current A/c deficit[a] (US$m)	138	288	394	321	265	376	359	426
5 Money Supply[b] (annual average % change)	20	26	18	29	32	34	31	43

Notes:
(a)   Current account balance after official transfers.
(b)   Money supply – broadly defined.

Source: IBRD, 1992, 1993; IMF, 1992; BOT, 1980, 1988, 1990.

to 400 in 1981 (Herbst, 1990). These parastatals did not operate commercially but made huge losses with liberal credit expansion to finance these losses which fuelled inflation (Rutihinda, 1991). The socialist policies caused capital flight while discouraging investment by the private sector (Green *et al.*, 1980). The government did not react to external shocks by adjusting its policies. The only 'adjustment' for several years was a dramatic compression of imports through licensing. Despite an imbalance in the external and internal accounts, government spending continued to rise rapidly. Since the widening fiscal imbalance was financed primarily from the central bank, money supply shot up and inflation continued to rise (Hyden and Karlstrom, 1993).

The emphasis in manufacturing was on import substitutes and not exports. This inward oriented industrial strategy placed the entire burden of foreign exchange earning on agriculture. Despite this, there was no strategy to increase agricultural exports (Wagao, 1992). Agricultural exports fell when they were required to increase to finance inputs for other sectors, because of a decline in investment in agriculture, villagisation, an overvalued exchange rate and supply-bottlenecks (URT, 1990c). Even more important, however, were pricing and marketing policies.

The decline in producer prices resulted mainly from increased official marketing costs and export taxes. The producer share of the sales price decline from 70.5 per cent in 1970 to 41.2 per cent in 1980; export taxes increased from 6.5 per cent to 19.9 per cent; and parastatal costs from 26 per cent to 37 per cent over the same period of time (Ellis, 1983). In the 1980s, producer prices continued to decline because of further increases in marketing costs and an over-valued exchange rate (Ellis, 1988). For food crops, the decline in producer prices caused an increasing amount to be sold through the parallel market and smuggled to neighbouring countries (Renkow *et al.*, 1983). Given the main focus of this chapter the following parts will devote attention to maize pricing and marketing policies.

III   MAIZE MARKETING POLICIES

Apart from a brief period after independence when free trade in maize existed, maize marketing was the monopoly of co-operatives and marketing boards from 1963 until 1988. In 1963 the National Agricultural and Products Board (NAPB) was formed and given monopoly of procurement from producers through co-operatives. The amount of maize that could be traded and transported across district boundaries was restricted to 360 kgs. Milling of maize was done by the National Milling Company (NMC). Private mills were nationalised in 1967. Despite controls on maize trade, a parallel market existed (Bryceson, 1993). The illegality of this channel, however, made it more expensive than it would otherwise have been (Smith and Spooner, 1990). When the NAPB was abolished in 1973 its activities were taken over by the NMC. Thus, beginning in 1973, the

NMC became responsible for both maize marketing and milling. The NMC was also given responsibility for managing the Strategic Grain Reserve (SGR) which was established in 1975 and acted as buyer of last resort on behalf of the government to stabilise prices. Before 1973 when the NMC dealt with milling alone it operated profitably. When it expanded its activities to cover all aspects of maize marketing it made losses. The NMC also dealt with a number of other food crops placed under public monopoly following the 1973/74 drought and undertook a number of activities which had no relationship whatsoever with its core food marketing activity companies (URT, 1991b).

The marketing arrangement involving co-operatives did not last long since co-operatives were abolished in 1976 and the NMC became responsible for maize marketing from the village level to the national level. This system implied countrywide coverage regardless of quantities available, causing transport problems and adding to NMCs own managerial and operational inefficiency. Thus the late 1970s and early 1980s were characterised by the NMC mobile teams' late arrival or failure to arrive for maize procurement and failure to transport purchased maize from areas of production to consuming centres (Bryceson, 1993). This led to an increase in parallel market activities and a decline in the NMC market share. The inefficiency of the NMC led to re-introduction of co-operatives in 1984. Co-operatives continued to suffer from problems identified as early as the 1960s. They have been formed from the top regardless of members' own needs, by a mere declaration in all areas of the country regardless of economic viability and continued to be subjected to political interference, in particular the requirement that they should be multipurpose organisations (Van Cranenburgh, 1990). They have, therefore, managed a large number of activities inefficiently rather than a few activities efficiently, thus incurring losses. Because co-operatives were established without an adequate capital base they depended entirely on guaranteed overdrafts from financial institutions for their crop procurement, as did NMC. By June 1990, outstanding overdrafts of co-operatives and marketing boards were equivalent to 13.3 per cent of GDP. They were in consequence a major contributor to money supply expansion, inflation and over-valuation of the country's currency. The share of commercial bank credit going to agricultural marketing increased from 20.8 per cent in 1970 to approximately 64 per cent in 1987 before it decline to 32 per cent in 1990 (BOT, 1981, 1991). This constrained the availability of credit to other sectors, particularly the private sector.

Maize Pricing Policies

Government intervention to control prices was more pronounced during the 1973–88 period. This was prompted by the 1973/74 drought which necessitated huge grain imports. Beginning in 1973/74, the government also provided a subsidy for maize flour to protect consumers while paying a uniform producer price, in all parts of the country.

This pan-territorial producer price compelled producers close to consuming centres to subsidise those in distant locations. In addition, supply side measures were adopted from the early 1970s which included: provision of free inputs and tractor services for maize producers in the Southern Highland regions, and (later) subsidised input packages (hybrid seeds, fertiliser and pesticides) (Bryceson, 1993). This contributed to increased production in the Southern Highland regions which are remote from the main areas of consumption. Public purchases from these regions rose from 18 000 tonnes per annum in the first half of the 1970s to an estimated peak of 437 000 tonnes during 1988 (Parsalaw, 1994).

Because of long distances to consuming centres and poor road conditions, transport costs from these regions are very high thus making the public sector the sole buyer. This increased the NMC marketing costs as the total volume of maize purchased declined, while it increasingly comprised maize from the remote Southern Highlands in the 1980s. The government fixed consumer prices for maize uniformly across the country, and lower than the NMC marketing costs, so that the NMC suffered losses. For example in 1980/81, the loss from selling maize was estimated to be 17.6 per cent of total maize sales that year (Suzuki and Bernard, 1987). The maize flour subsidy was sometimes not explicitly covered and the NMC accumulated losses from maize distribution and milling as well. Criticism of pan-territorial producer pricing and the high costs involved led the government to change. In 1982, the pricing system followed for maize was based on the regional production potential. High potential areas received a premium price. This pricing system, however, did not follow the principle of comparative advantage but what Bryceson (1991) calls 'climatic comparative advantage'. The Southern Highland regions are suited for maize production as regards soils and rainfall. Hence, the NMC transport costs were not reduced but increased by providing additional incentives for maize to be produced in areas with the highest cost of transport to the market.

During the second part of the 1980s, pan-territorial pricing was re-introduced. Although the maize flour subsidy was removed in 1984, the government retail price did not allow the NMC to cover its transport costs especially from the remote Southern Highland regions. For example, during 1989 the costs of purchase and transport of maize from Rukwa in the Southern Highlands to Dar was estimated at US$169/tonne while revenue was US$104/tonne. Together with overhead costs, the loss for one tonne of maize from Rukwa stood at US$73.7/tonne in 1989. The cost of moving the accumulated stocks of maize in different parts of the country by the end of 1989 and selling at the government price was estimated to have caused a loss of US $11.2 million in 1990 (ERB, 1990). This loss from maize alone is equivalent to 31.6 per cent of total NMC sales in 1990.

Another source of monetary loss for the NMC was operation of the Strategic Grain Reserve (SGR). The NMC operated the SGR without separate accounts from its commercial activities. There was, therefore, no way of knowing how much to reimburse the NMC for SGR operations. Moreover, government control over the SGR was weak and in the absence of separate accounts and explicit turnover procedures, the NMC mismanaged the SGR (URT, 1991b). Losses were covered by allowing the NMC unlimited access to bank borrowing. The government had to intervene in various years by agreeing to pay banks debts accumulated by the NMC. During 1981–88 period, the Treasury took over US$333 million of outstanding overdraft owed by the NMC to the National Bank of Commerce (NBC). Despite this, the NMC repayment history did not improve and by 31 May 1991, it had an outstanding overdraft of US$78.5 million.

The above review of maize pricing and marketing policies indicates that the inefficiency of the marketing system caused a decline in the volume of maze marketed through the official channel. Co-operatives and NMC made losses as a result of their own inefficiency and government pricing and marketing policies. These losses were accommodated through guaranteeing bank credit and sometimes explicit Treasury subsidies. They in turn became a source of monetary expansion and inflation in the economy. Beginning in 1988 the maize marketing system was liberalised to improve its performance as reviewed in the following part.

Maize Market Liberalisation in Response to Economic Problems

In response to its economic problems, in August 1986 Tanzania adopted a three year Economic Recovery Programme (ERP I). This programme was followed by ERP II 1989/90–1991/92 with the twin objectives of promoting growth and addressing the social dimensions of adjustment. The objectives of ERP I and II included:

(i)   To increase domestic production of food and export crops.
(ii)   To restore efficiency in utilisation and mobilisation of resources.
(iii)   To rehabilitate the physical infrastructure, in particular transport and communication in support of directly productive sectors.
(iv)   To restore internal and external balance.
(v)   To reduce inflation to below 10 per cent by 1991/92.
(vi)   To rehabilitate the industrial sector.
(vii)   To rehabilitate social services and enhance popular participation in them.

One of the policy instruments to achieve the objectives of increased domestic production of food crops, reduced monetary expansion and inflation, and lower food prices, was maize market liberalisation. Beginning in 1988 private traders were allowed to participate in maize trade, and the NMC and co-operatives were required to operate on a commercial basis. However, NMC was still required to manage the SGR, and to operate as buyer of last resort on behalf of the government to stabilise prices (URT, 1991b).

The following parts provide evidence on the impact of liberalisation on the structure, competitiveness and economic performance of the grain marketing system in the Arusha region. The results presented are based on field research carried out during 1991/92.

IV   THE IMPACT OF LIBERALISATION ON THE STRUCTURE AND COMPETITIVENESS OF THE MAIZE MARKETING SYSTEM IN ARUSHA REGION

In this research a sample survey of 150 maize traders was carried out during 1991/92 to assess the structure and competitiveness of the market in the Arusha region after liberalisation.

Organisation of Trade and Maize Flow Pattern

The intra-regional transfer of maize is mainly from markets in the surplus districts to the main consuming market in Arusha and deficit markets in other districts (Table 5.2).

Apart from the urban district markets indicated above and the regional market in Arusha, there are a number of rural periodic markets in surplus and deficit districts which trade with each other. Apart from intra-regional flows, markets in surplus districts also trade directly with rural and urban markets in the regions of Dodoma, Singida, Shinyanga, Tanga, Mwanza and Dar-es-Salaam (URT, 1991b). Estimates of intra and inter-regional trade in the 1980s are presented in Table 5.3.

The intra and inter-regional flow of trade is through two channels: private traders, and official channels comprising co-operatives and the NMC.

The Emerging Structure and Competitiveness of the Private Marketing System

After liberalisation of the grain marketing system, the number of private traders in the area of research increased sharply (Table 5.4). Evidence in other parts of the country documents the same trend of a sharp increase in private traders activity and market share in the second part of the 1980s (MDB, 1992).

Estimates of private traders' purchases indicate that private traders handled approximately 88 per cent and 93 per cent of marketed output in 1990 and 1991 respectively (Table 5.5).

Although there is improvement in the competitive structure of the marketing system, the market is dominated by a large number of small traders who are not specialised, who lack vehicles, trade finance and storage facilities. Thus they handle only small quantities and perform limited transport, storage and milling operations (Coulter, 1994).

Table 5.2   Intra-regional transfers pattern of maize in Arusha region in the 1980s

Surplus district	Main district market	Deficit district	Main district market
Babati	Babati	Ngorongoro	Loliondo
Mbulu	Mbulu	Monduli	Monduli
Hanang	Kartesh	Arusha	Arusha
Arumeru	Tengeru		
Kiteto	Kibaya		

Table 5.3   Estimates of intra- and inter-regional maize trade in Arusha region in the 1980s ('000 tonnes)

Year	Inter-regional transfers	Intra-regional transfers	Total marketed
1984	13	29	42
1985	71	31	102
1986	128	32	160
1987	102	33	135
1988	103	34	137
1989	81	35	116
1990	19	37	56
1991	7	38	45

Source: Adapted from Parsalaw (1994).

Table 5.4   Classification of maize traders on the basis of date of entry in Arusha region

Year	Number of entrants	Number of entrants as a % of total sample
Before 1984	17	11.3
1984–1987	36	24.0
1988–1991	97	64.7

Source: own survey, 1991

Table 5.5   Estimates of the amount of maize marketed through different channels in Arusha region in the 1980s ('000 tonnes)

Year	Total amount marketed	Official purchases	Official purchases % of total	Private purchases % of total
1985	102	39	38.2	61.8
1986	160	47	29.4	70.6
1987	135	69	51.1	48.9
1988	137	38	27.7	72.3
1989	116	61	52.6	47.4
1990	56	7	12.5	87.5
1991	45	3	6.7	93.3

Source: Parsalaw (1994).

Ownership Pattern of Market Facilities

Transport Facilities

Most maize traders in Arusha use hired trucks to transport maize from areas of production to the market and between different markets (Table 5.6).

Some vehicles owned are of small capacity and traders perform limited transport operations. For example, among the six traders who own vehicles, two are maize millers in Arusha town. They use their vehicles to distribute maize flour to

Table 5.6   Classification of maize traders on the basis of mode of transport used in Arusha in 1991

Mode of transport	Number of traders	Percentage of those who transported
Own transport	6	5.7
Hired trucks	63	60.0
Buses	15	14.3
Animal drawn carts and others	21	20.0
Total	105	100.0

Source: own survey, 1991.

retailers in Arusha town. Their vehicles are small. They rely on inter-market traders who hire lorries to supply them with maize. They also rely on some retailers close to milling plants to collect the produce and transport it using hired pick-up trucks and human pulled carts (*mkokoteni*).

The common practice observed among inter-market traders in Babati, Mbulu, Karatu and Kartesh is for more than one trader to hire a 7–10 tonne lorry to transport maize and share the costs among themselves. Traders who purchase maize from producers on the farm use hired pick-up trucks and lorries, while some use animal drawn carts. It is common for retail traders selling small quantities in open places in Arusha town to transport maize using buses from the surrounding rural markets of Ngaramtoni, Themi, Mbauda, TPRI, etc. and sell at the Arusha bus station and in other open areas in town.

Storage Facilities

For the 150 maize traders interviewed, none own a godown facility constructed for storage purposes. Traders use own houses, buildings and property they rent to store maize. Storage capacity available to most traders is very small, ranging from 0.9 to 27 tonnes for 148 traders, while the remaining two have a relatively large storage capacity of 450 tonnes each. Therefore, much storage takes place on the farm and traders conduct limited storage only. Other studies on Tanzania have indicated that it is farmers who carry out inter-seasonal storage of coarse grains (ERB, 1990; Coulter, 1994).

Milling Facilities

Only two among the 150 traders own milling facilities. These are small-scale hammer mills estimated to cost TSh. 2.5 million in 1991, with a processing capacity of one tonne/day. They differ from the industrial roller mills owned by the NMC in several respects:

(i)   They have a smaller capacity of one tonne/day compared to 60 tonnes/day for the industrial roller mill.

(ii) They cost TSh. 2.5 million in 1991 compared to TSh. 600 million for the roller mill.

(iii) The extraction rate of the industrial roller mill is high and it produces between superior and standard quality maize flour, while the small hammer mills produce low quality flour which needs to be milled twice to produce fine flour. The private sector commercial milling is, therefore, still rudimentary; this function is mainly done by consumers themselves.[1] However, one apparent effect of liberalisation has been to expose the NMC to competition from the small scale hammer mills which mill less refined products.

Size of Private Traders' Operations

The size of private traders' operations as measured by their storage capacity indicates that a large number of traders deal with small quantities of maize at a time (Table 5.7).

A large proportion of storage capacity is owned by a small number of traders, with 18 per cent of traders controlling almost 71 per cent of storage space. The typology of traders reinforces the capacity pattern revealed above. Among the 150 sampled traders 51 per cent operate as retailers, while 34 per cent operate as both retailers and wholesalers. Only 15 per cent of the sampled traders operate as permanent wholesalers (Parsalaw, 1994).

The trading structure results from inadequate capital for transport, storage and financing of stocks. Among the sampled traders, 84.7 per cent obtained the initial capital for trade from own savings, while 14 per cent obtained their initial capital as a loan from family and friends. Only 1.3 per cent of traders reported that they obtained a loan from commercial banks for trade (*ibid.*).

Choice of Market Channel

The channel preference for maize producers from 1988–1991, indicates that it was only during 1989 that the co-operative channel recovered some market share (Table 5.5). In that year, about 66 per cent of producers preferred the co-operative channel compared to 34 per cent who preferred the private market channel. Apart from 1989, the private channel attracted an increasing proportion of producers who sold maize. Producers who preferred the co-operative channel had a higher producer price as the prime mover. Other factors such as cash payment on delivery of produce, closeness and early starting of buying operations ranked lower. On the other hand, cash payment on delivery of produce ranked higher among reasons for producer preference for the private market channel. This is particu-

Table 5.7   Private traders' storage capacity in Arusha

Range of storage capacity (bags)	Number of traders	Total storage space (Tonnes)	Percentage of total storage space
10–30	25	56.7	2.8
31–50	58	233.1	11.5
51–100	40	302.4	14.9
101–300	25	540.0	26.6
> 300	2	900.0	44.2

Source: own survey, 1991.

larly important because in 1989 the private market channel producer and consumer prices were both lower. Despite a higher average price in the co-operative channel, some producers still preferred to sell through the private market channel. The dominant reason was the payment of cash on delivery of produce. Some producers also received a higher price from private traders. Since private traders paid a range of prices, some farmers were getting higher prices from private traders even though the average private prices were lower than the co-operative price.

Other factors which contributed to preference of the private channel included:

(i)   Private traders were buying maize on the farm so that producers did not have to incur additional costs of transport to the local market.

(ii) Private traders provided producers with empty gunny bags in exchange for their own gunny bags during purchase. In the co-operative channel, it is common for producers selling maize in 90 kg bags not to receive empty gunny bags in place of the ones containing produce.

(iii) Deductions made from the producer price, upon sale of maize to co-operatives, made producers prefer the private market channel to avoid these deductions.

Delayed payment by co-operatives results from a number of factors: first is inadequate working capital which makes them rely on bank overdrafts. Their application to commercial banks is made through the co-operative department, where the registrar of co-operatives has to approve a maximum credit limit for a co-operative union. There have been considerable delays in placing application forms and for application forms to pass through the various stages required before loans are approved. Another chronic problem facing co-operatives is failure to repay bank loans. This failure causes considerable delays in negotiating further credit for crop procurement. Delayed payment to producers did not solely result from inadequate capital and hence reliance on overdraft with consequent delays. Evidence elsewhere in the country and in Arusha, indicates that misuse of funds meant for crop procurement and outright theft are some of the reasons for lack of cash payment by co-operatives (URT, 1990a).

Barriers to Trade and Entry

Although at the national level, the official policy gives private traders freedom of entry and participation in grain trade, this policy is implemented differently at the local level. In 1991 for example, traders in Mbulu, Karatu, Kartesh and Babati were required to pay a fee of TSh. 0.21/kg to the co-operative union before they were allowed to transport maize to Arusha and other markets.

The main source of revenue for co-operatives is crop levy. The decline in co-operative market share in Arusha, particularly in 1990 and 1991 meant a decline in revenue from maize from TSh. 5.7 million in 1986 to TSh. 0.3 million in 1991.

There were also deductions from the producer price made by local authorities whose revenue partly depends on crop levy. These deductions were made despite a government directive issued in 1990 requiring all contributions from producers to be made voluntarily (*Daily News*, 31 March 1992). There was thus an impetus for the co-operative union and local authorities to team up and use the police force to ensure that private traders pay this fee, and there was evidence that this happened.

V   THE IMPACT OF LIBERALISATION ON ECONOMIC PERFORMANCE OF THE MAIZE MARKETING SYSTEM

The economic performance of the grain marketing system is expected to improve as a result of improved competition. This part provides results of the analysis of economic performance. The main objective in this analysis will be to observe performance trends over time after liberalisation while providing a comparison between the official market channel and private traders. The financial performance of co-operatives and the NMC will also be evaluated to determine whether liberalisation measures have been successful in reducing co-operative and NMC financial deficits.

Analysis of Margins

Table 5.8 indicates that the marketing margin as percentage of consumer price declined continuously from 1986 to 1990 before it rose in 1991.

Real consumer prices started to decline in 1986, a trend which can be explained by the fact that liberalisation was already under way before it became an official policy in 1988. The year 1991 experienced poor harvest in many parts of the country and it seems traders were able to increase their margin sharply in

Table 5.8   Maize marketing margin for private traders in Arusha
(constant 1997 TSh/kg)

Year	Producer price	Producer price as % of consumer price	Consumer price	Margin as a % of consumer price
1986	0.61	38.6	1.58	61.4
1987	0.61	48.8	1.25	51.2
1988	0.69	50.7	1.36	49.3
1989	0.55	51.4	1.07	48.6
1990	0.57	56.4	1.01	43.6
1991	1.06	46.3	2.29	53.7

Source: Adapted from Parsalaw, 1994.

that year, but (as a percentage of consumer price) to a point below the 1986 figure. This suggests an improved performance even to some extent in the unusual national demand and supply conditions of 1991.

Table 5.9 indicates that the official channel marketing margin declined in 1987, causing an increase in the producer price as a percentage of consumer price. Since 1987, the marketing margin as a percentage of consumer price kept on increasing with producer price as percentage of consumer price declining until 1990 before it rose in 1991.

Although the open markets in the country have generally been associated with higher consumer prices, evidence indicates that during the period of good harvest (1986–8), open market consumer prices in the country were lower than official retail prices (ERB, 1990: 85). It is also worth noting that the official retail price fixed by the government did not cover marketing costs of public marketing agencies with NMC operating at a loss partly as a result of this. Since the government had to intervene by agreeing to pay commercial banks' bad debts owed by the NMC (URT, 1991b), the consumer price that would provide a comparable basis with private traders' consumer price would be the one that would allow official channels to break-even. If this adjustment is made, the official channel producer price as a percentage of consumer price kept on declining from 1986 onwards as a result of increased margin, while that for private traders increased as a result of a decline in margin except in 1991 (Parsalaw, 1994: 315).

VI   ANALYSIS OF MARKET INTEGRATION

The impact of liberalisation on market integration was evaluated using regression analysis, spatial and temporal price analysis. The last two also indicate the marketing costs and profit levels for private traders.

Table 5.9   Maize marketing margin for official channels in Arusha (TSh/kg)

Year	Producer price (TSh/kg)	Producer price as % of consumer price	Consumer price	Margin as % of consumer price
1986	0.80	51.0	1.57	49.0
1987	0.77	63.6	1.21	36.4
1988	0.62	48.1	1.29	51.9
1989	0.61	46.2	1.32	53.8
1990	0.54	42.0	1.26	57.1
1991	1.10	57.0	1.93	43.0

Source: Adapted from Parsalaw, 1994.

Results of Regression Analysis

Regression coefficients for six markets in Arusha region are presented in Tables 5.10 and 5.11. To generate a stable series and reduce the possibility of spurious correlation, two obvious suspects were eliminated (seasonality and inflation).

The regression analysis used follows the model used by Ravallion (1986) on rice markets in Bangladesh. This is attained by regressing the supply market price against three explanatory variables as in the equation below:

$$P_{it} = aiP_{it-1} + b_{i0}(P_{lt} - P_{lt-1}) + b_{i1}P_{lt-1} + U_{ti}$$

where:
P_{it} = Supply market price at time t.
P_{lt} = Receiving market price at time t.
a_i = Measures the effect of lagged supply market price on current supply market price.
b_{i0} = Measures the proportional change in supplying market price caused by a change in the temporal margin of the receiving market (i.e., a change in price over time in the receiving market).
b_{i1} = Measures the influence of the lagged receiving market price level on the supplying market price.
U_{it} = Disturbance term.

A statistically significant b_{i0} indicates that traders in the supply market monitor changes in the receiving market price and adjust supply prices accordingly. It may, however, be possible that private traders fail to connect markets through commodity flows in the short-run. This led to construction of an index to measure short and long-run market integration. This is called the Index of Market Connection (IMC).

$$IMC = ai_{bi1}$$

The closer the index to zero, the higher the degree of short-run market connection. In principle, an index less than one indicates that markets are integrated in the short-run, while an index greater than one indicates poor connection across markets with past local market prices playing a dominant role in current local price formation (Lirenso, 1993).

Regression results in Table 5.10 indicate that the period between 1986–88 is characterised by very low R^2 indicating that the explanatory variables could only capture very little of the current supply market price. In all cases, Index of Market Connection (IMC) assumes very high values indicating that markets were poorly connected in the short-run. In all cases the lagged receiving market price (b_{i1}) is not statistically significant in explaining the current supplying market price developments. In all cases except one the receiving market temporal margin (b_{i0}) is not statistically significant in explaining the current supplying market price developments. The exception to this is Mbulu-Mondoli markets where the receiving market temporal margin is significant at 0.01 in explaining the current supply market price. Despite the significance of this temporal margin, together with the lagged supply market price, these two markets have only a middling R^2.

The regression results for the same pairs of markets during the 1989–91 period are presented in Table 5.11. The results indicate very high R^2 compared with the same variables during 1986–8. To varying degrees, the lagged receiving market price and the temporal margin are significant in a number of markets in influencing the supply market price during this period. The IMC in one case is

Table 5.10   Regression coefficients for six markets in Arusha (1986–88)

SU	RE	ai	bi0	bi1	IMC	R^2	Constant
BA	AR	0.316 (1.737)*	−0.133 (−1.009)	0.033 (0.347)	9.6	0.11	0.494 (2.465)**
MB	AR	0.347 (1.969)**	−0.031 (−0.283)	0.045 (0.423)	7.7	0.13	0.478 (2.397)**
MO	AR	0.766 (5.658)***	0.286 (1.520)	0.023 (0.152)	33	0.65	0.214 (1.235)
LO	AR	0.718 (6.212)***	−0.113 (−0.632)	0.182 (1.495)	4	0.62	0.157 (0.679)
KI	AR	0.468 (1.809)*	−0.176 (−0.171)	−0.174 (0.550)	2.7	0.28	0.764 (2.652)***
BA	MO	0.315 (1.809)*	−0.018 (−0.171)	0.044 (0.550)	7.2	0.13	0.494 (3.295)***
MB	LO	0.406 (2.326)**	−0.026 (−0.220)	−0.001 (0.006)	406	0.18	0.495 (2.633)***
MB	MO	0.553 (3.677)***	0.286 (2.869)***	0.085 (1.141)	6.5	0.39	0.280 (1.935)*

Notes: Figures in parentheses represent *t*-statistics.
         Significant at:- *** 0.01; ** 0.05; * 0.10

SU   Supply market
RE   Receiving market
BA   Babati
LO   Loliondo
AR   Arusha
KI   Kibaya
MB   Mbulu
MO   Monduli

Source: Adapted from Parsalaw (1994).

Table 5.11   Regression coefficients for six markets in Arusha (1989–1991)

SU	RE	ai	bi0	bi1	IMC	R^2	Constant
BA	AR	0.278	−0.145	0.482	0.6	0.93	−0.013
		(1.076)	(−0.981)	(3.154)***			(−0.238)
MB	AR	0.718	0.184	0.223	3.2	0.95	−0.042
		(7.067)***	(1.382)	(3.362)***			(−0.926)
MO	AR	0.677	−0.121	0.244	2.8	0.81	0.061
		(4.844)***	(−0.550)	(2.119)			(0.513)
LO	AR	0.693	0.063	0.474	1.5	0.96	−0.123
		(5.226)***	(0.414)	(2.615)***			(−1.294)
KI	AR	0.903	0.202	0.026	34.7	0.87	0.764
		(6.559)***	(0.811)	(0.224)			(0.754)
BA	MO	0.948	0.346	0.059	16.1	0.91	−0.001
		(8.360)***	(2.759)***	(0.690)			(−0.013)
MB	LO	0.639	0.204	0.179	3.6	0.95	0.054
		(5.221)***	(1.589)	(3.121)***			(1.117)
MB	MO	0.917	0.047	0.102	9.0	0.92	−0.016
		(8.002)***	(0.352)	(1.092)			(−0.255)

Notes:
Figures in parentheses represent *t*-statistics.
Significant at:- *** 0.01; ** 0.05; * 0.10

Source: Adapted from Parsalaw (1994).

less than one suggesting a strong short-run market integration. In other cases, although the IMC is greater than one, compared to the 1986–8 period they indicate an improvement in five pairs of markets.

Results of structural stability tests carried out using Chow procedure to determine whether the difference between the two regressions (1986–8 and 1989–91), are statistically significant for the eight pairs of markets indicates a significant difference between the two regressions for the three pairs of market of Babati-Arusha, Mbulu-Arusha and Babati-Monduli. Among the six markets under analysis, there are three surplus markets: Babati, Mbulu, and Kibaya. Due to long distances and poor road conditions, the market of Kibaya trades more with markets outside Arusha than those in Arusha. This leaves the markets of Mbulu and Babati as the main supply markets to the main receiving market of Arusha and the other deficit markets of Monduli and Loliondo. The results of structural stability tests indicate that there is an improvement in market integration between the two supply markets and the main receiving market of Arusha and the other deficit market of Monduli.

Although there are structural rigidities and administrative practices that restrict free trade, as explained, the above results show an improvement in market integration during 1989–91 compared to 1986–8, although not of statistical significance in a number of cases. A comparison of Tables 5.10 and 5.11 indicates high R^2 in every case during 1989–91; IMC improved in six out of eight pairs of markets; there are significant explanatory variables other than the lagged price in the same market (five cases) compared to one during 1986–8. The results of the structural stability test, however, indicate significant variation in 1989–91 over 1986–8 in only three pairs of markets.

Results of Spatial and Temporal Price Analysis

Spatial and Temporal price analysis using models as applied by Farruk (1970) and Hays and MacCoy (1978) were used to determine the profit levels and trends over time. In these models, the Price Spread (PS) is obtained after taking into account transport costs, handling costs and normal profits. The Net Seasonal Rise in Price (NSRP) is obtained after taking into account rent of storage facility, interest on capital tied down in stocks, physical loss during storage and depreciation of sacks. Computed PS and NSRP were above zero in all cases suggesting that profits earned by private traders in performing the storage and transport functions were above normal or that the analysis fails to capture some traders' costs (Parsalaw, 1994).

However, apart from one pair of markets (Babati–Mondulu), there is a decline in average price spread over the 1989–91 period for all pairs of markets. The average price spread declined from TSh 0.37/kg in 1986 to TSh 0.16/kg in 1991. This indicates that despite long distances, poor road conditions, inadequate capital, inadequate transport and residual attempts by local authorities and co-operatives to restrict private traders, there was an improvement in spatial arbitrage. In the case of NSRP, all markets indicate a positive seasonal rise in price. But if the drought year of 1991 is set aside, there is a pattern of decline in seasonal rise in price over 1988–90 period. The average seasonal rise in price as a percentage of expected price rise declined from 36.6 per cent in 1986 to 26.3 per cent in 1990. Moreover, although the seasonal rise in price is above what can be explained by storage costs, this cannot solely be attributed to private traders' profit. Evidence provided in this work and elsewhere (for example Coulter, 1994) indicates that on-farm storage is significant for inter-seasonal price variation.

VII CO-OPERATIVES AND NMC FINANCIAL PERFORMANCE

Grain market liberalisation measures introduced in 1988 were meant to improve the financial performance of public marketing agents by making them operate commercially in competition with private traders. Although the NMC was still required to maintain the (SGR) and stabilise prices, if there is separate accounting for these operations with the government adequately paying for their costs, NMC would still be required to perform commercially its role of buying, milling and selling grain. The following analysis attempts to establish whether this actually happened, and whether public marketing agents reduced financial deficits by operating commercially.

Financial Performance of Co-operatives in Arusha Region

The regional co-operative union[2] made after tax profits which peaked in 1987 (Table 5.12). After tax profits declined beginning in 1988 and by 1991 co-operatives incurred after tax losses of approximately TSh 2 million.

There are several reasons for this trend. First is the increase in co-operative overheads beginning in 1988. While overheads were increasing the co-operative market share for maize declined. The volume of maize handled by co-operatives declined from 20 500 tonnes in 1989 to 2 800 tonnes in 1991. As a result of this, revenue from maize declined from TSh 1.6 million in 1989 to TSh 0.212 million in 1991.

Contrary to expectations that co-operatives would reduce their over-extended roles after liberalisation in order to operate commercially, this did not happen. Thus, while there was a massive decline in revenue resulting from a decline in market share, there were losses incurred by various non-marketing operations (Table 5.13). These operations included: farming, transport, wholesale and retail selling of consumer goods.

A decline in revenue from maize, and losses from non-marketing operations made it increasingly difficult for the co-operatives to finance overheads, and they sustained annual losses. For example in 1989 revenue from maize for RIVACU could finance 40 per cent of overhead costs but in 1991 revenue could only finance 3.7 per cent of the co-operative overheads.

Table 5.12   Co-operative profits and losses (1986–91) (million TSh)

Year	Overhead costs	After tax profits
1986	3071	1629
1987	3102	4409
1988	3899	1675
1989	5527	1052
1990	5118	–372
1991	3538	–1973

Source: Parsalaw (1994).

Table 5.13   Co-operative losses from non-marketing operations ('000 TSh)

Year	Losses	Losses as a percentage of income
1986	50	5.9
1987	18	0.4
1988	1665	21.0
1989	2291	30.8
1990	2143	31.0
1991	1988	47.0

Source: Parsalaw (1994).

Financial Performance of the NMC

The NMC does not record its financial information by separate business activities and so it is not possible to make separate financial analyses of them. The following financial analysis of its accounts at the national level will, however, provide an insight into the trend in profits and losses before and after liberalisation in 1988 (Table 5.14).

The NMC continued to make losses after 1988 although the size of losses declined in real terms after 1988 (Table 5.14). There was a small fall in annual losses and a big fall in operating losses in 1989. This decline, however, did not result from improvement in efficiency. Because NMC made losses for every unit

Table 5.14   National Milling Corporation profit and losses by 31 July of each year (million TSh)

	1986	1987	1988	1989	1990	1991
Total sales	385	444	565	460	349	390
Total cost of sales	423	551	915	640	439	478
Gross profit (loss)	(38)	(107)	(351)	(180)	(89)	(89)
Total overheads	55	93	166	223	160	203
Profit (loss) for year	(72)	(180)	(496)	(372)	(232)	(262)
Net result for year	(92)	(183)	(496)	(372)	(232)	(262)
Bal. brought forward		(92)	(275)	(771)	(1143)	(1375)
Bal. carried forward	(92)	(275)	(771)	(1143)	(1375)	(1637)

Source: National Milling Corporation.

sold, the decline in sales in 1989 caused a decline in costs. Unit cost, however, increased from TSh 1.90/kg in 1988 to TSh 2.36/kg in 1989 (Parsalaw, 1994). In 1990 there was a big decline in operating and annual losses. This could be explained by the workers laid off, and the closure of some depots, branches and some retail shops in 1990, thus reducing overhead costs (URT, 1991a). In 1991, while operating losses stood at the 1990 levels, the annual losses increased as a result of an increase in overhead costs.

VIII   CONCLUDING SUMMARY AND RECOMMENDATIONS

Concluding Summary

There was an increase in the number of private traders after liberalisation, and there is evidence of a reduction in marketing margins during normal years in the private market channel. There is, however, evidence of a reversal of this trend in 1991, a year of poor harvest in other parts of the country. Public marketing agents did not reduce their marketing margin.

Despite a slightly higher producer price in the official channel, public marketing agents lost market share to private traders. Promptness of payment in cash by private traders, on-farm procurement, provision of gunny bags, early start of buying and higher price at different times of the year, made producers prefer the private market channel.

There was an improvement in market integration after liberalisation, with both spatial and temporal price spreads declining post liberalisation although still positive. Given the restrictions that still exist, together with poor roads and inadequate capital, these positive spreads may indicate above normal profits or the failure of models used to capture traders' costs and risk associated with operating in an uncertain and difficult environment.

Increased competition from private traders led to loss of public agents' market share. A loss in market share demands more cost cuts than there would otherwise have been needed if a parastatal was to be profitable with the same volume of business. Despite this, co-operatives and NMC continued their over-extended loss-making activities. They continued to receive overdrafts despite outstanding overdrafts with commercial banks. There was thus no incentive for them to operate efficiently.

Although at the national level government statements on liberalisation policy support free trade, implementation of this policy at the local level is different. There is evidence that when co-operatives lost their market share, instead of reacting by competing they resorted to coercive tactics directed against private traders. This involves colluding with local authorities who impose fees on private traders and use barriers manned by police to enforce this requirement. Uncertainty about the direction of implementation of the liberalisation process will undermine traders' confidence and they may hold back investment in transport, storage and processing all of which are vital for long-term efficiency gains from liberalisation.

Concluding Recommendations

The efficiency of the grain marketing system could be greatly improved if access to credit by private traders could be improved. This can be done by removing preferential access to public market agents and requiring them to repay outstanding overdrafts. It is argued that part of the reason for failure of commercial banks to provide loans for private marketing in Tanzania, is because so much credit is still outstanding to parastatals (Abbott, 1993).

Allowing NMC and co-operatives to cover their losses by guaranteeing them overdrafts will not make them operate commercially. To provide the necessary incentive to improve performance, preferential access to bank credit should be curtailed. Loans to NMC and co-operatives should only be approved by commercial banks after rigorous appraisal similar to that applied to private business.

Evidence provided in the study does not suggest total government withdrawal from the market, but points out areas where reliance on the market may not yield desired results, and government intervention may still be required. Government investment in infrastructure, particularly construction of trunk and feeder roads in rural areas, and possibly also in storage structures in public market places, will be required. One way to reduce private traders' storage problems might be to rent/sell storage facilities that will be available as a result of the reduced roles of NMC and other parastatals. But taking into account that there is considerable on-farm storage, a study on ways to improve traditional storage structures at the village level to minimise post harvest losses is also required.

The government will still need to intervene to protect low income consumers in times of food shortages, which would include operation of the strategic grain reserve. Intervention to support producers in remote areas and to cope with years of bumper harvest may also be needed. The capacity of the private sector to engage in such activities is either small or private traders are unwilling to undertake such activities. Continuous monitoring of the liberalisation programme is necessary to ensure that policies made at the top are implemented at the grass-roots level. Evidence indicates that official participants respond to competition by acting both as players and referees in the game. This requires prevention of coercive and predatory tactics.

Notes

1. The NMC industrial roller miller broke down in 1985 and it was not until 1991/92 that it resumed milling.
2. There was one co-operative union during 1986–88 but it split into two (ACU and RIVACU) beginning in 1989. The profits and losses are for both.

References

Abbott, J.C. (1987) 'Alternative Agricultural Marketing Institutions', in D. Elz (ed.), *Agricultural Marketing Strategy and Pricing Policy* (Washington DC: World Bank) pp. 15–21.

Abbott, J.C. (1993) *'Agricultural and Food Marketing Institutions in Developing Countries: Selected Regions'* (Wallingford: CAB International)

BOT (1980) *Economic and Operations Report*, June 1980.

BOT (1981) *Economic Bulletin*, 13 (1).

BOT (1988) *Economic and Operations Report*, June 1988.

BOT (1990) *Economic and Operations Report*, June 1990

BOT (1991) *Economic Bulletin*, 21 (3).

Bryceson, D.F. (1991) 'Food Pricing, Spatial Egalitarian Objectives and Urban Growth in Tanzania', Rural Development Studies: Research Seminar, Term I 1991–92 (The Hague: Institute of Social Studies).

Bryceson, D.F. (1993) *Liberalising Tanzania's Food Trade: Public and Private Faces in Urban Marketing Policy 1939–88* (London: James Currey).

Coulter, J. (1994) 'Liberalisation of Cereals Marketing in SSA: Lessons from Experience', *Marketing Series*, 9, (Chatham, Kent: Natural Resources Institute).

Ellis, F. (1983) *Agricultural Marketing and Peasant State Transfers in Tanzania*, Development Studies Discussion Paper No. 116 (Norwich: University of East Anglia).

Ellis, F. (1988) 'Tanzania', in C. Harvey (ed.), *Agricultural Pricing Policy in Africa: Four Country Case Studies* (London: Macmillan).

ERB (1990) *Tanzania Economic Trends*, 2 (3), 1989 and 2 (4), 1990 (Dar-es-Salaam, Tanzania: ERB, University of Dar-es-Salaam).

Farruk, M. (1970) *The Structure and Performance of the Rice Marketing System in East Pakistan*, Occasional Paper No. 31 (Ithaca, New York: Cornell University).

Green, R.H. *et al.* (1980) *Economic Shocks and National Policy Making: Tanzania in the 70s*, Research Report No. 8 (The Hague: Institute of Social Studies).

Hays, H.M. and J.H. McCoy (1978) 'Food Grain Marketing in Northern Nigeria: Spatial and Temporal Performance', *Journal of Development Studies*, 14 (2), pp. 182–92 (London: Frank Cass).

Herbst, J. (1990) 'The Structural Adjustment of Politics in Africa', *World Development*, 17 (5), pp. 949–58.

Hyden, G. and M. Karlstrom (1993) 'Understanding Structural Adjustment: Tanzania in Comparative Perspective', in M. Blomstrom and M. Lundahl (eds), *Economic Crisis in Africa: Perspectives on Policy Responses* (London: Routledge) pp. 41–60.

IBRD (1992) *World Tables 1992–93* (Washington DC: World Bank).

IBRD (1993) 'Problems of Marketing and Input Supply', in J.C. Abbott (ed.), *Agricultural and Food Marketing in Developing Countries: Selected Readings*, (Wallingford: CAB International) pp. 291–305.

IMF (1992) *International Financial Statistics, 1992 Yearbook* (Washington DC: International Monetary Fund).

Lirenso, A. (1993) 'Grain Marketing Reform in Ethiopia', DPhil Thesis, School of Development Studies, University of East Anglia.

MDB (1992) *Annual Review of Maize, Rice and Wheat*, MDB R1/92 (Dar-es-Salaam, Tanzania: Ministry of Agriculture).

Ndulu, B. and N.H. Lipumba (1991) 'International Trade and Economic Development in Tanzania', in Frimpong-Ansah *et al.* (eds), *Trade and Development in Sub-Saharan Africa* (Manchester: Manchester University Press) pp. 231–61.

Parsalaw, W. (1994) *Liberalisation of Maize Marketing in the Arusha Region of Tanzania*, unpublished DPhil Thesis, University of Sussex.

Ravallion, M. (1986) 'Testing Market Integration', *American Journal of Agricultural Economics*, 68 (1), pp. 102–9 (Worcester, Massachusetts: American Agricultural Economics Association).

Renkow, M. *et al.* (1983) *The Potential Effects of Alternative Structures and Pricing Policies in the Markets for Maize in Tanzania* (Washington DC: USAID).

Rutihinda, G. (1991) *Structural Adjustment, External Debt and Growth in Africa – Tanzania's Experience'*, in *Economic and Operations Report*, June 1991 (Dar-es-Salaam, Tanzania: Bank of Tanzania).

Smith, L.D. and N.J. Spooner (1990) *Sequencing of Structural Adjustment Policy Instruments in the Agricultural Sector*, Occasional Paper No. 6 (Glasgow: Centre for Development Studies, Glasgow University).

Suzuki, Y. and A. Bernard (1987) *Effects of Pan-Territorial Pricing Policy for Maize in Tanzania* (Washington DC: International Food Policy Research Institute).

URT (1990a) Report of Technical Task Force on Loan Recovery Problems in Tanzania (Dar-es-Salaam, Tanzania: Bank of Tanzania).

URT (1990b) *Economic and Social Action Programme* (Dar-es-Salaam, Tanzania: Government Printer).

URT (1991a) *Developments in Policy and Institutional Reforms since December 1989*, Report for the Meeting of Consultative Group for Tanzania in Paris (Dar-es-Salaam, Tanzania: Government Printer).

URT (1991b) *National Milling Corporation Restructuring Study Report* (Dar-es-Salaam, Tanzania: Ministry of Agriculture).

Van Cranenburgh, O. (1990) *The Widening Gyre: The Tanzanian One Party State Policy Towards Rural Co-operatives* (Leiden: Eburon).

Wagao, J. (1992) 'Adjustment Policies in Tanzania, 1981–89: The Impact on Growth Structure and Human Welfare', in Cornia *et al.*, *African Recovery in the 1990s: From Stagnation and Adjustment to Human Development* (London: Macmillan) pp. 93–115.

6 Structural Adjustment, Labour Markets and Employment Policy

John Toye

I INTRODUCTION

Since 1980, structural adjustment has changed from a policy of 'quick fix' aimed at correcting structural deficits in the balance of payments into a medium (or even long-term) process of economic and political reform in developing countries. What was originally designed as a swift and separable exercise of macroeconomic stabilisation has gradually become a persistent and diversified reform process which is hardly any longer distinguishable from development policy itself. It is not appropriate to give an account here of how this transformation took place (for this see Toye (1993)). But it is important to recognise it, because it has profound implications for those areas of development policy which are increasingly pervaded by the logic of structural adjustment. In the mid-1980s, the interface between structural adjustment and social welfare policies was raised as a major issue, in a wide-ranging debate on the 'social costs' of adjustment (Cornia, Jolly and Stewart, 1987). This paper discusses a particular aspect of this interface, between structural adjustment and employment policy, since it is now clear that for many developing countries employment policy must be adapted to the wider context of economic reform.

The practice of employment planning pre-dates the advent of structural adjustment, even in its original design as a macroeconomic quick fix. Employment planning was a specific elaboration of development planning, the technique used to produce economy-wide projections of planned investment and production targets, and a complementary set of economic policies (fiscal, monetary, commercial, etc.) to be implemented over a medium-term planning horizon. Employment planning has been an extension of this kind of development planning, integral to, and embedded in its overall technical framework (Amjad, n.d.: 1). The underlying philosophy of this approach has been expressed by Kornai (1975: 30–1), who argued that:

> a development planning model should demonstrate the consequences of different alternative economic policies on the whole life of the society in question

and that:

> there are no technical obstacles to adding variables and equations which describe income distribution, employment, education...

However, with due respect to Kornai, the attempt to integrate employment variables into development planning models did run into considerable practical obstacles. These arose partly from the problems of estimating appropriate coefficients and elasticities to make employment projections; and partly from the fact that *any* historical estimate will be inappropriate if a plan's aim is structural change. Nevertheless, the concern for the integration of employment objectives with development planning induced some useful research and action at a sectoral level on the promotion of efficient labour absorption.

One of the handicaps of the medium-term planning approach is its failure to address fully the recently increased level of uncertainty in the economic life of developing countries. Much of this uncertainty is external in origin, deriving from the fluctuating world prices of tradables, fluctuating world interest rates and currency movements and shifts in developed countries' policies on aid and trade. But some of it originates internally, from local weather conditions or changes in local political alignments that lead to shifts in policy. In these circumstances, the production of a single set of planning figures every five years (even if they are internally consistent) may well not be very helpful for the domestic decision-makers. Indeed, the need for structural adjustment policies, either of the short, sharp shock variety or the more pervasive kind, is itself evidence of the practical limitations of the medium-term planning mechanism. Employment planning has, therefore, increasingly come to include the short-term monitoring and forecasting of employment variables and the analysis of policy measures that affect them, outside the framework of large blueprint plans. As the time horizon shortens, then, employment planning changes into the more general category of employment policy.

The question to be addressed is how employment policy should best be conducted as part of the process of structural adjustment. This involves three subordinate questions. The first is how structural adjustment policies can be expected to affect employment and the functioning of labour markets. The second is whether governments undergoing economic reform have managed to deal appropriately with the employment dimensions of the reform. The third is whether a new specification of the tasks of employment planning can be written that will be consistent with the changing role of the state and the greater reliance on market processes that structural adjustment brings.

One set of answers to these three questions goes as follows. Structural adjustment either unnecessarily adds to unemployment and underemployment or lowers the real wage of labour, thereby adding to poverty and worsening the income distribution. Governments have, for various reasons, neglected these adverse employment, poverty and inequality outcomes of structural adjustment. In future they should turn back to the techniques of employment planning to ensure that this does not happen. Although this set of answers has the merits of clarity and popular appeal, it does need further refinement and elaboration. In the remainder of this paper, some refinements and elaboration of these responses will be proposed, which will try to do justice to the complexity both of the theory of economic reform and the empirical experience of it in Chile, Indonesia and Tanzania.

II   PRELIMINARY CONSIDERATIONS

Central to the complexities of the interface between structural adjustment and employment is the fact that 'structural adjustment' itself is a package of policies. The diagram at Appendix 6.1 illustrates this very clearly. At the simplest level of disaggregation, the adjustment policy package consists of both stabilisation measures and structural adjustment measures in the narrower sense. At the next level, stabilisation measures break down into devaluation and complementary monetary and fiscal policies, while structural adjustment proper breaks down into resource mobilisation, resource reallocation within the public sector, institutional reform and the liberalisation of a wide range of markets. Among the many markets to be liberalised is the labour market, with liberalisation meaning in this context the reduction in government-legislated regulation and the movement towards more market-determined wage and salary settlements.

This elaborate package of policies is also varied in both space and time. Despite the prevalent notion of structural adjustment as a standard policy package imposed on developing countries by the international financial institutions regardless of individual country circumstances, no two countries have *exactly* the same design of structural adjustment. Although designs are similar and show a 'family resemblance', they have to vary somewhat, if only because the initial conditions are never exactly the same. Within any one country, the content of the package also varies over time. The 'big bang' approach of implementing all the adjustment policies simultaneously is rather rare, although it was used in the Chilean case which we examine in later parts.

Most adjustment programmes involve designing a chronological sequence of adjustment measures, to ensure that they interact with each other in a beneficial rather than a counter-productive manner. In addition to the time-sequence that is planned, another factor that determines actual time variation is the extent to which policy implementation actually follows the sequence that is designed.

In the more elaborate form which it has now assumed in many developing countries, structural adjustment may usefully be thought of as a scaled-down development plan. The adjustment package of policies is plan-based, in the sense that it is related to a set of macroeconomic projections derived from the application of the World Bank's Revised Minimum Standard Model (RMSM), which itself is based on the dual-gap analysis familiar in the development planning literature. RMSM is, however, less technically sophisticated and covers a shorter period than the older development planning models (Tarp, 1993: 153–6). The balance between projections and policies has moved strongly in favour of policies. The SAL policies are more wide-ranging and different in content from those embodied in the typical development plans of the pre-1980 era. Moreover, their implementation is subject to much more explicit external monitoring, and external finance is more closely linked to progress in implementation, although the hardness of the policy conditionality can be exaggerated. With those important qualifications, therefore, an adjustment programme can be viewed as a development mini-plan.

If that is so, it is not surprising that the problems of evaluating the impact of structural adjustment programmes are very similar to those which arose earlier in the context of discussions of plan-fulfilment. The comparison of pre-plan with post-plan indicators tells us something, but not whether a better performance could have been achieved. The comparison of plan achievements with plan targets also is helpful, but raises the question of whether the targets were well-chosen at the start of the plan and remained feasible despite unforeseen events during the plan period. The success of a plan can be properly assessed only by comparing plan achievements with a hypothetical scenario of what would have happened in the absence of a plan. So it is with the evaluation of structural adjustment programmes (Toye, 1992). A 'counterfactual' scenario needs to be constructed to compare with what actually occurred during the adjustment period. This method has been applied to the Indonesian case (to be discussed in Parts IV and V) by Thorbecke and Associates (1992).

The evaluation of SAPs faces additional difficulties, however, because their objectives are directed at changing the policy environment rather than at simply increasing key variables (investment, output and employment, for example) within a relatively fixed policy framework. Policy change itself is more difficult to measure than plan expenditure, and it is important to net out the influence of the SAP finance on the target variables when determining the impact of the SAP policy changes *per se*. Despite these new problems, the old ones of controlling for the effects of weather and of changes in international economic conditions (terms of trade, world interest rates, etc.) still remain. It is important to remember that international economic conditions do not stand still while countries attempt to adjust their economies to them. They continue to change and, while some of these changes may be favourable and reduce the size of the adjustment problem, external conditions may have – and in the case of sub-Saharan Africa definitely have – deteriorated and increased the task to be accomplished. The problem of tracing the consequences of the SAP packages for any particular set of economic variables (such as wage levels or the number in employment) is, therefore, bedevilled by the prior problem of controlling for all the other non-SAP factors which affect those variables. So if unemployment has increased during the adjustment period, or the real wage fallen, this cannot be attributed automatically to the effects of the SAP. The same applies to employment increases or rises in real wages.

It is important to note that employment policies are to be found both outside and inside the SAP package. They are outside because some existing employment policies may be part of the initial conditions which the SAP package is designed to correct. For example, assume that a government has issued a directive to state enterprises to hire labour for social reasons, regardless of the financial losses which the enterprises incur thereby. Enterprise losses will be a significant contributor to the government budget deficit, which in turn fuels inflation, raises the real exchange rate and creates the balance of payments deficit that will call forth the SAP intervention. Employment policies which are incompatible with macroeconomic balance, such as the one just cited, are part of the problem which structural adjustment is supposed to remedy. For simplicity, such inappropriate employment policies may be designated as 'macro-incompatible' policies.

Where macro-incompatible employment policies already exist, it is likely that employment policy conditions will also be included inside the SAP package. This may be in the form of a simple reversal of existing policy – in the form of a condition that the offending directive should be withdrawn. Or it may be in more indirect and less visible ways, perhaps by a requirement that state enterprises be re-constituted as fully autonomous commercial corporations. The detail of the inside policies is irrelevant to the general point that employment policies as a category can act either as an obstacle to macro-economic adjustment, or as a catalyst of it. Which it does depends on the nature of the policy, and whether it is macro-compatible or not.

For the stabilisation component of the adjustment process to succeed, two changes must be brought about. Domestic spenders (households, firms and the government) must change their pattern of demand, so that they want to buy fewer tradables (i.e. goods that are traded or could easily be traded). At the same time, domestic producers have to change their pattern of output, so that they want to produce more tradables. A simultaneous 'double-switch' has to be achieved which attacks the deficit both on the import and the export side. Devaluation of the domestic currency is the standard measure to achieve this, by changing the price incentives for importers and exporters in the appropriate directions. Long experience, however, has shown that devaluations are not always effective, for a variety of reasons.

III   THEORETICAL ASPECTS OF SAPS AND LABOUR MARKETS

Before examining further the obstacles to the successful implementation of adjustment policy, it will be helpful to analyse how stabilisation measures of devaluation combined with fiscal and monetary restraint could theoretically be expected to change the levels of wages and employment. In order to do this, we must first specify an analytical framework. Following Knight (1976), we assume that the context is of a small, open economy with the following features:

(a) the relative price of importables to exportables remains constant, permitting analysis in terms of a composite good called 'tradables' whose price is determined in world markets;

(b) the prices of non-tradable goods are determined by supply and demand in the domestic market;

(c) tradables and non-tradables are final consumption goods, so that intermediate goods, for purposes of simplification, do not appear in the analysis;

(d) in the short run, capital is locked into its sector, while labour (treated as homogeneous) is mobile across sectors.

Under these assumptions, fiscal and monetary restraint supplemented if necessary by a devaluation, will raise the price of tradables relative to non-tradables, causing producers to switch resources that are mobile (in the short run, only labour) out of non-tradables and into tradables.

This short-run reallocation of labour leads to the establishment of a new wage level throughout the economy. Since the relative price of tradables has increased while the price of non-tradables has fallen, the real consumption value of the new nominal wage level will depend on the composition of the workers' consumption basket in terms of tradable and non-tradable goods. A fall in the real consumption wage is more likely, the more tradables relative to non-tradables that workers consume (Addison and Demery, 1993: 137). The overall effect on poverty in the economy, however, does not depend merely on whether the real consumption wage does fall. If poverty is concentrated in the non-tradable sector, and the switch of labour to the tradable sector is large enough, poverty will not increase. The effect on the poverty index of switching labour into the less poor sector can more than compensate for the fall in the real consumption wage. Some suggest that this is an unlikely outcome, however (Stewart, 1993: 29–30).

The assumption used so far that labour is freely mobile between sectors in response to short-run changes in product prices is, however, an unrealistic one. As has already been suggested, most governments in countries which adopt SAP programmes will have in place at least some employment policies which are macro-incompatible, i.e. which act as obstacles to the smooth market-based adjustment which the simple theory describes. Examples might be a minimum-wage law which sets a floor to the permitted decline in nominal wages; or a system of wage indexation which prevents a permanent decline in the level of real wages. A further complication is that such macro-incompatible employment policies, when they exist, do not affect all parts of the economy equally. In developing economies, labour markets are normally taken to be segmented or dualistic. On the one hand, there is a formal sector which is subject to the sway of official policies – concerning taxation, location of industry, company reporting, investment and so on, as well as employment regulations. On the other hand there is an informal sector where the official writ does not run, and where employment regulations (and all the others) are rarely effectively enforced. To the extent that government policies are sources of imperfections in the labour market, it will be the informal sector where the labour market is fully competitive, and the formal sector where it is less so.

To carry the analysis further, it would be necessary to specify the relationship that connects the division between tradable and non-tradable sectors, and the division between formal and informal sectors. At the extremes, two possible connections can be specified. One scenario is where all non-tradables are located in the formal sector, because of the existence of a large and inefficient public sector, while tradables are produced by an informal agricultural and small-scale industrial sector. The other is where tradables are produced in the formal sector by efficient firms, either private or public, and the informal sector produces inferior foodstuffs and local handicrafts. Without going into the detail of the analysis here, it can be stated that neither of these limiting cases gives results which overturn the findings from examining the simpler case of a fully competitive labour market. These are that for a small, open economy, defined as we have defined it, 'the poverty effects of employment and wage changes under adjustment cannot be predicted without country-specific information on some of the key parameters, in particular the consumption basket of workers' (*ibid.*: 142).

The small open economy model therefore seems to support an agnostic approach. It does not provide the grounding for a general presumption that the stabilisation component of the adjustment package will cause unemployment to rise, or the real wage to fall. They will do so if workers have a strong preference for consuming tradables, but not otherwise. It does not demonstrate that, for stabilisation measures to succeed, the real consumption wage has to fall in all sectors.

The small open economy model discussed above has a number of features which limit its relevance to adjustment situations, apart from those already mentioned. Unemployment is modelled as search unemployment only. The model assumes that all unemployment is accounted for by workers in the process of moving between jobs. It rules out by assumption Keynesian unemployment which arises because the goods market is quantity-constrained. Any excess of tradable goods caused by the reduction of domestic absorption is supposed to be able to be exported. But in the short run this may be unrealistic. Various types of investment in production and marketing may be a necessary condition of the expansion of tradables. Recall, however, that in the model, investment is held constant. Thus episodes of Keynesian unemployment, as Meller (1992: 64) argues occurred in Chile in 1982–3, cannot be explained within this theoretical framework. Nor can the relationship between actual unemployment and the real wage level.

Beyond this world of simple theory lie complications which are real enough in the experience of adjustment, but very hard to model. It is to these practical problems of policy-making that one must look when analysing the success of stabilisation policies, and not merely the predictions of theory. Simple theory does not deal with problems of expectations, for example. Consumers and producers will not react to a new set of price signals if they believe them to be only temporary. Particularly in the case of devaluation, where it is an instrument which governments of developing countries have not used for many years, and indeed publicly criticised and foresworn, the first resort to it may fail simply because the relevant economic actors expect a swift reversal of policy. The speed with which governments can make their stabilisation policies credible, and therefore effective, is more a matter of political than of economic calculation.

On the economic side, it is always possible to choose the correct policy instruments, but then to miscalculate the pressure with which to apply them. Even if one chooses a pair of nutcrackers, rather than a steam hammer, to crack a walnut, it is still possible to use excessive force and smash the nut. The percentage of the devaluation may be mis-judged in either direction, and fiscal and monetary policy may be set too lax – dissipating the incentive effects of the devaluation – or too tight, causing *avoidable* unemployment, bankruptcies and poverty. These kinds of implementation errors cause secondary costs to the economy which are not inherent in the policies themselves (Killick, 1993: 153–5).

A third important cause of real-life failure of stabilisation measures is that the relevant elasticities of demand and supply are too low. In principle, all the supply-side measures in the structural adjustment programme are designed to avoid this particular cause of failure. But if they are pursued too slowly in practice, their benefits will be delayed and the response to devaluation will be too weak. Microeconomic policies, especially in the labour market, must be made macro-compatible, if the entire package of structural adjustment measures is to succeed. The new role for employment policy is to ensure that this happens. And if it is right to describe structural adjustment programmes as development mini-plans, then this definition of the new role for employment policy is nothing more than a reiteration of the old requirement for consistency between plan and policies, although now revived in a modern guise.

IV   CHILE, INDONESIA AND TANZANIA: BASIC COMPARISONS

Empirical cases studies of the adjustment experience of a variety of countries can help to improve understanding of the negative and positive aspects of employment policy inhibiting or facilitating the adjustment process. In choosing countries for such detailed analysis, a wide geographical spread will be advantageous. The sources of wage inflexibility, and its consequence labour market segmentation, differ considerably in different developing regions of the world.

Unionisation has been stronger in Latin America than in Africa or Asia. The typical forms of government intervention also differ markedly between the three continents. The case studies to be discussed here – of Chile, Indonesia and Tanzania – capture some of these continental contrasts in the institutional context of structural adjustment.

The three case studies also provide important contrasts along other dimensions. One such is the previous history of macroeconomic management, especially whether it included recent successful episodes of stabilisation or not. Another is the nature and severity of the economic crisis to which adjustment has to be made. A third is the duration and intensity of the adjustment process – how radical and extensive has it been, and how deeply it has been affected by design and implementation errors.

Chile after 1973 provides the purest case of a monetarist stabilisation pro- gramme evolving into a drastic and radical economic re-structuring on free market lines. It was intended to be a classic real-life experiment to test the conservative economic doctrines emanating from the University of Chicago (Foxley, 1983: 4). It served as a prototype for many other structural adjustment programmes of the early 1980s, and that in Turkey in particular. The political basis for this experi- ment was the violent overthrow of the Allende government of 1970–3 by a highly authoritarian military regime under General Pinochet. Previous recent experiences of monetarist stabilisation had either failed (1956–8) or been aborted (1968–70). The programme of social transformation pursued during the Allende years had by 1973 created substantial imbalances in the Chilean economy.

Indonesia had already undergone a radical change of political-economic regime in 1966, when the Sukarno government was overthrown by the New Order movement of President Suharto. The macroeconomic mismanagement of the 1950–66 period was reversed by US-trained technocrats who largely succeed- ed in stabilising the economy by 1969. The adjustment that was required in response to the post-1981 oil price decline was undertaken in a less politically- traumatic context than existed in post-Allende Chile, since trusted economic tech- nocrats were already in place, although sharing influence with 'engineering' technocrats who distrusted full liberalisation (Azis, 1993).

Since independence, Tanzania has never undergone a regime change as thor- ough going and violent as those in Chile and Indonesia. The erosion of the social- ism of President Nyerere and the transfer of power to chosen successors have been very gradual. Some of the key institutions created during the Nyerere period con- tinue in being with little modification. As economic difficulties increased through the 1970s, the pressure for economic change increased, and various home-grown measures of economic liberalisation were adopted in the early 1980s, although with insufficient internal austerity and external financial assistance.

The Chilean economic crisis of 1973 resulted from the rapid changes intro- duced by the Allende government. In particular, the mobilisation of trades unions with official encouragement had brought about a rapid redistribution of income, an expansion of public sector employment as private enterprises were nationalised and an accelerating inflation which reduced real wages by 40 per cent. The fiscal deficit rose to 25 per cent of GDP, while the money supply growth rose to 350 per cent per annum. The effect of inflation was to create a huge balance of payments deficit and rapidly falling foreign exchange reserves. The deteriorating economic situation was a reflection of a fierce social struggle, conducted with little regard for the economic consequences.

The post-1981 crisis in Indonesia was very different. It was caused largely by a single large external shock, the collapse between 1981 and 1986 of the world oil price. This had serious consequences for an economy which had achieved rapid growth in the 1970s by managing successfully the investment of large oil revenues. The balance of payments deficit ballooned, while real income per head declined. Confronting these consequences remained an economic problem, whose solution was made easier because it was not located within more extensive social and political upheavals.

By 1985, Tanzania was facing more than just an economic problem. External pressures, notably war and the 1970s oil price shocks, undoubtedly played a part in de-stabilising the Tanzanian economy. But the economic organisations of 'Tanzanian socialism' had already demonstrated poor economic performance, including financial irresponsibility and openness to corrupton. The crisis of the mid-1980s was centred on the need for internal organisational change as well as economic policy reversals, and the difficulty of bringing this about in a one-party political system where Nyrere's influence, both official and unofficial, remained strong. If in Chile the scope for economic policy change was too wide open, in Tanzania it was too restricted. The symptoms of imbalance were the usual ones. Negative growth of GDP per head after 1977 was accompanied by inflation accelerating to the 30+ per cent per annum level, plus an annual trade deficit regularly at the $500 million mark.

When each of the three countries embarked on the adjustment process, they exhibited marked differences in the structure of employment. Chile's labour force of around three million people showed only 4.8 per cent of open unemployment, and of those employed, 77 per cent had jobs in the non-agricultural sectors. Two-thirds of these non-agricultural jobs were in the formal sector, while the remainder were either in the informal sector (26 per cent) or domestic service (7 per cent). Even if agriculture were classified as entirely informal in character, that would imply an informal sector (excluding domestic service) absorbing just over 40 per cent of those in employment.

Indonesia had a labour force of nearly 60 million in 1982, with an unemployment rate of 3 per cent. Only about one-third of these were in waged employment, the rest being in various forms of self-employment or family-based work. The largest component of wage employment was in the public services, followed by agriculture and forestry and manufacturing. This suggests that the Indonesian informal sector absorbed a much larger share of the labour force than did the Chilean.

Comprehensive figures of the Tanzanian labour force were first collected for the year 1990–91, some five years after a serious adjustment process began. They show about 11 million people, of whom about 8 per cent were either unemployed or under-employed. Of the fully employed, only 10 per cent were in wage employment, divided roughly in half between the public sector (the government and parastatals) and the private sector. Although only 182 000 were in waged employment in the private informal sector, the great bulk of the employed labour, some 90 per cent, was working in the informal sector of traditional agriculture.

These contrasts in the structure of the employed labour force reflect the broader economic differences between the three case study countries, especially in levels of income per capita, the diversification of productive activities and the degree of involvement in foreign trade. In addition, one would expect them to be related to differences in the institutions of the labour market, and particularly to the role of trades unions and modes of government regulation of that market. Is this indeed so?

In Chile during the Allende years the rate of unionisation among those employed rose sharply from 23 to 30 per cent. The trades unions exerted their pressure through a system of centralised bargaining, winning substantial increases in nominal (but not real) wages. This power was extended as about 250 private enterprises were nationalised. The system of bargaining was legally established under the Chilean Labour Code. The Pinochet coup immediately suspended all trade union activity and the application of the Labour Code, which had provided procedures to govern the hiring and dismissal of labour. Union power was effectively curtailed during the rest of the 1970s, and when official figures of union membership reappeared in the early 1980s, the rate of unionisation had fallen to 12 per cent. Unions were greatly weakened but not destroyed.

In Indonesia in 1981, an authoritarian system of industrial relations was already in place. The official labour union, SPSI, was very much a creature of the government and played little role in wage-setting or in safeguarding workers' rights. Some unofficial unionisation may exist, but workers' actions in defence of wages and conditions, such as it is, is either spontaneous and unorganised, or possibly responsive to various kinds of direct political manipulations.

Despite its socialistic stance, Tanzania – unlike Chile under Allende – never permitted the operation of independent trades unions. The main trades union body, JUWATA, was an organ of the one legal political party, the CCM, until 1992. Until then, JUWATA acted merely as a liaison body between the CCM-led government and the workforce. It had no local branch organisation and the whole set-up remained highly centralised. Sporadic attempts at local strikes against non-payment of wages were put down by military force (Sender and Smith, 1990: 122–8). In these respects, Tanzania differed little from other 'socialist' economies in low-income sub-Saharan Africa, such as Angola and Mozambique.

The modes of government intervention in the labour market showed considerable divergence, the Chilean mode being the distinctive one. After the 1973 coup, wage rates were no longer negotiated with trades unions, but determined on the basis of government recommendations to the private sector (1973–79) and later of legal directives (1979–82). Until 1982, the government implemented a policy of complete wage indexation to past levels of inflation. A minimum wage law also remained in force throughout the whole of this period.

Indonesia, too, had minimum wage legislation in which the wage was calculated according to 'minimum physical needs'. But unlike Chile between 1973 and 1979, Indonesia had in place an employment code specifying procedures to deal with redundancy, although the extent of its enforcement was partial. There was no overt government determination of the level of money wages, because rates were kept down by apparently unlimited supplies of labour at the prevailing wage. The Tanzanian situation basically resembled that of Indonesia, and contrasted with that of Chile.

A final basic contrast between Chile, Indonesia and Tanzania is to be found in the duration and intensity of the adjustment experience. Chile clearly stands out because of the prolonged and comprehensive nature of its adjustment process. As is shown in the next part, it has lasted for the best part of two decades, with three distinctive main phases. In Indonesia, the adjustment period lasted about eight years (1981–9) and stopped short of a thorough-going economic liberalisation. Tanzanian efforts at adjustment are relatively recent, have been undertaken very gradually and some of the more important measures remain prospective rather than actual. The three cases under examination here are thus widely dispersed along the spectrum of possible adjustment experiences. In Chile, adjustment was maximal; in Indonesia, it was middling and in Tanzania, to date, it has been rather mild.

V   SUMMARY OF THE ADJUSTMENT PROCESSES

Chile

During the first main phase of Chilean adjustment (1973–81), macroeconomic stabilisation was undertaken simultaneously with an attempt at the complete deregulation of all product and factor markets. The deregulation policies in the labour market have already been mentioned above. The stabilisation component consisted of an initial period of fiscal austerity, during which unemployment rose to around 20 per cent. This was accompanied, and then followed by progressive deep cuts in the average nominal tariff rate, which was reduced to 10 per cent (from 105 per cent) by 1980. But during this period the peso was not effectively devalued in real terms. Rather, various different tactics of exchange rate management were designed to squeeze out inflationary expectations. These tactics produced a substantial upward revaluation of the peso in real terms by 1981. The combination of deep nominal tariff cuts and a higher real exchange rate discouraged investment in tradables. Although inflation was successfully brought down to 9.5 per cent and exports continued to grow, a balance of payments deficit of 15 per cent of GDP remained, which was financed by foreign borrowing of banks and enterprises after internal deregulation. By 1981, serious imbalances in the macroeconomy still persisted despite rapid economic growth and the virtual victory over inflation.

During the second main phase of adjustment (1982–84), the Chilean economy was adversely affected – like other Latin American economies – by a combination of rising international interest rates and deteriorating terms of trade. Given the imbalances remaining in 1981, these external shocks had serious negative effects on growth, import absorption and unemployment, which climbed to 30 per cent. Real interest rates reaching 48 per cent per annum failed to attract further foreign lending and the government was finally forced into two major devaluations in mid-1982, plus the reimposition of foreign exchange and capital controls. In addition, financial deregulation in the 1970s permitted an unsound structure of debt to be built up within the banking system. Very high real interest rates plus devaluation precipitated a massive banking crisis, which the government was forced to bail out at a huge cost to public funds.

During this time, Chile entered into an IMF–World Bank adjustment programme, which reassured foreign creditors, and permitted debt re-scheduling. The severity of the crisis in terms of falls in output and investment shook domestic confidence so badly that response to the devaluations of 1982 was very slow to emerge. No significant supply response from the tradables sector emerged until 1985, when a new, more pragmatic policy regime was introduced.

This third phase of adjustment was characterised by continuing IMF–World Bank programmes and external debt re-scheduling and debt-equity swaps. The real exchange rate was permitted to decline substantially, which in combination with raised nominal tariffs finally prompted a robust growth of tradables. Public investment was permitted to grow significantly from 1983 to 1989 and proved to be complementary with private investment in stimulating output growth. This growth was assisted also by higher copper prices, the benefits of which were passed through to the private sector. This sector's increased prosperity permitted a successful re-privatisation of banks and the sell-off of some traditional state enterprises. In this final phase, economic growth averaged 7 per cent a year.

Indonesia

The Indonesian adjustment programme after 1981 had three main elements – a tightening of fiscal policy; changes to key prices in the economy and deregulation and institutional reform. The gradual increase in fiscal stringency was brought about not by reducing expenditure in real terms, but by considerable improvement in domestic revenue-raising. This was assisted by tax reforms in 1984/85 which removed many (but not all) of the 'tax expenditures' which pervaded the existing tax legislation in the form of 'incentives' and other discretionary tax exemptions. At the same time the tax system was simplified and tax collection mechanisms were improved. One spectacular example was the privatisation of the collection of customs duties by using a Swiss company to certify dutiable items and receive payments.

Key prices in the economy were also subject to significant changes. In 1983, the real rate of interest was negative: by 1991 it had been raised to the extremely high level of 14 per cent per annum. The rupiah was steadily devalued, losing 44 per cent of its 1985 value by 1991 in terms of its real effective exchange rate. The combination of regular nominal devaluations with a low and slightly decelerating rate of domestic inflation resulted in a substantial improvement in Indonesia's external competitive position.

Financial deregulation was taken forward in a major way in 1988, with the removal of many of the existing barriers to entry to the banking business and the phasing out of schemes of subsidised credit. The rapid growth of banks and bank assets required tighter monetary policy and new prudential regulations by 1991. Protection of domestic industry has been reduced by the conversion of quantitative restrictions to tariffs, the lowering of average nominal tariffs from 22 per cent in 1985 to 10 per cent in 1991 and the reduction of non-tariff barriers to trade. Investment licensing has been scaled down until new entry is prohibited virtually only in the services sector. Policy towards foreign investors has become much less restrictive. Regulation of maritime transport has been greatly reduced, leaving the government as a residual operator. A start has been made on the reform of state enterprises. Despite all of these changes, Indonesia has by no means completed the deregulation of its economy.

During the adjustment period, Indonesia's aid receipts multiplied sixfold at current prices. By 1991/92, they exceeded the government's revenues from the corporation tax on the oil companies. In spite of this, the economy's debt service ratio declined from 40 to 30 per cent, while growth proceeded between 1987 and 1991 at 7 per cent a year. An important source of this growth (apart from aid) was non-oil exports, and within this category exports of manufactures such as plywood, clothing, textiles, and footwear. The growing economy also reduced its key macroeconomic imbalances substantially, with both the fiscal deficit and the current account deficit being halved as percentages of GNP.

Tanzania

Tanzania's adjustment period began effectively with its IMF agreement in 1986, which was quickly followed by debt-rescheduling and the resumption of IMF-World Bank credits. Since then, the Tanzanian shilling has undergone a regular series of devaluations from a value of TSh 17.47 per US dollar to TSh 290 by April 1992. At that point Foreign Exchange Bureaux were permitted to operate, and traded at TSh 400 to the dollar. The long term aim is to unify the official and bureaux rates. The legalisation of forex bureaux put an end to a wide range of restrictions on access to foreign exchange.

Although Tanzania moved from large negative real interest rates in 1986 to slightly positive real interest rates by 1991, this measure had very limited impact. Inflation has remained high at around 28–30 per cent and borrowing at rates slightly above that is a risky undertaking. In addition, the financial sector remains in considerable disarray, so opportunities even for this kind of credit remain very restricted for most of the private sector.

Deregulation has proceeded on a number of different fronts. Extensive price control on final and intermediate products was dismantled, except for petroleum products and fertilizers (to which a subsidy still applied). Restrictions on the sale of agricultural products were greatly eased, although marketing boards retain residual functions for coffee, cotton and cashew sales. Import restrictions were scaled down by adopting an open general licence system, with a small negative list. Finally, a more liberal code for foreign investment was adopted in 1990.

Fiscal policy has been tightened in Tanzania since 1985/86, when the budget deficit equalled about 21 per cent of expenditure, to reduce it to an average of 7.6 per cent at the end of the 1980s. However, taking the public sector as a whole shows a somewhat different picture, as the government has increased its grants and loans to the parastatal enterprises, while the state-owned banks have also given parastatals extensive credit. These arrangements have led to growth in the money supply and inflation has continued throughout the period since 1986 at around 30 per cent a year. Not until 1992 was a commission appointed to recommend reforms of the parastatal sector. Retrenchment in this sector would be larger and more politically hazardous than the 1985 retrenchment of 12,750 civil servants, especially as many of these were subsequently re-engaged.

Tanzania's economic performance since 1986 has been a decidedly mixed one. The overall growth rate has been raised to a steady 3 per cent per year, at least some of which must be attributable simply to the resumption of aid flows. Export earnings have increased only slightly, despite a 7.5 per cent a year growth in export volumes – some of which may represent merely a redirection into official channels of previously illegal exports. As a result, the current account deficit has increased. So far the adjustment process has provided no solution to the problem of the falling world prices of Tanzania's traditional export crops. Finally, as has been noted, the reduction in the budget deficit has not made any impact on the rate of inflation, because of failure to press ahead sufficiently with the reform of the financial sector and the parastatal enterprises. Tanzania's adjustment was, by the early 1990s, perhaps half complete.

Inter-Country Comparisons of Adjustment

What lessons for policy can be drawn from these summaries, necessarily sketchy, of adjustment under radically different circumstanes? The most successful experience seems to be that of Indonesia. Compared with that of Chile, it is shorter and unmarked by any deep crisis and subsequent policy reversals, but achieved similar end-states of economic growth and macro-economic stability. Compared with the Tanzanian reform process, Indonesia's appears to be more purposive and more radical, as well as faster, especially in the key areas of mobilising domestic resources and stimulating the supply of non-traditional exports. But Indonesia's relative success has to be judged against the background of two problems which it did not face, but both Chile and Tanzania did. The first concerns the difficult political environments in which the Chile and Tanzanian government had to pursue reform. This contrast has already been drawn out in Part IV. The second concerns adverse external economic conditions. These played a part in exposing Chile's economic fragility in 1982–83, and in depriving Tanzania of increased export earnings in the second half of the 1980s. By contrast, Indonesia enjoyed both political stability and political support for its economic reform, and, after the initial oil price shock, freedom from adverse international economic trends while the economy was adjusted.

But having made due allowance for these differences in political and economic circumstances, it would appear that between 1973 and 1981, Chilean policymakers made serious and avoidable policy errors. These errors stemmed from a profoundly ideological commitment to extreme free market theories of economic policy. Such theories are utopian. The attempt to apply them to a real economy without regard to its specific institutional structures is to invite policy inconsistency and economic disaster.

Three major policy errors marked the first phase of the Chile adjustment programme. The first was the total replacement of the existing institutions of wage-bargaining by a government-imposed system of wage indexation to past levels of inflation. This method of 'disciplining labour' in order to reduce inflation introduced an unnecessary rigidity into the labour market, and left the government to look to exchange rate management to control the inflation rate to which wage levels automatically adjusted *ex post*. The freezing of the exchange rate in 1979 to eliminate inflation via the working of expectations and the 'the law of one price' was the second mistake. This permitted a 30 per cent real revaluation of the peso which went unnoticed by the authorities, the effect of which was a widening trade deficit financed by volatile foreign private capital inflows. An import-led boom in the non-tradables sector generated fast economic growth, but this was unsustainable. The third mistake was failure to regulate a stock market boom that was engineered by large conglomerate firms getting preferential credit from banks which they owned in order to bid up their own share prices. This boom also inevitably came to bust (Taylor, 1988: 117–20).

The Chilean failures of 1973–81 underline the need to maintain a realistic real exchange rate and the importance of well-judged devaluations as an instrument of successful adjustment. A 50 per cent devaluation after 1982 produced (after a long lag) a supply response in tradables production. Gradual devaluation, but with a large cumulative impact, played its part in the Indonesian adjustment package. Tanzania, which had resisted any but minor exchange rate changes until

1986, has now made very large adjustments while enjoying steady, if still slow, economic growth.

The financial sector can be seen to be a critical danger area in the adjustment process. It is fatally easy to assume that, once state intervention in setting interest rates and controlling credit is removed, financial intermediation will take place in textbook fashion. In Tanzania, such a withdrawal has yet to take place, so the private sector still faces a liquidity squeeze. But the early Chilean experience shows the natural tendency of unrestrained private enterprise to rig financial markets to acquire short-run unearned profits. Adequate supervision and regulation of banks and financial markets is essential to the promotion of a healthy climate of private enterprise. Even in Indonesia, deregulation produced links between conglomerates and banks similar to those in Chile, leading to the financial problems of the Summa Bank in 1992.

Our main concern in this paper, however, is with employment policies, to which we return in Part VII, after comparing the wage and employments trend in the three case study countries.

VI   TRENDS IN WAGES AND EMPLOYMENT

Chile

A general assessment of trends in wages and employment during Chile's adjustment period is that they were unfavourable. The Chilean case also shows a sequence in which strongly adverse trends during the initial phase of extreme free market economic policies was followed by a significant recovery after 1985, when more pragmatic policies were adopted. If 1970 is taken as a normal year, because it preceded the pumping up of public sector employment under Allende, one index shows unemployment in 1990 as no lower than 1970 (at 5.7 per cent), while another index gives a rate of 9.2 per cent. At the height of the 1982 economic crisis, however, the rate had according to both indices soared to 20 per cent, or 25 per cent if those on the government's emergency employment programmes are included. The detailed figures on employment are given in Table 6.1.

The raw employment figures can be misleading due to the numbers of hidden unemployed involved in emergency employment programmes (EEPs) and the reductions in hours worked. The employment programmes were in one sense a form of social security rather than true work, often involving part time duties of limited duration. Wages were well below the minimum wage and positions lacked employment entitlements such as national insurance contributions. Between 1975 and 1981 the number in EEP's represented a highly significant per cent of the economically active population, 1.9 per cent in 1975 and almost 6 per cent in the period 1976–7. For this reason the unemployment figures are best considered in conjunction with adjusted figures which include those in emergency

Table 6.1 Employment and unemployment in Chile 1970–1990
(thousands of persons; percentages)

	Labour force	Employment	EEP	Unemployment (%)	Adjusted unemployment (%)
1970	2932.2	2766.1		5.7	5.7
1971	2978.8	2865.6		3.8	–
1972	3000.8	2907.8		3.1	–
1973	3039.0	2893.1		4.8	–
1974	3066.8	2784.7		9.2	
1975	3152.9	2727.3	71.5	13.5	15.5
1976	3216.4	2705.0	172.5	15.9	20.6
1977	3259.7	2796.8	187.5	14.2	19.2
1978	3370.1	2891.5	145.8	14.2	18.0
1979	3480.7	3000.4	133.9	13.8	17.2
1980	3539.8	3122.1	191.0	11.8	16.5
1981	3669.3	3269.3	175.6	10.9	15.1
1982	3729.5	2971.5	226.8	20.4	25.7
1983	3797.1	3091.2	502.7	18.6	30.1
1984	3937.1	3185.1	336.3	19.1	22.9
1985	4071.8	3420.3	324.3	16.0	20.9
1986	4160.3	3582.0	233.5	13.9	18.0
1987	4288.3	3748.0	148.5	12.6	15.2
1988	4455.0	3911.5	46.2	12.2	13.1
1989	4620.6	4163.2		10.1	10.1
1990	4815.8	4369.9		9.2	9.2

Note: EEP is numbers employed engaged on government emergency employment programmes.

Source: Garcia, 1992, Table 2.

employment programmes. (The method of adjustment assumes that 88 per cent of those in EEP were effectively unemployed.)

Trends in real wages during the adjustment period are given in Table 6.2. Real wages contracted by 40 per cent in 1973 and 15 per cent in the following two years, informal incomes reducing similarly. Average real wages then grew between 1975 and 1981 at an average of 6 per cent per year, partly as a result of full indexation in a period of decelerating inflation. This rate exceeded productivity increases and discouraged hiring. During the 1982–3 crisis, the improvements of the late 1970s in average real wages were completely reversed, and a rising

Table 6.2   Indices of real wages in Chile, 1970–1990

Years	Minimum wage	Index of remuneration	Wage of manufacturing
1970	81.0	109.7	97.1
1971	106.8	134.1	106.6
1972	101.7	119.0	101.2
1973	46.2	73.1	68.4
1974	90.6	70.2	62.2
1975	105.1	62.5	58.3
1976	100.1	78.9	78.6
1977	84.6	79.9	78.6
1978	97.4	85.0	87.4
1979	98.3	92.0	94.2
1980	100.0	100.0	100.0
1981	110.0	108.8	115.5
1982	122.2	108.6	110.7
1983	93.2	97.0	102.9
1984	82.1	97.1	99.0
1985	74.3	93.0	97.1
1986	78.8	95.0	101.9
1987	66.9	93.1	103.2
1988	74.2	98.6	109.8
1989	82.5	100.5	113.4

Source: Garcia, 1992, Table 4.

trend did not begin to emerge again until 1986. The ambit of wage employment expanded, its growth being focused on large and medium enterprises in the private sector. The relative scope of informal sector employment contracted, diminishing the impact of a slower recovery in average informal incomes than in wages.

Indonesia

The general assessment of employment trends during the Indonesian adjustment experience is that the latter has been 'employment-friendly'. The economy has been able to absorb a slightly larger proportion of the growing labour force, so unemployment has fallen a little below its 1982 rate of 3 per cent. The decline has not been entirely smooth, however; it showed a temporary reversal in 1988–9 before falling again. The figures are in Table 6.3.

Table 6.3   Unemployment in Indonesia, 1982–1990 (percentages)

Year	Unemployment rate
1982	3.0
–	—
1986	2.6
1987	2.5
1988	2.8
1989	2.9
1990	2.5

Between 1986 and 1990, wage employment rose by nearly 5 per cent per annum. The largest increase was in the trade and services sector, closely followed by manufacturing, reflecting the labour absorption of labour intensive export industries such as timber processing, textiles, clothing and footwear. Employment in public services was held virtually constant. The sectoral growth of wage employment is presented in Table 6.4.

Over the whole of the adjustment period, real wages remained flat, with the more or less constant real wage encouraging the steady recruitment of new labour into employment. There was little difference between the behaviour of real wages in agriculture and industry, as is shown by Table 6.5.

Real consumer wages in most sectors followed a pattern of a steep rise between 1983 and 1985, then a fall for the following three years beginning to rise

Table 6.4   Wage employment by sector in Indonesia, 1986 and 1990
(thousands of persons; percentages)

	1986	1990	1986–1990 Average annual growth (%)
Agriculture, Forestry, etc.	3,531	4,876	8.4
Manufacturing	3,105	4,296	8.5
Trade and Services	789	1,169	10.3
Public Services	7,283	7,300	0.1
Other	2,872	3,435	4.5
Total	17,580	21,076	4.6

Source: BPS, *Labour Force Survey*, 1986 and 1990.

Table 6.5   Real wages indices in Indonesia, 1983–1991

	Real producer wages (agriculture)	Real producer wages (industry)
1983	100	100
1984	104	113
1985	114	116
1986	111	107
1987	108	101
1988	103	99
1989	109	101
1990	109	102
1991	110	–

again after 1988. By 1992 real wages experienced a further boost due to falling inflation. Data for hoeing, weeding and planting from BPS Farmers Terms of Trade Survey follows this pattern, as does data on the construction industry. Manufacturing wages appear to follow the pattern, rising to 1985 and falling to 1988, although data past 1990 are not available. Women gained more industrial employment growth during the structural change, although on average they still earn less than half the male wage.

Tanzania

The lack of availability of relevant employment and wage statistics for Tanzania makes it impossible to provide comparable series to those presented for Chile and Indonesia, even for the small proportion of the economically active labour force employed for wages and salaries. Standard series on employment and wages published by the government Bureau of Statistics still end in 1984 or earlier. As previously mentioned, the first comprehensive labour force survey relates to 1990/91, well after the adjustment process began in 1985/86. A substantial information gap exists precisely for the period during which adjustment began in earnest.

An ILO estimate of unemployment among heads of households in 1982 provided an estimate of 3 per cent for unemployment. The Ministry of Labour survey for 1990/91 gives a figure of 2.6 per cent unemployed, plus 2.9 underemployed. It seems fair to conclude (albeit on thin evidence) that the Tanzanian adjustment programme is unlikely to have brought about great changes in the pattern of wage employment, but has succeeded in keeping up with the growth of its labour force. The main effects of the measures so far are likely to be a reduction in underemployment in informal rural agriculture, and a redistribution of jobs in the waged sector away from the public and towards the private sector.

Inter-Country Comparisons

In the absence of comparable data for Tanzania, comparisons must be confined to Chile and Indonesia. The contrast between the overall wage and employment trends in these two cases is clear enough. Declines over a long period in both real wages and employment characterise Chile, while rough constancy of real wages and persistent employment increases characterise Indonesia. But how are these trends to be linked with their adjustment programmes? It is necessary here to recall our earlier cautionary remarks about problems of evaluation. Unless all the non-policy influences on economic performance can be controlled for, it is invalid simply to assert that performance outcomes are the results of the policies adopted. In Chile, for example, the most adverse outcomes belong to the second phase of adjustment, when deteriorating external conditions greatly exacerbated the problems which had been allowed to build up during phase one.

Inter-country comparisons are additionally vitiated by the fact that the initial conditions which set the tasks for policy-makers engaged on structural adjustment differed markedly between the two cases. Chile faced much more serious inflationary pressures and was institutionally adapted to inertial inflation in a way that Indonesia was not. One of the factors which makes inflation inertial is a highly mobilised labour force, which Indonesia certainly did not have. The proper test for the value of a set of policies is, therefore, not whether another country derived better results from adopting a similar set of policies. It is whether the country in question would have done better or worse if it had adopted different policies from those that were in fact chosen.

Thorbecke and Associates (1992) have attempted to answer this question for Indonesia. The basic message which emerges from the Thorbecke study is that the Indonesian economic technocrats calculated the strength of its stabilisation measures very well to meet their balance of payments, growth and income distribution objectives. In their programming of public expenditure, the chosen policies were not optimal, when judged from a long-term perspective. But every government has to make political as well as economic decisions. Although it is hard to be definite about this, it may well be the case that sub-optimal expenditure programming was necessary to sustain the political support for the entire programme. Even authoritarian governments, like Indonesia, require support from some quarters, and cannot be expected to act as pure and disembodied executives of liberal economic rationality. It is, however, much easier to manipulate the composition of expenditure to meet both political and social objectives when the total of public expenditure is held firmly within a macroeconomic framework where the imbalances have been reduced to manageable proportions, as in the case of Indonesia. It is, moreover, easier to maintain a sustainable macroeconomic framework when, as also was true in the Indonesian case, the government did not withdraw precipitately from all forms of microeconomic interventions.

Two general points are worth making on the basis of the data in this part. The first is that the results from Indonesia seem to support the propositions derived from the theoretical discussions in part III. Given the absence of any obvious improvement in external circumstances, they reinforce the agnostic conclusion derived from economic theory, that adjustment policies do not inevitably depress the level of real wages or destroy employment. Structural adjustment that is employment-friendly is at least possible, although it may require the rather special circumstances that prevailed in Indonesia in order to be realised.

The second point is that the choice of policy instruments within the broad context of a structural adjustment operation remains crucial. After allowing that the 1982–83 crisis in Chile had important external determinants, it is implausible to argue that better results could not have been achieved – not only for employment, but also for production and foreign exchange reserves – under different policies. The third phase of adjustment embodied better policies, as well as a fillip from the copper price.

VII   THE EFFECT OF EMPLOYMENT POLICIES

No doubt there are good bureaucratic reasons for having a separate government department to regulate employment law, industrial relations and wage bargaining. The policies of such a department can be thought of as 'employment policies'. But this bureaucratic definition of employment policy is a rather narrow and conventional one, and can be misleading. For in reality, policies as they affect employment and wages are a seamless web. The impact of policy on employment and wages derives from the interaction of 'employment policies' in the bureaucratic sense with a much broader set of policies. The former cannot be properly designed except in explicit conjunction with the design of the latter. That is why good employment policies are those which are 'macro-compatible'. Or, to give a more precise definition, good employment policies are those which maximise remunerative employment subject to the constraints of balance of payments and fiscal stability. This perspective implies that there cannot be an ideal package of employment policies (in the bureaucratic sense), which can be recommended for general adoption by employment ministries in adjusting countries. The act of separating out one sub-set of policies for general prescription as an ideal package involves disregarding the essential requirement of macro-compatibility.

Evidently, a different approach is needed. The approach taken here is to try to illustrate the idea of macro-compatibility by considering examples of employment policies and asking whether they are likely to frustrate, fail to influence or facilitate the pursuit of macro-economic stability. Policies that tend to frustrate the search for stability are termed negative; those that fail to influence it one way or the other are termed neutral; and those that facilitate stabilisation are termed positive. The examples used are chosen from the three case studies. The allocation of the examples to the three categories remains qualitative and judgmental – inevitably so.

Chile's adjustment history provides a rich store of examples of negative, neutral and positive employment policies, and of an eventual shift from negative to positive. During the first phase from 1973 to 1982, errors in economic policy inflicted more heavy costs in terms of employment losses and real wage declines than were necessary. On top of these, however, its employment policies (in the bureaucratic sense) compounded these errors. The suspension of existing labour laws created an institutional vacuum in the labour market which both permitted very heavy shedding of labour and discouraged new hiring of labour, because it raised uncertainty about what employers' future obligations to labour would be. A better policy would have been to maintain the existing Labour Code but to replace specific provisions in it as required.

The Pinochet government was continuously surprised by the depth of the impact of its policies on unemployment. Well able to monitor employment trends as they unfolded, it was unable to predict at all accurately future employment trends, which it always expected to improve at what proved to be an unrealistic pace. The consequence of this was that its counter-measures were either inadequate or ineffective. Its Emergency Employment Programme, large though it was, was unable to prevent a very rapid decline in the wages share of GNP. No scheme for labour re-training was adopted. A subsidy scheme to promote the hiring of labour was entirely neutral in its impact.

Not until the 1982–83 crisis finally dented essentially ideological beliefs in the magic powers of the free market did more pragmatic employment policies begin to be tried. Not until 1990, after the election of President Aylwin, were positive employment policies accorded a central and fully legitimate place in the structure of economic policy. The social democratic civilian government actively sought a sustainable public consensus. This consensus embodied a restoration of labour and trades union rights within an agreed framework of productivity growth and industrial peace. The adverse distributional effects of adjustment were now addressed by social expenditures directed towards the poorest and supported by new taxes for their finance. These measures have been rewarded by continuing growth and some decline in poverty indicators (Schkolnik, 1992; de Kadt, 1994).

The role of employment policies in the bureaucratic sense was much smaller in Indonesia than in Chile. Because the structural adjustment measures proved themselves quite quickly to be employment-friendly, employment creation by specific ancillary measures never became an objective of the Indonesian government. Because in an authoritarian system, labour had never in recent years been mobilised, the government was under no pressure to alter its modes of regulation of the labour market. Much employment planning in Indonesia, therefore, falls squarely into the neutral category. It proceeded in the realm of development planning exercises which had little impact on policy. It had undoubted defects, but they did little harm since planning was disconnected from policy-making. The same difficulty of predicting the employment response to measures of structural reform as had occurred in Chile, was manifest in Indonesia. But in the latter case, unlike the former, it was the creation of jobs rather than their destruction which went unanticipated, and it is far from clear whether, if job destruction had been predicted, policy-makers would have acted differently from the way in which they did.

The technocrats who were guiding the reform programme may have mis-judged the employment effects of their policies in some instances. The public works schemes which provide guaranteed employment may have been allowed to decline too swiftly in the late 1980s. More spending on such schemes could have been undertaken, perhaps, provided that complementary anti-inflation safeguards had been put in place. Had this been done, there might have been no reversion to dirigiste policies announced by the President, against the grain of technocratic opinion, to address equity concerns. Quotas of bank lending for small enterprises and quotas of equity of large enterprises to be transferred to co-operatives look like populist gestures in the face of anxieties about the distributional results of adjustment. Ironically, such gestures could have been counter-productive and have had negative consequences for employment and distribution.

The examples of positive employment policies in the Indonesian experience were very few. This is not because international agencies and technical assistance projects did not research and propose such policies. It is rather because the evi-dence suggests that the proposals made did not percolate upwards sufficiently to influence policy, against a general background in which the employment conse-quences of adjustment were never perceived as a major issue of political economy. The Indonesian economy might, however, have performed even better than it did, if its reasonably good supply of employment statistics and policy advice had been put to use instead of being somewhat complacently neglected.

Despite considerable inputs of external technical assistance during the 1980s, the formulation of employment policies remains at an early level of development in Tanzania. Departmental responsibility is primarily with the Planning Commission, while the Ministry of Labour handles labour disputes, safety at work, conditions of service and similar matters. The current Plan fails to focus on economy-wide employment issues, which is hardly surprising, given the absence of planning models, historical data and general analytical capacity in the employ-ment area. The main focus of policy concern is on the retrenchment of civil ser-vants and parastatal employees. For obvious political reasons, the government has approached this task very circumspectly. Much of the planned retrenchment remains in the future and details of the compensation packages and resettlement facilities (e.g. re-training and credit access) have yet to emerge fully. As well as the political difficulties (which are perceived officially as being intensified by the introduction of a multi-party political system), the costs of retrenchment have to be met through new budgetary expenditure without breaching ceilings given by macroeconomic constraints. Apart from this question of public sector labour shedding, where the requirement of macro-compatibility is very evident, policy attention is slowly focusing on the possibility of emerging skill shortages in the longer term, and the need for private finance to be channelled into education and training. In Tanzania, then, structural adjustment has neither been greatly helped or hindered by existing employment policies. Such policies are still largely in the formulation stage.

VIII   THE SCOPE FOR MORE POSITIVE ACTION

The search for better employment policies during structural adjustment should be based on the main conclusions which can be drawn from the foregoing discussion. The summary of these starts from the theoretical implication of the small open-economy model that the stabilisation component of structural adjustment will not necessarily reduce employment or real wages in all sectors of the economy. The role of employment policy is not, therefore, inevitably that of trying to counteract a general loss of employment and reduction in real wages. Structural adjustment can be 'employment-friendly' both in theory, and in reality, as evidenced by the Indonesian case. But it can also be 'employment-hostile', particularly when the design of the macro-economic policies of stabilisation and adjustment is flawed, as was evidently the case in Chile during 1973–81.

In the broadest perspective, the best route to improving employment and wages outcomes under adjustment is to improve the design of macroeconomic policies. One particular area of difficulty in policy design concerns the sequencing of the different elements in the adjustment policy package. The economic theory of sequencing is still very primitive, much of the accumulated wisdom in this area consisting of common sense, rules of thumb and weakly based empiricism (Greenaway and Morissey, 1992: 22–8). Nevertheless, a strong sense of pragmatism can, while sequencing theory is being refined, be immensely helpful in avoiding policy errors that cost much in terms of lost employment and incomes. It is only when initial conditions are so dreadful that policy errors could not possibly worsen the situation that the neglect of sequencing is justified, and a simultaneous pursuit of all elements of the policy package could be recommended. The 'big bang' approach to adjustment is a desperate remedy and should only be attempted when the conjuncture is truly desperate.

The programme of economic liberalisation is most endangered, and most likely to fail, when it is pursued in the context of fierce social and political struggles. In such contexts, the economic objectives of the programme become entangled with, and distorted by, political objectives, such as destroying the power base of political opponents and building up the power base of political allies. So it was in Chile under Pinochet, and so it is still in many parts of Eastern Europe and the former Soviet Union. Successful liberalisation is also endangered by an ideological conviction of the invincibility of freely operating market forces and the inevitability of economic liberalisation being accompanied by increases in economic welfare. Socio-political conflict and free-market ideology in governments together make a potent policy cocktail which induces a reckless resort to 'big bang' liberalisation strategies, with consequent economic crises. The opportunity to learn how the economy responds to initial measures, and to adjust implementation accordingly is thereby thrown away. This could only be done by policy-makers who believe that they have nothing to learn, but everything to lose by delay.

These are large considerations, beyond the ambit of employment policy in its more limited definition. But even in this narrow sense, the ability of policy-makers to learn from their previous action and respond flexibly remains of paramount importance. Two types of difficulty obstruct this, of which the country experiences surveyed here give ample evidence. The first is found in the Indonesian situation, in which quite good quality statistical information exists on employment and wages, but is not drawn on by the relevant policy-makers when taking decisions. The remedy here is essentially an educational and promotional one, assuming that the economic technocrats would prefer to be better informed. The other type of difficulty is found in the Tanzanian situation, in which, policy-makers appear to be inhibited by distributional considerations in pushing ahead with structural adjustment, but as yet lack even basic data and analytical skills to provide information that would probably reassure them if they had it. This appears to be the more deep-seated problem and perseverance in, and expansion of existing technical assistance programmes seems to be the appropriate course to follow.

To say this is not to imply, however, that all would be well if only existing sorts of knowledge could be connected up with the policy process. New areas of relevant information remain to be pioneered in all the countries studied. In general, available statistics contain only the most elementary male/female disaggregations, and in some countries, even these are absent. This makes it very difficult to understand the differential impact of structural adjustment on men and women workers, their respective flexibilities of response to altered price signals and the possible need for special training, credit and other policies to mitigate constraints on womens' participation in the labour force. Closely linked with these gender questions are questions about the movement of labour between the formal and informal sectors. Statistics on these two sectors tend to be collected by different methods, and to be non-comparable in timing and depth of coverage. Inferences about movement between them, which is a classic mode of labour force adjustment (especially in Africa) can only be weakly based. Finally, data is everywhere weak in relation to the key theoretical concepts of the adjustment mechanism: these are the amount of labour in sectors which produce tradables and non-tradables and the proportions in which different categories of workers consume tradable and non-tradable products. Without reasonable estimates of these key magnitudes, it is impossible to make empirical estimates of the likely employment and wage consequences of the macroeconomic policies which countries adopt. Here then are three critical areas where information improvements – if these could then be fed into policy making – could improve the macro-compatibility of employment policies.

The very notion of the macro-compatibility of employment policies narrowly defined excludes the possibility of prescribing an ideal package of such policies, to serve as a model for adoption in all adjusting countries. To that extent it is unhelpful to technical assistance agencies which seek to do more than simply recommend ways to improve the information base and the local capacity for relevant policy analysis. On the other hand, this notion does point towards a superior policy-making process, which has proved itself capable, in fortunate circumstances, of reconciling the legitimate aspirations of labour with the limits on them set by the macroeconomic conjuncture. This process is variously known as 'social dialogue' or 'social compact'. It consists of national governments engaging in high-level discussions with nationally representative labour organisations in order to explain the economic rationale of their adjustment policies, the current and expected performance of the economy and the distributional implications of this. The ultimate aim is to accommodate the demands of labour as far as possible within an economic framework that promotes growth based on increased productivity. Social dialogue has been a feature of the final years of the Chilean experience, and has also been successful in the latter stages of Mexico's recovery from its debt crisis. It is most immediately applicable in Latin America, where labour institutions have been reconstituted and empowered to participate responsibly.

For Asia and Africa, the Latin American example indicates what might be possible in the future rather than what can be started straight away. But at the very least, it indicates the urgent need for Asian and African countries which have not already done so to include in their agenda for economic liberalisation the removal of government restrictions on the construction of representative institutions for labour and their legitimate activities. Labour market de-regulation which fails to encompass safeguards for the free association of labour gives evidence of a partial and asymmetric liberalism. It also defers indefinitely the start of any real social dialogue, which is the best route to achieving compatibility between the evolving macroeconomic reality which a country faces and the welfare and productivity of its labour force.

References

Addison, T. and Demery, L. (1993) 'Labour Markets, Poverty and Adjustment', *Journal of International Development*, 5 (2), March–April.

Amjad, R. n.d. 'ARTEP's Experience in Short and Medium Term Employment Planning', mimeo, New Delhi, ILO (ARTEP).

Azis, I.J. (1993), 'The Politics of Economic Reform and the Role of Technocrats'. Draft paper for conference on 'The Political Economy of Policy Reform', held at the Institute for International Economics, Washington DC, on January 14–16, 1993.

Cornia, G.A., R. Jolly and F. Stewart (1987) *Adjustment with a Human Face* (Oxford: Clarendon Press for UNICEF).

Foxley, A. (1983) *Latin American Experiments in Neo-conservative Economics* (Berkeley: University of California Press).

Garcia, N.E. (1992) 'Structural Adjustment and the Labour Market', mimeo, PREALC/ILO.

Godfrey, M. (1993) 'Employment Planning within the Context of Economic Reforms: A Case Study of Indonesia', mimeo, Jakarta.

Greenaway, D. and O. Morissey (1992) 'Sequencing Lessons from Adjustment Lending Programmes', *CREDIT Research Paper*, 92/11, University of Nottingham.

Hodd, M. (1993) 'Employment Planning within the Context of Economic Reforms: A Tanzanian Case Study' (London: SOAS).

de Kadt, E. (1994) 'Poverty-focused Policies: the Experience of Chile' in J.D. MacArthur and J. Weiss (eds), *Agriculture, Projects and Development* (Aldershot: Avebury).

Killick, T. (1993) *The Adaptive Economy* (Washington DC: Economic Development Institute of The World Bank/London: Overseas Development Institute).

Knight, J. (1976) 'Devaluation and Income distribution in less developed economies', *Oxford Economic Papers*, 28.

Kornai, J. (1975) 'Models and Policy: The Dialogue Between Model Builder and Planner', in C.R. Blitzer, P.B. Clark and L. Taylor (eds), *Economy-wide Models and Development Planning* (Oxford: Oxford University Press for the World Bank).

Meller, P. (1992) *Adjustment and Equity in Chile* (Paris: OECD Development Centre Studies).

Schkolnik, M. (1992) 'The Distributive Impact of Fiscal and Labour Market Policies: Chile's 1990–1 Reforms', Innocenti Occasional Papers, EPS 33, mimeo.

Sender, J. and S. Smith (1990) *Poverty, Class and Gender in Rural Africa: A Tanzanian Case Study* (London: Routledge).

Stewart, F. (1993) 'The Impact of Adjustment Policies on the Incomes of the Poor – A Review of Alternative Approaches', mimeo, Queen Elizabeth House, Oxford.

Tarp, F. (1993) *Stabilisation and Structural Adjustment* (London: Routledge).

Taylor, L. (1988) *Varieties of Stabilisation Experience* (Oxford: Clarendon Press for WIDER).

Thorbecke, E. and Associates (1992) *Adjustment and Equity in Indonesia* (Paris: OECD Development Centre Studies).

Toye, J. (1992) 'The Appraisal and Evaluation of Structural Adjustment Lending: Some Questions of Method', mimeo, IDS, Brighton.

Toye, J. (1993) 'Structural Adjustment: Context, Assumptions, Origin and Diversity', mimeo, IDS, Brighton.

Appendix 6.1   A schematic representation of structural adjustment policy

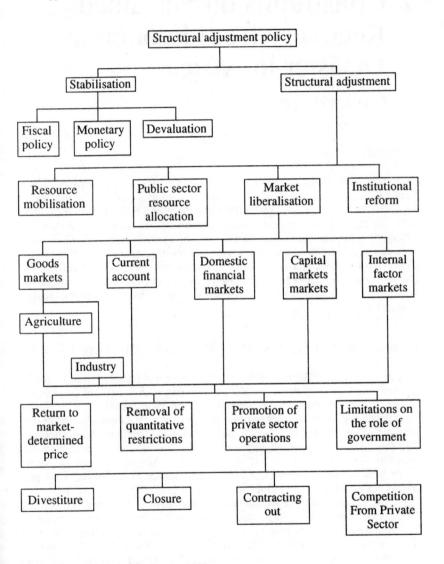

Source: Smith and Spooner, 1992.

7 Constraints on Sustained Recovery from Economic Disaster in Africa

Charles Harvey

I INTRODUCTION

This paper argues that governments of African countries recovering from economic disaster have increasingly accepted that they must persist with the macroeconomic polices demanded by the IMF and the World Bank. However progress with structural reform has been more difficult; it has been slow to start (for example, seven or eight years in the case of banking reform in Ghana and Uganda) and doubtful of success. Yet a recovery of private sector investment is essential for sustained recovery, once existing capacity becomes full utilised with the greater availability of foreign exchange; and private sector investment cannot be expected to recover while the civil service, the banks and parastatals remain unreformed.

II BACKGROUND: THE PROBLEM AS IT WAS IN THE LATE 1980S

In a previous paper (Harvey, 1990), it was argued that recovery from economic disaster required persistence by the government with a new set of policies, namely those agreed with or imposed by the World Bank and the IMF.[1] Persistence was necessary because the first year of a structural adjustment programme was invariably difficult. The new policies were normally deeply unpopular, especially non-marginal increases in the cost of foreign exchange and therefore the cost of imports, and in interest rates. Any supply response, which might have increased income and employment, tended to be delayed while producers waited to see if investment in increased production would be profitable. Governments were also required to do other unpopular things, such as restricting credit, removing subsidies, increasing taxation and cutting government spending. The first year of an adjustment programme was always, therefore, extremely difficult politically, and the second year was often not much better. This political difficulty was compounded by the fact that the promised increase in aid, supposed to follow from agreement with the IMF and the World Bank, was invariably delayed for at least six months and often for a year. Neither the bureaucracies of recipients, nor the bureaucracies of aid donors, were capable of managing a sudden large increase in the flow of aid. The only immediate increase in aid flows was the first tranche of a loan from the IMF, and the first tranche of a loan from the World Bank. There was thus a strong tendency for governments not to persist with economic reform programmes, but to abandon them early in their life.

The interesting question in these circumstances was why some governments persisted while others did not. It was clearly not interesting to say that persistent governments had sufficient political will. It was important to try and discover, if possible, whether persistent governments had factors in common. The most significant factor appeared to be the degree to which the government had debated internally the issues in making a major change of economic policy. This was particularly important where a government was not only required to change its economic policy, but also required to make a complete reversal of an entire strategy of development. The greater the previous commitment to socialism, the greater the difficulty in being convinced of the need to adopt structural adjustment policies.

In this context, it also helped if a new government came to power without a commitment to a long history of previous economic policies, even if the new government was also committed to socialism or otherwise antagonistic to the IMF and the World Bank. The contrast between Ghana in 1983 and Zambia in 1985 is extremely striking on this point. The second Rawlings government in Ghana took office strongly opposed to the ideology of the Washington institutions. During its first eighteen months, the new government became convinced of two basic facts. The first was that recovery was impossible without external finance; the second was that it would not find that finance from the Communist bloc, despite extensive efforts to obtain it. The government therefore devised a change of economic policy which would be so neo-liberal that the Bank and the Fund would have to agree with it. Thereafter the Ghanaian government persisted with its new policy despite extreme political difficulties, including seven coup attempts in three years.

In contrast, the new policy which was introduced in 1985 in Zambia, was sprung on the government by President Kaunda with very little internal debate or preparation. It was in fact only supported by the President himself, and by two other ministers. It was opposed publicly and consistently by the remainder of the Cabinet and the Central Committee of the ruling party, in almost daily speeches up and down the country. In those circumstances, producers would have been extremely foolish to invest significant resources in increased production in the expectation that the policy would be sustained. Moreover, it became rational to buy not only current needs for foreign exchange but future needs as well, in the expectation that the availability of foreign exchange would be restricted when the policy was reversed. This became a self-fulfilling prophecy.

There were other factors which seemed to affect persistence with structural adjustment policies across a number of countries. Among the positive factors were the response of tax revenue to devaluation, since if tax revenues increased faster than government spending as a result of devaluation then it became easier to control the budget deficit and therefore inflation. It was difficult for Sierra Leone to make a success of adjustment, therefore, because of the dominance of alluvial diamonds in exports. Alluvial diamonds are produced by small scale operators, are exceptionally easy to smuggle, and are therefore particularly difficult to tax.

The response of tax revenues to structural adjustment policies was not just a matter of the structure of the economy, and therefore luck. It was also a matter of policy. For example, the Ghanaian government made a substantial effort to improve the collection of taxes after 1983, including forcing the daily collection of taxes from informal urban traders, and managed to increase the real value of tax revenue by four times in three years. This change was so successful that the Uganda government actually hired Ghanaians to try and attempt the same change in Uganda.

Another common factor in success and failure was whether food was subsidised or not. Once a government has taken the political credit for subsidising food and keeping its retail price down, it becomes increasingly difficult for the government to accept the political blame for reducing or removing that subsidy. As inflation continues, the gap between the subsidised price and what would be the free market price becomes larger so that the shock and the political cost of removing the subsidy becomes greater over time. This was a major factor in the abandonment of a number of attempts at structural adjustment in Zambia, because the maize subsidy was so difficult to reduce. It was only eventually reduced during the honeymoon period after a change of government. In sharp contrast, the Ghanaian and Ugandan governments never subsidised food. Although the subsidisation of food is the most common source of this particular difficulty, the subsidy on petrol in Nigeria played a similar role. In 1993, petrol cost US 3 cents per litre in Nigeria, and an attempt to raise it by 6 per cent caused riots. The subsidy cost approximately N.60 billion annually, equivalent to 70 per cent of federal revenue in the 1993 budget. It was also, of course, extremely profitable to smuggle petrol to neighbouring countries which increased the cost of the subsidy and benefited non-Nigerians.

III   CHANGES IN THE EARLY 1990S

The role of previous failed attempts at structural adjustment changed gradually. In the 1980s, the failure of previous adjustment programmes was a clear negative factor. For example, in Uganda in 1988, it was difficult to find anybody in government who thought that the structural adjustment programme would work, on the apparently logical grounds that previous programmes had failed. By the end of the 1980s, and in the early 1990s, the failure of previous programmes was overtaken by the failure of attempts to adjust without the international financial institutions (IFIs). Governments realised that whether previous programmes had failed or not, they had no choice but to accept the conditions imposed by the Washington institutions.

The accumulated experience of failure to recover without external assistance was not the only factor that changed. Most of the countries being discussed here, namely those trying to recover from extremes of economic decline, became increasingly dependent on aid. Among the seven countries, this applied to all except Nigeria. Oil exports in Nigeria remain extremely large, despite the relatively low oil price in recent years, so that aid receipts are a very small proportion of total exports and imports and may explain in part why Nigeria does not at the time of writing have an agreed IMF programme. This is shown in Table 7.1 below, where net disbursements of Official Development Assistance (ODA) are compared with imports for 1991. As can be seen, ODA paid for more than half of imports in six out of the seven countries. The percentages would be slightly lower if imports of services were included with imports of goods, but the picture of overwhelming dependence on aid inflows to maintain imports would not be substantially changed.

A further factor increasing the dependence of the other six countries on Western aid is the end of the Cold War. Whereas it was once possible to reject agreement with the IMF in favour of seeking alliance and assistance from the Soviet Union and other Eastern bloc countries, that option is no longer available.

As a result of these changes, reversion to the old economic strategy of controls over prices and foreign exchange, and all the other policies objected to by the World Bank and the IMF, has become less frequent and less likely to recur. In the

Table 7.1 Net ODA as a proportion of imports, 1991

	Net ODA	Imports	Net ODA as a % of imports
Ghana	724	1418	51
Mozambique	920	809	114
Nigeria	262	6525	4
Sierra Leone	105	163	64
Tanzania	1076	1381	78
Uganda	525	550	95
Zambia	884	1255	70

Source: World Bank, *World Development Reports*, 1993 and 1994.

mid-1990s, the issue is not so much whether countries will persist with devaluing their currencies according to market forces, and the other macroeconomic changes associated with IMF programmes, as to whether they will persist with the structural changes which take longer but which are also essential for eventual recovery. Persistence with policy changes concerning fiscal, monetary and exchange rate policies may be necessary, but is clearly not sufficient.

Structural changes are required for two main reasons. The first is that the success of macroeconomic policy changes is endangered if the budget deficit is not controlled, and the budget deficit is itself affected significantly by structural changes. One of the major contributors to budget deficits is the excessive size of the civil service. Another is the deficits of parastatals. A third is the very high cost of writing off the bad debts of commercial and development banks, and recapitalising them in order to allow them to continue to lend.

The second reason why structural changes are necessary is that the private sector is seriously inhibited from recovery while reforms have not taken place. Clearly, private sector recovery of output and investment requires a functioning banking system, providing as an absolute minimum normal banking services of deposit, cheque clearing, and safe custody of cash. In addition, recovery requires a banking system able to lend for increases in working capital. Parastatal reform is also necessary, because the private sector will be unable to recover quickly so long as it is required to buy low quality and high cost services from parastatal corporations. Civil Service reform is also necessary for private sector recovery, because governments in the past hired such a high proportion of the educated and skilled manpower in the economy, and recovery seems unlikely while so many of these scarce manpower resources are inefficiently deployed in partly neglected civil servant jobs and part-time employment in the informal sector. It is also necessary for the government to be able to manage the economy and supply government services efficiently, which is impossible while civil servants are paid too little to be able to do their official jobs full time.

Unfortunately, these structural reforms have proceeded much more slowly than was originally envisaged in structural adjustment programmes, have cost more than was expected, and in some cases appear to be making no progress at all. Not only is this damaging to private sector recovery in the ways already described, but the slowness of progress and in some cases the complete lack of it has seriously undermined the credibility of governments' expressed commitment to the private sector, with damaging effects on producers' willingness to invest in production.

IV   REFORM OF THE CIVIL SERVICE

The basic problem with civil service employment in most of the sample countries is that wages are too low and employment is too high. This results in a wage bill which the government cannot afford, but in people being paid so little that they cannot afford to do their jobs properly. Civil servants have to seek alternative sources of income in order to survive. Governments therefore end up with a large civil service which delivers very few government services, because civil servants are occupied during working hours working in the informal sector. In addition, government resources such as offices, telephones and transport are used to support the business activities of civil servants, adding to government expense without adding to the supply of government services. Income in kind, most importantly housing, compensates only partially for the loss of real income from wages and salaries, but explains to some extent the extreme reluctance of civil servants to relinquish their jobs.

Some of these points can be illustrated with statistics from Zambia. During the post independence period, the real wage of the lowest paid government workers remained about the same, the index remaining at 100 from 1966 to 1975. During that period, a reduction in differentials was already taking place, so that the index for an under-secretary fell from 149 in 1966 to 100 in 1975 with similar but slightly smaller falls for lower ranking professional civil servants. Thereafter, the index for upper rank civil servants fell to 11 or 12, and for the lowest paid to 38. The impact on upper rank civil servants was not quite as bad as is implied by these figures, because allowances increased to some extent to compensate. It was estimated that allowances were approximately equal to the value of salaries by 1990. Nevertheless, the real value of government employment fell to 20 per cent of its 1975 value by 1990. (Chiwele, 1994: 156–7). A secondary effect of the drastic fall in the real wage of senior civil servants was not just that they sought alternative sources of income within Zambia, but that many left the country to earn higher pay in such African countries as Botswana and South Africa, in the United Nations system, and in the rest of the world.[2]

It was essential, therefore, to reduce the size of the civil service by a large amount, in order to pay the remainder a wage that would enable them to do their civil service jobs. It was also necessary to raise wages for skilled employees in order to retain them in government employment, and if possible to induce them to return from abroad. It was also necessary, as with other forms of structural change, that progress should be made on what had been promised in order to sustain the credibility of the adjustment programme.

As might have been expected, the record in reduction of civil service employment is very different from the promises made to the Washington institutions. For example, Zambia announced plans to cut the civil service from 80 000 to 60 000 in early 1986. This was to be done by a combination of reducing the retirement age by five years and by redundancy. There was also a freeze on all recruitment, except professionals. Later in 1986, 5000 daily paid workers were reported as having been laid off. Later that year, the retirement of 2000 civil servants was delayed while better terms were worked out. Meanwhile the ruling party recommended the creation of more than 500 new posts. In 1987, there were further announcements of the need to cut government employment. In 1987, after a break with the IMF, the government announced a new set of measures which included public works schemes which would of course increase government employment. There was no further public announcement of the intention to reduce government employment, while the government pursued its own economic policies independent of the IFIs. When overt discussion resumed with the IMF in 1989 there was talk of the need to cut the real level of government expenditure, but not explicitly of the need to cut government employment. A new agreement with the IMF was reached in late 1989. This involved the publication of a Policy Framework Paper (PFP) which called among other things for cuts in the number employed in the civil service together with an increase in salaries especially for the more senior staff. Nothing was done however, and in September 1990 there was a general increase in civil service pay and allowances which doubled the budget allocation for salaries in the 1991 Budget. In 1992, a new PFP was published, which again called for civil service reform, including a reduction in numbers. There was no progress with this part of the programme, however, because by then the government was very unwilling to do anything unpopular in the lead up to a general election involving several parties for the first time since the 1960s.

This was a fairly typical story of promises made but not implemented. The government of Zambia was frequently willing to 'agree' to a plan to reduce the numbers of civil servants drastically, but apparently without any serious intention of implementing its promises. There were of course genuine difficulties in reducing the number of civil servants, both in Zambia and elsewhere. Many governments did not actually know how many people they employed, so that some sort of census of public sector employment had to be made before a redundancy programme could be implemented. However, this provided a perfect excuse for delay, and other genuine reasons could always be found for further delay. Furthermore, it was always going to be difficult to implement a redundancy programme when the people implementing it were those whose jobs were under threat.

Whatever the reasons, the results have generally been very meagre. Three of the sample countries are listed by the World Bank (World Bank, 1994: 124) as having had a decrease of 5 per cent or more in civil service personnel between 1985 and 1992. Information is not available for Mozambique and Nigeria, and Tanzania is listed as having had an increase in civil service personnel of more than 5 per cent. While a decrease of any amount is a considerable achievement, and one bought at considerable political cost, the decreases that have taken place have been quite inadequate to the scale of the problem. Salaries, even at the top end of the scale, have been as low as $25 a month.[3] While it may not be necessary to restore the real value of salaries to the level they were at in the 1960s, when salary structures were inherited from the colonial period, the amount that is needed to enable people to work full time at their civil service jobs and to induce professionals to return from foreign countries is clearly much more than the savings that might accrue from a 5 per cent reduction in civil service personnel.

In the nature of things, it is extremely difficult to know how much people are earning in the informal sector when moonlighting from their civil service jobs. Some indication of orders of magnitude are available, however.

Where donors have installed expatriate personnel in government ministries, they have in some cases introduced 'allowances' for local personnel to enable them to be at their desks. In one of these projects, a maximum of $130 a month was enough to procure full time attendance from local employees, including senior civil servants. Their informal sector earnings must therefore have been less than this. It is not possible to say whether $130 a month was more than was necessary to achieve this result, so it is only possible to say that the supply price of labour was somewhere between $25 and $130 a month. It seems unlikely, however, that the price being paid was very much more than was necessary. Even supposing that it could have been reduced to $100 a month, this would imply paying four times the local wage. Logically, this implies that the civil service would have to be reduced by three-quarters if those remaining were to be paid an adequate wage, assuming an unchanged structure of relative pay. Such a reduction would be of a quite different order of magnitude to anything that has been achieved in any country in Africa. Moreover, many of those cuts which have taken place have been largely 'ghost workers', namely workers who never existed but whose salaries were collected by somebody else, with the possible exception of Ghana and Guinea in which significant numbers have been cut among those who were actually employed (World Bank, 1994: 123). And in those countries where significant numbers of government employees have been retrenched, most of those losing their jobs have been the lowest paid, namely daily paid workers. Clearly, even more daily paid workers must be dismissed in order to pay professional civil servants their supply price, than if cuts were made right across the board. More recent information from Uganda reinforces this point. The civil service has been cut (in numbers) by approximately one-third; the savings have been used to increase the pay of those remaining, and additional funds have been provided so that the government wage bill has gone up, not down. Nevertheless, wages are still below the Uganda government's own target of a minimum living wage of USh 70 000 or $77 a month at the September 1994 rate of exchange (Barya, 1994; interviews, Kampala, September 1994). Similarly, the civil service in Sierra Leone is reported to have been cut by one-third, but salaries remain inadequate (EIU, 1994/2).

It seems apparent that no government is capable of making the cuts that are necessary in civil service employment simply by compulsory methods of retrenchment. Something much more drastic and radical is required. If a sufficiently attractive cash redundancy package were offered, the numbers offering to accept it could in principle be very large. The cost is not as high as might be expected, precisely because the real value of government wages has fallen so far. Moreover, there is less need to provide training, credit, and specific alternative employment opportunities for those made redundant precisely because they already have alternative sources of income to which they can devote themselves full time. Indeed, some schemes for the retraining of civil servants made redundant have had a low take-up, for example in The Gambia. In Uganda, the government has only provided a retraining scheme for retrenched soldiers, because of the danger for civil order of large numbers of redundancies among men whose training is in violence. This is no similar scheme for civil service retrenchees, and the large cuts in employment have occurred with negligible political protest (Interviews, 1994).

Although the cost has had and will have to come out of other uses of government revenue and aid flows, it is difficult to see how structural adjustment can proceed successfully without cuts at least as large as those in Uganda. Moreover, if even very large cuts in the civil service do not enable the government to pay an adequate wage, then a full recovery of the quantity and quality of government services depends on further increases in tax revenue and aid.

V   REFORM OF PARASTATALS

Parastatal corporations were created in Africa in order to reduce economic dependence on foreign capital, and in order to invest in areas where it was thought that the private sector would not venture. As is well known, the results were disastrous. In many cases, parastatals did not produce annual accounts so that the first problem, as with civil service reform, was a serious lack of information on which to act. Among the sample countries, Zambia was a partial exception to these strictures. For example in the late 1980s and early 1990s the companies held by Indeco, the industrial holding company, were mainly profitable. In 1988/89 Indeco made a profit of K 703 million, and only two out of its 42 subsidiaries made a loss. However, it was not possible even in Zambia to know whether the profitability of parastatals was as result of their efficiency, or as a result of their monopoly position in the economy. Their ability to charge high prices was enhanced by the shortage of foreign exchange for competing imports, and, in some cases, a granting of exclusive import rights to the company making a particular product.

Reform of the parastatal sector is therefore essential. Moreover, it has been argued that reform of parastatals, for example through the negotiation of management contracts on performance with the government, is not sustainable in practice without the incentives associated with private ownership. Few reformed parastatals have made sustained progress, and some have had to be reformed two or three times. With hindsight, it should not be surprising that weak governments, lacking the expertise and strong political backing necessary, should not have been able to enforce performance contracts. This means that privatisation in the sense of transferring parastatals to the private sector, or closing them down and allowing the private sector to supply the services and goods they previously provided, becomes even more essential. It also means that delays in privatisation are costly and damaging.

In all cases, delay has been extensive. There are two types of reason for delay. Firstly, there are genuine technical difficulties. Where accounts have not been properly kept, an audited balance sheet and profit and loss account are essential before privatisation can take place. In addition, privatisation must be as transparent as possible, because of inevitable suspicions that the sale will be made at artificially low prices. This would endanger the whole process by creating public hostility.

There are also technical problems peculiar to particular countries. For example, in Uganda many properties were confiscated from the Asian community by the government of Idi Amin. The Museveni government which came to power in 1986 promised to return confiscated properties, but it proved a lengthy task to establish among other things the ownership of any improvements and investments which had taken place since confiscation. In Ghana, a major problem concerned redundancy payments to workers in parastatal corporations. During the period when government provided more or less unconditional financial support to the parastatal sector, trades unions negotiated extremely generous redundancy payments. This made it difficult in Ghana to close down formally even those parastatals which had ceased to produce anything, because former employees were able to establish legal claims to redundancy payments, and it was impossibly expensive or any potential buyer to make a parastatal profitable if that required (as it usually did) a reduction in the labour force.

In nearly every country there were other fears which tended to delay the privatisation process. Governments were not only afraid of selling parastatal corporations for less than they were worth, but were also nervous of selling to foreigners or to ethnic minorities within the country; and in some cases as for example in Zambia, the government was not willing to sell profitable corporations. This eliminated of course the candidates which would have been most easy to sell to the private sector, and left the government trying to sell parastatals which fewer people wanted to buy. Political fears included an unwillingness to allow concentration of ownership, where domestic buyers could be found. Finally, domestic finance for the purchase of parastatals was limited, and in several countries the Stock Exchange was too small or non-existent, so that new legislation had to be passed and a new institution created before any public sale could be undertaken by means of a public share issue whose shares could be traded subsequently. In Zambia, these factors contributed to the fact that in mid-1994 only 12 out of 160 parastatals listed for privatisation in the first two tranches had been sold and none via the Lusaka Stock Exchange; the privatisation revenue account was being used to revive parastatals already closed; the ruling party was planning to buy some parastatals in order to prevent sale to foreigners; and the Ministry of Agriculture was planning to delay until 1997 the sale of 'at least' 15 statutory bodies in order to allow time to find 'acceptable' bids (*Times of Zambia*, 8, 15, 24 June, 1994).

In the circumstances, it is not surprising that there were everywhere long delays before privatisation was started, and also long delays between the announcement of a privatisation policy and the first real progress. Moreover, in general privatisation was initially of small companies. 'Divestiture is proceeding slowly among small and medium sized firms and scarcely at all among large enterprises – not surprising since most big enterprises were classified as strategic' (World Bank, 1994: 103).

The countries in our sample fitted this pattern quite closely, although of course there were some country by country variations. There was invariably quite a long delay, of several years, after the reaching of agreement with the IMF and the World Bank on a programme before a privatisation programme was started. There was then further delay before a significant number of firms were actually privatised. Of the seven sample countries, only Ghana and Mozambique were classified as having privatised as much as 10 per cent to 25 per cent of parastatals by 1992, and a much smaller proportion by value because the first firms to be privatised were small or medium scale. Ghana was the first country in the sample to embark (in 1983) on a sustained programme of structural adjustment, and did so with an unusual degree of persistence and political commitment. Mozambique was extremely unusual in that privatisation began before there was a structural adjustment programme, and indeed before the government joined the World Bank and the IMF in 1984. No doubt this was because Mozambique was forced to nationalise a large number of private businesses at independence when 90 per cent of the Portuguese expatriate population left. An agreement was only reached with the IMF in May 1987, following a programme of structural adjustment introduced by the government before agreement was reached, yet between 1985 and 1988 47 large and 40 small firms were already privatised. Thereafter progress was very much slower. All of the remainder with the exception of Nigeria (see below) had privatised less than 10 per cent of their parastatals by 1992 (*ibid.*).

Arguably, the problem is greatest in Tanzania. In the 1980s there were more than 400 parastatals, and they were notorious for overstaffing, inefficiency, needing government subsidy, and borrowing a high proportion of bank credit. It was clear in 1986, when the structural adjustment programme was started, that very little progress would be made if something was not done about parastatal deficits, and that this required large scale redundancies. Yet it was announced at the time that no party member would lose his or her job, while it was well known that parastatals had employed large numbers of party members. Managers were appointed by the ruling party, often from the civil service, so that loyalty was more to the party than to any concept of profit maximising or efficiency. It is also argued that donors were partly responsible for the soft budget constraint on parastatals, since nearly all parastatals got donor support and cost consciousness was lower in donor backed parastatals (Eriksson, 1991). The Tanzanian government was not only anxious not to remove its supporters from parastatal employment, but was also very fearful of selling parastatals to the Asian business community which would have been very unpopular politically. As a result, there was a small number of closures of parastatals, but little else was done. The Policy Framework Paper in 1991 said that a privatisation policy would be announced by the end of that year, and a Public Corporations Act was passed in 1992. By 1993, four parastatals had been turned over to joint ventures with foreign corporations, two had been partly sold and seven had had management contracts with private sector interests. There was some increase in the 1980s and early 1990s in competition from the private sector, and some evidence that parastatals exposed to such competition had become marginally less inefficient. Nevertheless, some seven years after the introduction of what is said to be a relatively successful structural adjustment programme, the impact of the privatisation programme was extremely small in relation to the size of the problem. Moreover, failure to improve the disastrous parastatal sector made it almost impossible to reform the banking system, because the main government commercial bank (which had 90 per cent of the market) had most of its loan portfolio in lending to insolvent and loss making parastatals.

Nigeria is an exception to this picture of lack of progress in privatisation. The structural adjustment programme which began in 1986 was implemented with rather more vigour in Nigeria than in most other countries. Partly this was because of the extraordinary public debate which took place prior to the implementation of the programme, which although it resulted in a resounding rejection of the idea of borrowing from the IMF nevertheless enabled the Nigerian government to go ahead with IMF-type policies provided that no money was actually borrowed. Most unusually, the government simply abolished the parastatal agricultural marketing boards almost immediately, handing over agricultural marketing entirely to the private sector. By the end of 1990, 54 out of 110 parastatals had been sold, although as always the larger ones remained in public ownership. At this point the privatisation programme had raised $31 million which was, in Nigerian terms, a relatively small sum (it was only 2.5 per cent of government consumption in that year, for example). By early 1992, the number of companies sold had risen to 78, and the amount of money raised to $89 million; and by the end of 1992 $101 million had been raised, leaving only 30 parastatals still in government hands. By the standards of other African countries this was a remarkably rapid achievement even though it had taken seven years from the introduction of the structural adjustment programme in 1986. Even in Nigeria, however, the main utilities remained in public hands, and remained inefficient. For example electricity supply was extremely unreliable. Moreover, it was reported in late 1993 that there was virtually no new investment, either domestic or foreign. This illustrates the point that privatisation may be necessary in creating a good investment climate, but it is clearly not sufficient.

Overall, its seems that there was a slow start to privatisation, but that after four or five years some significant progress was achieved. Despite this progress, the largest and most important parastatals remained almost everywhere in government ownership and this included the key utilities which continued to provide inefficient and expensive services to the private sector. It is also significant that the one country which had never really pursued a socialist economic strategy, namely Nigeria, was the one that had made most progress. The number of listed companies on the Nigerian Stock Exchange rose from approximately 100 to 141 by 1991 and there were more than 600 000 individual shareholders. Nothing remotely like this was achieved in any of the other sample countries. The next most successful privatisation programme was in Ghana, where 14 companies were listed on the Stock Exchange and turnover was very low. A particular reason for this was the very restrictive rules regarding foreign participation, which only began to be improved in 1993, some ten years after the structural adjustment programme began. Moreover, the sums of money raised for the government by selling off parastatals were negligible, and may indeed have been negative once account is taken of the costs borne by government in preparing parastatals for sale. Not only did debts have to be written off and rehabilitation undertaken, but large sums were spent on accountancy and legal services in order to update accounts and clear up other problems which were necessary before a sale could take place.

It is clear that expectations of privatisation were far too optimistic. The process took much longer than expected, and when it did begin to make progress the firms privatised were mainly small ones leaving large parastatals whose reform was difficult to implement, and even more difficult to sustain while they remained in public ownership. Understandably, governments have been unwilling to see large scale closure of parastatals after having invested so much in their creation. Nevertheless, the benefits of privatisation programmes are as much in the ending of subsidy and inefficient high cost supply of goods and services as in any financial benefits to the government. As noted by many writers, closure is not a total loss to the economy provided that the assets can be sold for use by some other producer. If they cannot be sold, that must mean that they have no economic use. Meanwhile, as much can be gained from ending the monopoly of parastatals and allowing legal private sector competition as from the actual sale of parastatal corporations.

VI   FINANCIAL SECTOR REFORM

The first stage of financial liberalisation has normally been to raise nominal interest rates. However, in the 1980s, African governments generally failed to raise nominal interest rates above the level of inflation when inflation was at all high. Indeed, the higher was inflation the further were nominal interest rates below inflation. The real costs of borrowing, and the real returns to bank deposits, were even more negative if account is taken of the fact that the interest cost of borrowing is tax deductible and the interest on bank deposits is normally taxed (Harvey and Jenkins, 1994). There were many reasons why governments were unwilling to impose very high nominal interest rates, including the impact on the budget of a high cost of government's own borrowing. In addition, high nominal costs of borrowing impose a risk on business. In theory, borrowing at 50 per cent nominal when prices are rising at 50 per cent imposes no real cost on the borrower. However, the higher the rate of inflation the greater the likelihood of variation in inflation, so that using the current rate of inflation as a proxy for expectations of the future rate is extremely risky. It is more than possible that inflation will fall while nominal interest rates remain unadjusted. Moreover, whereas the costs of a business include a wide range of goods and services and are therefore likely to rise with the general rate of inflation, the items that a business sells are relatively few in number and may not move in the short or even the medium term in line with inflation. In other words, there is a strong risk of a shift in the terms of trade against a business which at times of high inflation would impose very high costs on a business borrowing at a high nominal rate of interest. Whatever the reasons, African governments did not succeed in using monetary policy in the 1980s to achieve positive real rates of interest.

These generalisations apply fully to the countries being considered in this paper. Using annual data, and adjusting for the fact that the interest cost of borrowing was tax deductible in every country, there were only three years in which the post-tax cost of borrowing was positive in real terms. This is shown in Table 7.2 below.

Even if it is assumed that firms borrowing from banks did not pay tax, so that interest rates were positive simply when the nominal cost of borrowing was above the rate of inflation, there were only 15 instances where annual data

Table 7.2   Real interest rates, 1980–92
(adjusted for interest cost being tax deductible)

	Number of years positive	*Number of years negative*	*Inflation when interest rates positive (per cent)*
Ghana	1	12	10
Nigeria	2	11	6 to 7
Sierra Leone	0	13	
Tanzania	0	13	
Uganda	0	12	
Zambia	0	13	
TOTAL	3	74	

Note: No data for Mozambique in *IFS*.
Source: *International Financial Statistics (IFS)*.

showed the cost of borrowing to be higher than the rate of inflation, compared with 62 instances where the cost of borrowing was below the rate of inflation. Most of the occurrences of interest costs being above the rate of inflation were in recent years. For example, the four cases in Tanzania were in the most recent four years, the same applies to Ghana, and to Uganda. Almost invariably, interest rates above the rate of inflation were achieved only in years where inflation was relatively low. In other words, the governments of these countries were not willing to raise nominal interest rates to very high levels when inflation was also high. A partial exception to this was Zambia in 1993, a year not covered in the Tables, when the average cost of borrowing rose as high as 113 per cent. However, inflation was even higher in that year, at 188 per cent. These points are illustrated in Table 7.3 below.

Deposit rates were of course normally below lending rates, so that real deposit rates were even more negative than the cost of borrowing. Interest rate policy did not make it possible, therefore, for savers to obtain a real rate of return on their savings in the 1980s. However, it would not necessarily have been of benefit for banks to attract more savings, because the banking system in several of these countries was dominated by a government owned commercial bank which had a high proportion of bad debt in its loan portfolio. Attracting more deposits into these decayed commercial banks would have resulted in a mal-distribution of savings rather than the more efficient allocation which is assumed in the theory of

Table 7.3   Real interest rates 1980–92
(unadjusted for tax)

	Number of years positive	Number of years negative	Inflation when real interest rates positive (%)
Ghana[a]	3	10	10 to 25
Nigeria[b]	6	7	6 to 13
Sierra Leone	0	13	
Tanzania[c]	4	9	20 to 26
Uganda[c]	2	10	28 to 33
Zambia	0	13	
Total	15	62	

Notes:
a Positive in 1989, 1991–92.
b Positive in 1982, 1985–87, 1990–91.
c Positive in 1990–91.

Source: *International Financial Statistics (IFS).*

Table 7.4   Market share and bad debts of government-owned commercial banks in Ghana, Mozambique, Tanzania, Uganda and Zambia prior to restructuring

	Share of market[a]	Bad debts percentage
Ghana: GCB	50%	70%[b]
Mozambique: BM	95%	large[c]
Tanzania: NBC	90%	60% to 80%
Uganda: UCB	50%	33%[d]
Zambia: ZNCB	20%	small[e]

Notes:
(a)   Share varies according to whether it is measured by deposits, assets or capital. Figures given are orders of magnitude only.
(b)   Prior to reform and recapitalisation, which was completed in 1991.
(c)   See text.
(d)   Based on a 30 per cent sample of loans by value at end-1989, this being the sum needed to 'clean up the portfolio'.
(e)   Small, meaning that it is within commercially acceptable limits, if it is assumed that loans with government guarantees are not bad debts.

Source: Interviews and World Bank financial sector reviews.

financial liberalisation. The extent of the dominance of government owned commercial banks with a high incidence of bad debts is shown in Table 7.4 above.

The problem in Nigeria was slightly different. In 1986, there were some 40 commercial banks in Nigeria so that there was a high degree of competition. Between 1986 and 1991 the number of commercial banks rose to 114, with 60 further applications in process. The main reason for this proliferation of commercial banks was the management of the foreign exchange market. The formation of a commercial bank entitled it to apply for an allocation of foreign exchange at the official exchange rate, and this provided large profits because the foreign exchange could be sold in the unofficial market at a much higher price. This system of providing foreign exchange quotas to commercial banks ended in 1992. This endangered the 80 or so new banks created since 1986, because they had few other sources of profit. The extent of bad debts was largely unknown, because bank supervision and regulation did not require provision against bad debts before 1990, and because the very rapid increase in the number of commercial banks made it impossible for the Central Bank to supervise banks properly. A sample of 62 commercial banks revealed that 41 per cent of loans were uncollectable, with N 9 billion of bad debts. The estimate for all banks was some N 20 billion, which was greater than the capital base of all banks combined. The worst offenders were reported to be the 20 commercial banks owned by state governments, which had bad debts amounting to 64 per cent of their loan portfolios (EIU, 1990/4). In 1989, the government did change the management of the 12 banks in which it had a controlling interest, but it also started a new People's Bank which was already in trouble two years later. The People's Bank was set up to offer low interest rate loans to low income borrowers, but it set up a nation-wide network within a very short period and, for that reason alone, was bound to run into trouble quickly. Further evidence of bad debts came from the annual report of the Nigerian Deposit Insurance Corporation (1990) which recorded that nine commercial banks were 'distressed' with a ratio of uncollectable loans to capital of 5482 per cent, which was 73 per cent of total loans. Six out of nine of these banks were owned by state governments. Another 26 (of which 23 were owned by state governments) were classified as problem banks, because classified assets were greater than shareholders funds. The bulk of non-performing loans were to or guaranteed by, the owners (namely state governments) or to contractors working for state governments. By 1994, some one-third of the 120 commercial banks could be described as 'distressed'. Their problems were likely to get worse, because the dual foreign exchange rate system which had been so profitable had been abolished.

Not only was the problem of bad debts in government owned commercial banks extremely large, but reform took a very long time to implement. For example, it was some eight years after the structural adjustment programmes started in Ghana that Ghana completed the formal rehabilitation of commercial banks, in 1991. The Ghana Commercial Bank (GCB) was able to exchange some 58 per cent of its loan portfolio for government bonds, amounting to C 12.7 billion of bad debts. The Bank retained a further 12 per cent of its portfolio in bad debts in the form of smaller loans, loans to individuals, and loans to farmers. The Bank acquired a new managing director, a new board of directors with only one of the previous board remaining, sacked 2000 employees and closed a few branches. However, the managing director was the only senior employee recruited from outside the Bank. The restructuring was enough to make the Bank profitable after losses in the previous year, but the slowness of privatisation of parastatals, to which the Bank lent much of its money, made it likely that bad debts would re-emerge as a problem.

A similar strategy was followed in Tanzania, where bad debts were also transferred to a new government agency and replaced by government bonds. In addition to getting rid of TSh 75 billion of bad debts, the government granted a further TSh 50 billion to NBC to settle its debts with the Bank of Tanzania. However, it was reported that delays in privatisation were leading to new bad debts in the NBC's portfolio. In addition, it was reported that 3500 of the NBC's 9500 staff were in excess of requirements (EIU, 1993/3). As with Ghana, this whole process of banking reform was long delayed, reaching the stage described some seven years after the structural adjustment programme started.

In Uganda, the restructuring of Uganda Commercial Bank (UCB) was taking place in 1994, also seven years after the start of the structural adjustment programme. It remained to be seen whether a new managing director from the Central Bank, the appointment of four expatriates immediately under him, large scale branch closures and staff retrenchment and the issue of government bonds to replace bad debts as in Ghana, would result in sound lending. The problem was a great deal less serious in Zambia, both because the government-owned Commercial Bank (ZNCB) had only 20 per cent of the commercial bank market, and because the ZNCB was reported to be sound in the early 1990s. However, the more rigorous pursuit of stabilisation in 1993 meant that inflation at a much higher level than the cost of borrowing was no longer available to bail out imprudent borrowers. The consumer price index in Zambia increased by only 3.6 per cent in the final quarter of 1993, while lending rates remained at between 80 per cent and 100 per cent. This contributed to many parastatals becoming financially unsound and endangered the loan portfolio of the ZNCB.

In Mozambique, central and commercial banking were combined in one institution, the Bank of Mozambique. In 1992, this was split into a central bank and a commercial bank. The first ever audit of the banks was not expected to take place until 1994, and because commercial and central banking were combined there was no bank supervision. As a result, there are no firm figures of the extent of bad debts in the banking system. Most lending was to parastatals, whose losses were covered by a combination of government grants and guaranteed borrowing from the banking system. A review of loans to the 30 largest borrowers from the banking system showed that, in 1993, 99 per cent of loans to parastatals were non-performing. Between 1988 and 1992 the government took over bad debts amounting to Mt 116.9 billion, which was 48 per cent of 'claims on the economy' in 1989. This sets a minimum to the extent of bad debts, which was certainly much larger, but to an unknown extent. Meanwhile, parastatals continued to borrow while the privatisation programme proceeded extremely slowly. As in Tanzania, privatisation and reform of the banking system had to be undertaken simultaneously, which made the entire process even more difficult than it would otherwise have been.

Overall, it is clear that reform of unsound financial institutions takes a long time. The record is that several years after structural adjustment begins are required before reform is even initiated (seven to eight years in the cases of Ghana and Uganda), while reform in the form of the writing-off of bad debts and the recapitalisation of unsound banks, is not in itself a sufficient guarantee that new lending will avoid a repetition of the problem. The difficulty of reforming unsound financial institutions is not confined to distressed economies. For example, the doubtful condition of the Gambia Commercial and Development Bank (GCDB) was revealed as early as 1983, and confirmed by a series of subsequent studies. By 1991, the Bank had still not been reformed and reform was being vigorously resisted by the Gambian Government (McPherson, 1991). Similarly, the Botswana National Development Bank (NDB) began to accumulate significant bad debts in 1979 following the appointment of a new managing director. Total lending increased by 622 per cent in three years. The problem was first recognised officially in 1983, and continued to be referred to in a series of National Development Plans and Budget Speeches. Ten years later, the 1993 Budget Speech announced that a series of corrective measures would be taken, and there was some prospect that action would actually follow. Meanwhile, during those ten years a large amount of bad debt had been written-off without succeeding in rendering the NDB sound (Harvey, 1993). If successful reform of unsound banks takes so long, and is so difficult to make successful in rapidly growing economies which have avoided economic disaster (the GDP of Botswana, for example, grew at 14.5 per cent a year from 1970–80, and at 10.1 per cent a year from 1980–92), then it is very predictable that reform should be so delayed and prove so elusive in the least successful economies discussed in this chapter.

VII   CONCLUSIONS

In the 1990s, persistence with structural adjustment in economies recovering from disaster has become the norm with the single exception of Nigeria. Progress has been a great deal slower than was originally envisaged by the IMF and the World Bank, but African governments have learnt to persist with economic reforms at a sufficient pace to satisfy the donors. Even Sierra Leone, despite a serious problem with civil war, actually completed a Rights Accumulation Programme (RAP) although this did not result in an immediate increase in aid because of failure to make progress with democratic reforms and human rights.[4]

What this means is that governments now persist with devaluation to the point where most exchange rates are now more or less market determined. Progress has also been made in lowering rates of inflation so that real exchange rates as well as nominal rates are devalued. This has required drastic control of budget deficits, or finding ways of financing those deficits in non-inflationary ways. Two countries, Uganda and Zambia, resorted to monthly cash budgets in order to control their deficits. This had dramatic effects in reducing rates of inflation. However, it seems unlikely to be sustainable in Zambia where the cash receipts out of which spending was allowed included receipts from large issues of Treasury Bills at exceptionally high nominal interest rates. This may prove unsustainable for two reasons, firstly because it diverts a large amount of bank credit from the private sector to the purchase of Treasury Bills, and secondly because without a reduction in the budget deficit it is resulting in very rapidly increasing interest payments by the government.

Nevertheless, even in those countries where macro economic policy has been successful in reducing inflation, and sustained growth has resulted, as in Ghana,

Tanzania and Uganda, there is little sign of a recovery of private sector investment. Some recovery of output has been possible financed by increased aid inflows and the greater use of existing capacity as foreign exchange has become more readily available. In the longer term, however, private sector investment is essential for sustained economic growth even if aid inflows continue at their present level. Aid can restore infrastructure and, to a lesser extent public services, but does not flow in significant quantity to the private sector. There has been some inflow of foreign investment, but only into enclave projects such as gold mining in Ghana. There are also some indications in Uganda of the return of flight capital, but its seems that this is going mainly into housing rather than into productive investment. It has been argued in this paper that a sustained recovery of private investment, whether domestic or foreign, must depend on much greater progress with structural reform, including especially reform of the civil service, parastatal sector and the banking sector. The evidence is that reform has been slow to start, difficult to implement, and uncertain in its results. Most governments have failed to cut their civil service significantly, and even where this has taken place it has been insufficient to enable the government to pay the remaining civil servants an adequate salary. Privatisation of the parastatal sector has been equally slow and difficult, privatisation of the larger corporations has hardly proceeded at all, and reform where it has taken place has proved difficult to sustain. Reform of decayed banks has been equally slow, and equally uncertain to result in sound lending.

While efforts to implement structural reforms clearly have to continue, the slow rate of progress suggests that more radical alternatives should also be considered. In civil service reform, this would require the redirection of aid to buying out very much larger numbers of civil servants. In reform of the parastatal sector, it would require giving greater weight to the option of closure of loss making parastatals and allowing the private sector to compete away their markets, rather than to takeover of the corporations themselves. In banking, it would require consideration of drastic reduction in the size of decayed banks, or their closure; the risk in trying to reform decayed banks is that they will be expensively restructured and re-capitalised only to develop bad debt portfolios again.

It is also possible to argue that progress with structural reform is likely to be slightly quicker in the future than in the past. Just as it took some time for governments to realise that there was no alternative to persistence with structural adjustment policies at the macroeconomic level, because of the impossibility of doing without donor support, there is some evidence that governments are beginning to realise that structural reform cannot be delayed indefinitely and that they are beginning to pursue structural reform with greater determination. For example, the Uganda government was, as noted already, extremely reluctant and unenthusiastic about structural adjustment in 1987. The contrast now is quite striking. So long as donor support continues, and an increasing number of countries can point to economic growth as a result of adopting structural adjustment policies, it is possible that more governments will develop a similar level of enthusiasm and therefore pursue structural reforms more seriously.

Notes

1   The earlier research concerned seven African countries namely Ghana, Nigeria, Sierra Leone, Somalia, Tanzania, Uganda, and Zambia. Each suffered during the 1980s from severe macroeconomic imbalance, as shown by a non-marginal increase in the cost of foreign exchange of 100 per cent or more within a period of three months. The present research concerns all of the previous group of countries except Somalia which has been dropped because of the war situation, and Mozambique which has been added.

2   In the late 1980s, there were so many professional Ugandans working in the homelands in South Africa, that the ANC sent a delegation to Kampala to discuss the problem with the Ugandan government.

3   The average government wage in Sierra Leone was $14 a month before the 1992 coup, and these were frequent reports of even these wages not being paid (EIU, 1992/2).

4   The IMF has set up Rights Accumulation Programmes in countries with arrears on previous IMF borrowing. The borrowing country then agrees to IMF Conditionality, and this allows the country to re-negotiate its official debts and to receive aid from other donors.

References

Barya, John-Jean (1994) 'The Politics of Civil Service Reform in Uganda' (mimeo, paper for research commissioned by European Commission at IDS).

Chiwele, Dennis (1994) 'Stabilisation, the Real Wage, Employment and Welfare: The Case of Zambia's Formal Sector Employees', unpublished DPhil thesis, IDS, University of Sussex.

Economic Intelligence Unit (EIU) Quarterly Reports.

Eriksson, G. (1991) 'Economic Programmes and Systems Reform in Tanzania', Stockholm School of Economics, for SIDA.

Harvey, Charles (1990) 'Recovery from Macroeconomic Disaster in Sub-Saharan Africa', in C. Colclough and J. Manor (eds), *States or Markets? Neo-Liberalism and the Development Policy Debate* (Oxford: Oxford University Press).

Harvey, Charles (1993) 'The Role of Government in the Finance of Business in Botswana', *Institute of Development Studies, Discussion Paper*, 337.

Harvey, Charles (1993) 'The Role of Commercial Banking in Recovery from Economic Disaster in Ghana, Tanzania, Uganda and Zambia', *Institute of Development Studies, Discussion Paper*, 325.

Harvey, Charles and Carolyn Jenkins (1994) 'Interest Rate Policy, Taxation and Risk', *World Development*, 22 (12).

McPherson, Malcolm, F. (1991) 'The Politics of Economic Reform in the Gambia', *Harvard Institute for International Development, Development Discussion Paper*, 386.

World Bank (1994) *Adjustment in Africa: Reforms, Results, and the Road Ahead.*

8 Constraints on the Effectiveness of Structural Adjustment Packages in the Production and Availability of Pharmaceutical Products in Kenya

Pius Owino

I INTRODUCTION[1]

According to the orthodox adjustment programmes, depreciation of the real exchange rate (*RXR*), *ceteris paribus*, induces price incentives in favour of the production and export of Tradable (*T*) goods relative to non-tradable (*N*) goods. Trade liberalisation is supposed to reduce protection and improve economic efficiency, while reduction in government spending offsets the inflationary impact of devaluation. In practice, however, many constraints offset these intended objectives. This chapter aims to highlight these constraints by examining the impact of these three policy instruments on the production and availability of pharmaceutical products (PPs) in Kenya. To start with, we examine whether price incentives make the production and export of *T* goods including PPs more profitable relative to *N* goods.

Price Incentives and the Manufacture of Tradable Goods in Kenya

Using Gross Domestic Product (GDP) statistics by industry of origin we examined whether or not depreciation of the *RXR* as measured by P_n/P_t induces price incentives in favour of the production and export of *T* goods relative to *N* goods. In the first instance, Kenya's GDP data were re-classified into *T* and *N* goods sectors, and thereafter, sectoral relative prices of the two sectors calculated. Changes in the profitability between *T* and *N* goods sectors was determined using the relative ratio of the contribution of the *T* goods sector (C_t) to *N* goods sector (C_n). Our a priori expectation is that a depreciation in the *RXR* as measured by P_n/P_t increases both the profitability in the *T* goods sector, and *T*-sector's relative contribution to GDP (C_t/C_n).

As shown in Figure 8.1, changes in the relative prices P_n/P_t did not make the production of *T* goods in Kenya more profitable, except for 1984. In part, the expansive macroeconomic policy accompanied by a fixed exchange rate, and import restrictions before 1980, led to low profitability in the production of *T* goods (Julin and Levin, 1992; de Groot 1991).

After 1980, Kenya pursued a series of nominal devaluations under structural adjustment but still this did not change the profitability of the *T* goods sector, mostly because the expansionary macroeconomic policy remained unchanged. The increase in the profitability of the *T* goods sector between 1981 and 1983, was partly because of increased protection behind high tariff and non-tariff barriers (World Bank, 1990). Kenya's shift to a more restrictive macroeconomic policy between 1983 and 1986, accompanied by various nominal devaluations under structural adjustment led to an increase in the profitability of the *T* goods sector, and an increase in C_t/C_n in 1984. However, the 1984 drought led to a slight decline in C_t/C_n in 1985 and 1986, both directly and via its effects on export earnings and industrial inputs. After 1986, Kenya's terms of trade improved and the authorities shifted from a restrictive to a more expansionary macroeconomic policy. Also, Kenya's trade liberalisation had

Figure 8.1   Price changes and contributions to GDP

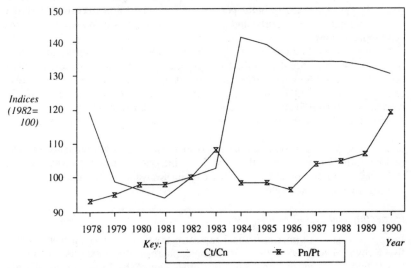

Source: Kenya: *Statistical Abstracts* (various issues).

gained momentum leading to removal of monopolies, increased supply, and allowing more competition. These events decreased the price of T goods relative to N goods making the production of the former less profitable.

Moreover, in the case of Kenya's pharmaceutical industry, the impact of a depreciation in the RXR is relatively small because of the high import content (75–93 per cent)[2] of Kenyan produced PPs and the limited degree of substitutability of such imports. As noted by Killick (1990: 17), and Velasco (1988: 19), under such circumstances, devaluation increases the cost of producing exportable PPs via its effects on the prices of imported inputs, and this in turn offsets a large part of the gains from devaluation on the price received from exports.

Notwithstanding these facts, *ceteris paribus*, exporters of T-goods (including PPs) should still have had the incentive to export so long as export prices were increased relative to the domestic prices. In the next part, we explore whether exports of PPs at the aggregate and firm levels responded to price incentives.

Price Incentives and Exports of Pharmaceutical Products from Kenya

More than 75 per cent of Kenya's pharmaceutical exports go to the Preferential Trade Area (PTA), with Uganda and Tanzania accounting for more than 50 per cent of the export market (Owino, 1993: 179). Exports have performed poorly as evidenced by the sharp declines in 1979–82 and 1986–90 (see Figure 8.2). The figure also shows that changes in pharmaceutical exports and the RXR as measured by P_n/P_t are to some extent related as predicted by theory. For instance, a rise in P_n/P_t (appreciation), in the periods 1979–82 and 1986–90 corresponds to a fall in pharmaceutical exports; and pharmaceutical exports increased when P_n/P_t fell (depreciation).

Similar to these findings, our analysis using a simultaneous equilibrium model[3] revealed that price incentives influence aggregate pharmaceutical exports, though not significantly (Owino, 1993: 183–5). Still, changes in the bilateral real exchange rates (BRXR) and pharmaceutical exports were found to be positively related (but insignificant) for Uganda, Tanzania and Burundi, and negatively related and also insignificant in the case of Zambia, Rwanda and Mauritius (*ibid.*).[4]

The general conclusion that emerges is that price incentives influence exports of PPs, though not significantly. Firm level interviews provided many reasons (both price and non-price factors) that explain Kenya's pharmaceutical exports, and these are presented below.

Ownership and Size of Firms

Poor performance of pharmaceutical exports is not unusual in an African country like Kenya (Foster, 1993: 296). On average, pharmaceutical exports account for less than 10 per cent of firms' sales in Kenya. Out of the 16 firms studied, only three medium-sized local firms were relatively more active in the export market

Figure 8.2 Price changes and pharmaceutical exports supply

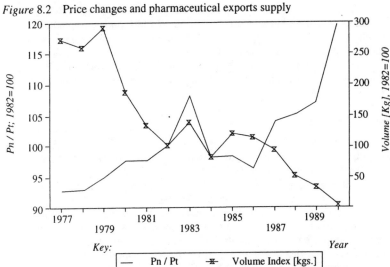

Source: Kenya: *Statistical Abstracts; Annual Trade Reports* (various issues).

as judged by their increase in exports (as share of total sales) from 13 per cent in 1988 to 20 per cent in 1990. Exports by the multinational corporations (MNCs) in the sample declined successively between 1988 and 1990 partly because such firms were avoiding competition from associate companies. Except for one firm, the small-scale local firms exported nothing between 1988 and 1990 because the cost of finding out about a market was too high, as were other overheads of exporting. That left only medium-scale local firms (Kenyan Asians) who responded to price incentives and were large enough to tackle the export market.

According to the active exporters, the major PTA trading member countries expedited the issue of import licenses to would-be importers if quotations were made in the Kenyan Shilling, rather than in hard currency. To increase their competitiveness following a depreciation in the RXR, the active exporters cut the foreign exchange price while maintaining the same profits in local currency. It was also found that the active exporters (all Kenyan Asians) were more active because they had stronger ties with the business community within the PTA.[5] In part, this explains why this group reacted much faster to exchange rate depreciations than the MNCs who did not have a 'ready' market.

The shifts i) to generic prescriptions; and ii) from buying drugs using brand names, to bulk buying using generics by many countries within the PTA (Kanji *et al.*, 1992) also provided the active exporters with an added advantage. Considering that the MNCs rarely participate in public tenders using generic names,[6] these changes decreased their potential to export to the PTA, while at the same time favouring pharmaceutical exports by the indigenous medium-scale firms who specialised in the production of generic PPs. Our investigations further revealed that the active exporters performed much better in: i) the liquid preparations widely used in the essential drugs programme (EDPs) within the PTA; and ii) relatively more sophisticated PPs like injectables which are less developed in the region.

Delays in Payments by the Government

The government of Kenya (GOK) was the major buyer of PPs manufactured in the country in the early 1980s with a share of about 60 per cent of the entire market (Table 8.1). However, this share fell to 30 per cent in the period 1985–90. Correspondingly, the share of sales to the government by the firms investigated fell – in one extreme case from 80 per cent in 1984 to 10 per cent in 1990.

Because of financial constraints, the GOK used to pay the drug suppliers late, typically nine to 18 months after signing the contracts – at original price, without interest. In addition, the GOK hardly ever honoured the devaluation clause.[7] As a result, many firms that participated in GOK drugs supply contracts had less working capital, and their production activities were adversely affected. Such firms were thus prompted to shift to the private sector and export markets where payments were made instantaneously.

Poor Administration of Export Incentives

Export incentives should make exports more profitable and if paid to the manufacturers they should induce an increase in export supply. However, for Kenya, the export incentives worked badly throughout the SAP period (Owino, 1993; World Bank, 1990; Mosley, 1991). In the first instance, the export compensation scheme was poorly managed, and caused corruption. Virtually all firms in Kenya's pharmaceutical industry treated gains from the scheme as a temporary windfall, mostly because the claims were hardly ever honoured. Secondly, though the manufacturing-under-bond and export processing zones (EPZs) are fairly recent, their performance up to the time of research was not encouraging. All but three firms were against using EPZs to promote exports because of the fear of losing the domestic market which accounts for a larger proportion of their sales. Overall, the poor administration of the export incentives means a decline in the profitability of exports and subsequent low exports.

Political Environment

Kenya's political status with Uganda and Tanzania (key export markets) has been erratic since the collapse of the East African Community (EAC) in 1977, and on several occasions the common borders between these countries have been closed.

To this end, the price incentives did not necessarily operate as expected. It was found that the fall in Kenya's pharmaceutical exports after 1986 was caused partially by the strained political relationship between Kenya and Uganda immediately President Museveni came into power. The active exporters asserted that Uganda's trade policies shifted in favour of barter trade, which did not benefit pharmaceutical trade. Again, Uganda increased duties on imports from Kenya including the PPs.

Preferential Treatment

Kenya and its trading partners offer preferential price treatment to local PPs because of, among other factors, the need to increase self sufficiency in the most basic drugs such as antimalarials, and anticipated quick response and more flexible delivery times especially during an epidemic (MOH *et al.*, 1984: 17). It was found that preferential price treatment in several countries, notably Zambia and Tanzania, blocked the penetration of Kenya's pharmaceutical exports even in instances of favourable price incentives.

Foreign Exchange Shortages

Countries in Sub-Saharan Africa (SSA) have faced various macroeconomic crises, including foreign exchange constraints since the late 1970s. Among Kenya's key export markets, Tanzania and Zambia were cited as the worst hit by foreign exchange shortages especially in the early 1980s. As a result, these countries were compelled to rely on external donor support to supplement drug supplies. In many instances, the donors tied the drug purchases to parent countries, or relied on well established (and much cheaper) international organisations such as the United Nations International Children's Emergency Fund (UNICEF), and non-profit organisations like International Dispensary Association (IDA) – thus denying Kenya part of its traditional pharmaceutical export market.

Price Incentives and Use of Local Inputs

Depreciation of the RXR, *ceteris paribus*, raises the price of foreign currency, and in effect increases the price of imports including intermediate and capital goods used by the manufacturing sector. These movements should favour the use of relatively more domestic inputs compared to imported inputs.

Our analysis of input usage of selected firms in Kenya's pharmaceutical industry between 1985 and 1990 provides various pointers. One, it reaffirms the high import intensity in this industry with the imported input content averaging about 75 per cent of total cost of production. By allowing for the import content of locally purchased inputs, the figure could be as high as 93 per cent (World Bank, 1987: 52). Two, wide variations exist in the use of the available local inputs. Generally, the indigenous firms used relatively more domestic inputs than MNCs, but between 1985 and 1990, there was a greater shift to use of local inputs, by MNCs who were using much less before. Whereas the domestic inputs intensity for the local manufacturers rose marginally from 33 per cent in 1985 to 37 per cent in 1990, it doubled for the MNCs studied, from 9 per cent to 20 per cent. Our study revealed a series of factors which influence the substitution from imported to domestic inputs. These factors are discussed below, starting with scarcity of foreign exchange.

Scarcity of Foreign Exchange

The substantial increase in the use of domestic inputs by MNCs was apparently because such firms had easier access to foreign exchange before 1985, whereas the local firms did not, and so had to adjust sooner. The adjustment was however confined to products already being produced in Kenya, and of a low technology kind, and products not jealously guarded by multinational monopoly producers. These included products such as packaging material, binders, flavours and colours.

Substitutions in the use of chemical inputs were very limited and relatively insignificant. Out of the 16 firms studied, only three firms used more local chemicals between 1985 and 1990. The indigenous firms claimed that they had almost reached their limit of substitution, and the remaining imported inputs could not be substituted. Elsewhere, indigenous firms in Zimbabwe were also compelled to switch to using more local inputs much earlier because of scarcity of foreign exchange (Muzulu, 1993).

Non Availability of Active Ingredients

The firms in Kenya's pharmaceutical industry did not switch to using more active ingredients between 1985 and 1990 because such inputs were not available locally. Like other developing countries (LDCs), Kenya does not have a comparative advantage in the production of new active ingredients for the pharmaceutical industry. Also, 'already developed' active ingredients are not manufactured presumably because the inventors take out patents or otherwise protect their monopoly, or because production requires a high technology industrial base which Kenya does not have. As noted by, among others, Ballance *et al.* (1992) the global pharmaceutical industry is highly secretive, and its research concentrated in a few industrialised countries.[8]

Kenya's capital base is very weak to support any intensive Research and Development activities required to develop and market a pharmaceutical product. In addition, the country does not have: i) active and adequate experimental and clinical research programmes; and ii) an advanced ancillary industry to support the development of a strong chemical base industry. Similar to these findings, Muzulu (1993) also found constraints in switching from imported to local inputs either because of non-availability or lack of inputs in sub-sectors such as textiles, industrial chemicals and metal fabrication in Zimbabwe.

Expensive and/or Poorer Quality Inputs

About half of the firms investigated claimed that they continued buying domestic inputs not because they are of superior quality or cheaper, but because someone started making them. On the other hand, for instance, it was asserted that the local maize starch: i) has a high micro biological content which reduces the efficacy of drugs; and ii) is more expensive than imports, though convenient because of greater availability and accessibility. In another incident, despite government's policy to encourage the use of local sugar, some firms (especially the MNCs) still regarded the product to be unsuitable for pharmaceutical use.

Back in 1985, the local manufacturers complained about the cost and quality of bottles manufactured in Kenya. The bottles were considered to be more expensive and the rejection rate was high (10–37.5 per cent) because of broken necks or rough surfaces (Owino, 1985). In this survey, the complaints seemed to be focused on the cost rather than the quality. EMCO, previous local producer of glass bottles went bust. The new firm, Central Glass, concentrates on beer bottles, regarding making medicine bottles as marginal. The glass bottles obtained from Central Glass (the only local manufacturer), were twice as expensive as similar imports from Europe or Asia. At the time of research, some firms were considering buying bottles from Tanzania and South Africa because of cost considerations. However, there were many obstacles inhibiting the moves, particularly the documentation process at the border.

Restrictive License Agreements

Restrictive license agreements which specify source(s) of supplies may prevent local manufacturers from responding to price incentives. In Kenya's pharmaceutical industry, some firms, especially MNCs or firms sub-contracted by them, were compelled to buy inputs from the parent companies or specified sources approved by the MNCs. Though agreements of this kind are useful provided they are intended to provide such benefits as quality assurance and regular supply of inputs at reasonable costs, they constrain increased use of domestically sourced inputs. Furthermore, the agreements provide avenues for transfer pricing in Kenya (Owino, 1985: 87).

Trade Liberalisation and Manufacture of Pharmaceutical Products

Trade liberalisation in Kenya's pharmaceutical sector has been implemented in various stages. Initially, removing the 40 per cent duty on finished PPs in 1981, and then, reducing tariffs on pharmaceutical inputs widely used in the sector. Thereafter, there was a gradual waiver, and reductions in the range of tariffs on other less used active ingredients such as vitamins, vegetable alkaloids and glycosides. By June 1992, import duties on all PPs were eliminated with the exception of white cotton wadding, first-aid boxes and one category of infusions.

The remarkable changes in the level and dispersion of tariffs were not however accompanied by an increase in the volume of imported pharmaceutical inputs, and finished PPs as would have otherwise been expected. Imports of pharmaceutical inputs trended downwards slightly with large fluctuations especially between 1981 and 1986. However, on average, the imported inputs have been more available than in 1981 and in particular in 1982, 1984 and 1986–89.

Figure 8.3 also reflects a gradual decline in the quantity of imported finished PPs between 1982 and 1989. In part, this shows that the gradual decrease in the level of tariffs as part of trade liberalisation did not lead to an increase in the availability of imported PPs. This could be explained by various factors. Firstly, *import substitution* – the share of imported finished PPs in total drugs consumption in Kenya fell from about 80 per cent (1980–85) to 44 per cent (1986–90), and the relative share of consumption of locally produced PPs increased (in particular after 1986).

Secondly, *change in donor policy* – the indigenous manufacturers contracted by Kenya's EDP asserted that from 1985, the donors (SIDA and DANIDA) shifted from imports towards buying more local drugs where available and of acceptable quality to support the local industry. Thirdly, the *depreciation of the RXR* which is advocated under SAP made the imports of finished PPs more expensive leading to a gradual fall in their importation.

Figure 8.3   Liberalisation of pharmaceutical imports

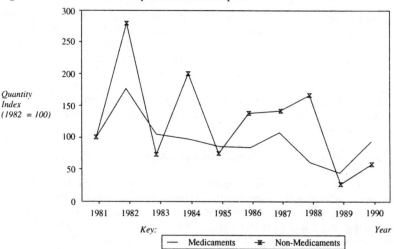

Source: Kenya: *Annual Trade Reports* (various issues).

Fourthly, *the non-tariff barriers were not reduced* – Kenya's pharmaceutical sector remains heavily protected through non-tariff measures. The effective rates of protection[9] for importable (ERP_m) and exportable (ERP_x) PPs, were found to be 74 per cent and 85 per cent respectively before 1982. Thereafter, ERP_m and ERP_x reduced to 11 per cent and 23 per cent respectively in 1988, before they rose gradually to reach 21 per cent and 31 per cent in 1991. Although the ERPs between 1988 and 1991 are much lower than the ERPs pre-1982 these did not result in a significant reduction in protection.

The re-classification of PPs from schedule one to a more restrictive schedule two in 1988 gave the MOH more control over the sector, and these powers were used to block some firms wishing to enter pharmaceutical production in Kenya. In addition, there exist other non-tariff barriers in Kenya's pharmaceutical industry: i) legislation introduced in April 1984 that requires all drugs marketed in the country to be registered by the Ministry of Health (MOH); ii) authorisation to manufacture, distribute, export and import can only be granted by the MOH; iii) the government, through its respective departments has the mandate to monitor closely the manufacture, distribution and advertisement of drugs to assure safety and adherence to laid down procedures by the Government. Depending on how these powers are used they could become major non-tariff barriers.

Furthermore, GOK provides preferential price treatment (especially in government tenders) to the local manufacturers as noted earlier. Ministry of Health *et al.* (1984: 16–17), support such protection on the basis that it is difficult for local manufacturers in developing countries like Kenya to compete with imports of generics because of: i) small production runs; ii) high unit costs; and iii) insignificant foreign exchange savings given that more than 50 per cent of the production cost of the PPs is accounted for by imported active ingredients and other inputs.

Apart from the methods of protection highlighted so far, the pharmaceutical industry is typically protected through other forms of control which are unlikely to be reduced under SAP. One, product development rather than low prices determines the nature of competition in this industry.[10] Immediately new drugs are discovered and developed, the compounds are patented even before they are declared fit for use in the market. Through the patents, the process technologies are safeguarded, and the manufacture of new products is only undertaken in-house at the innovators' headquarters to ensure that the technology does not leak to outsiders.[11] Other manufacturers willing to manufacture or distribute the same products are legally bound to seek permission from the innovators, mostly MNCs. Once the permission is granted, a license agreement has to be reached to utilise the scientific and technological knowledge developed. Apart from providing security for the inventions, such agreements stipulate terms such as: process technology, source of inputs, method of distribution and limitations on exports. In most cases, the MNC subsidiaries or approved vendors are the preferred source of inputs.

Two, government policies and legislation not related to tariffs and quotas can protect the existing producers against competition. For instance, through national health programmes, a government can influence the type and quantity of drugs bought by the public sector, manufactured, distributed and imported by the country. For instance, Nigeria de-registered all pharmaceutical products in 1991, and thereafter re-registered only those drugs in the essential drugs list. Thus, only these drugs could be imported, manufactured and distributed in the country making the economy entirely dependent on generics (Ballance *et al.*, 1992: 49). In the USA, several insurance companies notify policy holders the type of drugs to be considered for reimbursement under health insurance cover.[12]

Many of these controls are not likely to be reduced under SAP. Unfortunately, it is difficult to quantify the effects of the non-tariff barriers as also documented by Laird and Yeats (1988).

Simultaneous trade liberalisation with other elements in SAP such as reductions in government spending may lead to a decline in public sector demand for drugs, and drug shortages. This provides the central thrust of our discussion in the next part.

Government Expenditure and Availability of Essential Drugs in Kenya

Apart from SAP policy instruments like trade liberalisation, the availability of essential drugs in Kenya's Rural Health Facilities (RHFs) is influenced by, among others, changes in: GOK expenditure, MOH expenditure, allocations towards drugs and dressings, procurement decisions and donor support. In this respect, we examine these factors to provide a basis upon which to analyse the adequacy of provision of essential drugs in Kenya.

GOK expenditure (in US$)[13] declined successively between 1980 and 1983, and rose thereafter, on average by about 12 per cent annually (except for the declines in 1985 and 1989). Correspondingly, MOH expenditure declined by about 7.2 per cent per annum between 1980 and 1985, and rose subsequently through 1990 by about 8.8 per cent per annum, except for the decline in 1989.

As a proportion of GOK expenditure, health spending declined gradually from 6.7 per cent in 1980 to 4.7 per cent in 1990 (Table 8.1). Though Kenya's aggregate health spending increased in the late 1980s, the country's rapid population growth rate estimated at 3.8 per cent led to a fall in per capita health spending from an average of 7.4 US$ per annum (1980–85) to 6.3 US$ (1986–1990). Table 8.1 also shows the trend in GOK expenditure on drugs and dressings (in US$) between 1980 and 1990, and the split of such spending among the various public health facilities. As a proportion of MOH recurrent expenditure, spending on drugs and dressings fluctuated widely between 1980 and 1990: generally rising between 1980 and 1984 (except for 1983), falling sharply between 1984 and 1988, and recovering thereafter through to 1990. The sharp increase in drug expenditure allocations in 1984 is partly due to an exceptional grant to the Central Medical Stores under the new drugs management system (Segall *et al.*, 1989: 37).

Table 8.1   Health expenditure indicators, 1980–90

Year	GOK Exp (m.Ksh.)	MOH expenditure (m.Ksh.)	MOH expenditure % of GOK exp	Per capita (in US$)	Expenditure on drugs (m.Ksh.)					% of MOH Rec.exp.	GOK share (%) of drugs consumption#
					PHs	DHs	RHFs	Others+	Total		
1980	19440	1306	6.7	10.5	30	50	32	39	151	14	54
1981	22440	1422	6.3	9.1	32	86	32	41	191	16	61
1982	23814	1394	5.9	7.0	54	70	40	47	211	17	56
1983	25156	1526	6.1	6.1	42	60	22	53	177	14	63
1984	30694	1654	5.4	5.9	45	67	24	140	277	19	74
1985	33114	1854	5.6	5.5	49	75	29	60	213	14	51
1986	41770	2206	5.3	6.4	50	80	46	59	235	12	35
1987	44552	2358	5.3	6.3	50	80	49	62	241	12	24
1988	59334	2780	4.7	6.5	40	131	49	65	285	12	31
1989	63130	2878	4.6	5.8	49	149	74	83	355	15	36
1990*	79932	3742	4.7	6.5	60	201	94	103	459	17	26

Notes:

GOK expenditure on drugs/Total drugs consumption.

*   Estimates, Rec. Exp. – recurrent expenditure.

+   Kenyatta National Hospital, Rural Health Demonstration Centres, Psychiatric Services, Training Colleges Spinal Injury Unit, Public Health Control Department.

PHs   Provincial Hospitals.

DHs   District Hospitals.

RHFs   Rural health facilities.

Year   Financial Year, e.g. 1980 is FY 1980–81.

Sources: GOK: *Appropriation Accounts*, IMF; *IFS 1992, Statistical Abstract, Economic Surveys*.

In part, because of financial constraints, GOK's share of total drugs consumed in Kenya declined between 1980–84 and 1985–90 as shown in Table 8.1. Out of GOK expenditure on drugs between 1980 and 1990 (Figure 8.3), the District Hospitals received the largest share (38 per cent), followed by Provincial Hospitals (18 per cent), then the RHFs (18 per cent), Kenyatta National Hospital (14 per cent), and lastly, the remaining health institutions (12 per cent). Normally, decisions on these allocations are determined centrally by the treasury, and as noted by Segall *et al.* (1989: 44), the MOH has little influence. As a result, the ministry's stated priority for rural, preventive and promotive services is hardly ever depicted in the matching expenditure allocations, despite strong donor support. Drug expenditure allocations to the RHFs declined sharply from 4.3 million (US$) in 1980 to 1.65 million (US$) in 1983. However, there was some recovery from 1984 to 1990.

Drug Expenditure Allocations and Availability of Essential Drugs in the RHFs

The declines in GOK, MOH expenditures, and health spending per capita (in US$) in the early 1980s correspond to the inauguration of SAP which required reductions in government spending. The RHFs shouldered a large portion of the cuts in health spending. Whereas the district hospitals were more successful in protecting their budgets, those of the RHFs fell sharply in the early 1980s, particularly between 1983 and 1985. As a result, the donors tried to put more pressure on the government to release more financial resources to the RHFs in the early 1980s, but by reducing their support if matching government funds were not forthcoming. The combination of these factors adversely affected the availability of essential drugs in Kenya, and this perhaps led to an increase in health spending by the GOK and donors in the late 1980s. It could therefore be argued that structural adjustment had adverse effects on the availability of drugs in Kenya in the early 1980s, and this led to improvements in GOK and MOH spending in the latter part of the 1980s.

The increases in GOK drug expenditure allocations to the Essential Drugs Programme (EDP) from 1985 did not meet the targets agreed with the donors (Owino, 1993), and were inadequate to sustain essential drugs supplies. We investigated the extent to which drug shortages existed in Kenya's RHFs under the EDP between 1987 and 1991. As shown in Table 8.2, the actual distribution of drug kits was much lower than the requirements. Out of the total drug kit requirements of the RHFs between 1987 and 1991, only 54 per cent and 62 per cent of health centre and dispensary kits were bought and distributed respectively. For the health centre requirements, 60.7 per cent kit 1's and 46.9 per cent kit 2's were distributed. Similarly, for dispensary kits requirements, 63.5 per cent kit 1's and 60.2 per cent kit 2's were issued.

As can be seen, the peak of drug shortages was in 1989, and the supply of kit 2's wholly bought by the GOK have been lower than kit 1's bought jointly by the

Table 8.2   Actual distribution of drug kits as a percentage of requirements
(percentage in bracket)

	1987	1988	1989	1990	1991	1987–91
HC1	3964	4240	4690	5867	4467	23228[+]
	(80%)	(56%)	(56%)	(68%)	(51%)	(60.7%)[++]
HC2	3221	4543	3099	4141	5168	19554[+]
	(65%)	(60%)	(37%)	(48%)	(37%)	(47.4%)[++]
D1	8412	11029	7060	8914	9379	44794[+]
	(78%)	(80%)	(49%)	(57%)	(59%)	(63.4%)[++]
D2	8336	7458	6484	10864	9313	42455[+]
	(77%)	(54%)	(45%)	(69%)	(59%)	(60%)[++]

Notes: [+] drug kits distributed; [++] kits distributed as percentage of requirements.
Source: Ministry of Health and SIDA (various).

GOK and the donors.[14] A further investigation of selected RHFs in five districts in Kenya also revealed inadequacy in the supply of essential drugs between January 1991 and April 1992[15] (Owino, 1993: 287).

Our survey showed that during periods of drug shortages, the zonal depots and district hospitals opened the kits, and issues the drugs as loose items, thereby increasing incidences of pilferage and mishandling. Shortages also caused irregular distribution of drugs which created additional problems such as frequent movement of health personnel from the RHFs to the zonal depots or district hospital stores, and additional walking distance for the patients as they sought drugs from other RHFs. In other cases, drugs meant for RHFs were still being used at district hospitals despite warnings against this by the Director of Medical Services as early as 1987.

On the whole, Kenya's EDP worked badly throughout the 1980s mainly because of the inability of the GOK to keep up with its share of costs. Even after ten years' support by foreign donors the government has been unable to take full control of EDP. This has compelled the donors, particularly DANIDA to continue supporting the EDP after the end of their initial contract period in June 1991.[16] The EDP would have collapsed in the early 1980s if it were not for the extended donor support.

Corresponding to lack of adequate funds, the MOH has been delaying payments to the suppliers, or effecting partial payments. This has evoked various reactions. Many suppliers have been unwilling to provide additional credit to the GOK. Others took the GOK to court over non-payment of bills (CAG Report, 1985–86: 49). Still, other suppliers threatened to halt supplies unless they were paid compensation for losses arising from devaluation. Yet in other cases, some firms took advantage of delays in GOK payments to defer delivery of drugs to the Medical Supplies Co-ordinating Unit (MSCU) hoping to gain in the event of a devaluation (CAG, 1982/83: xxxiii). When firms awarded contracts failed to honour their delivery schedules the GOK was on many occasions compelled to re-tender the contracts on emergency basis and at much higher prices.

Continued financial constraints threaten the survival of Kenya's EDP. Firstly, the EDP *lacks adequate pharmaceutical technologists* to monitor the use of drug kits issued to the RHFs. At times the kits are distributed to the RHFs by drivers (based at the zonal depots or district hospital stores) who are not technically well informed about the drugs. As a result, such persons are unable to solve on sight immediate problems such as withdrawing expired drugs, or are slow in moving drugs to most needed areas.

Secondly, *poor transportation* – the EDP relies heavily on vehicles based at the national office and zonal depots. It was found that these vehicles were inadequate (in number and type) for the distribution, monitoring and supervising of drug kits issues to the RHFs as also noted by MOH and SIDA (1988a: 41–2). As a result, some rural health workers coming for drug kits at the District Hospital stores are compelled to use 'matatus' because of lack of official transport (MOH and SIDA, 1988c: 89). Apparently, the government vehicles which are supposed to support the EDP are very old (thus requiring a lot of finance to maintain), or are grounded due to lack of funds to buy spare parts and petrol. As a result, drugs may be available at the stores but cannot reach the RHFs.

Thirdly, *proper storage* is vital for the drugs because risks of spoilage increase once the drugs are exposed to bad weather. Due to limited finance the GOK has been unable to provide adequate storage at some stations,[17] and at times the drugs are kept in poorly ventilated houses, or in stores with limited space. Of the regions covered by our study, Kajiado district was the most affected by poor storage. In the first four months of 1992 alone, three facilities in Kajiado district could not use about 20 000 paracetamol and mebendazole tablets because the drugs were exposed to excess heat.[18] About 30 per cent of the ointments were also damaged because of exposure to excess heat.

Fourthly, the RHFs cited *anomalies in the distribution* of drug kits to be a major factor causing drug shortages. Out of 40 cases of anomalies highlighted, 16 related to tampering and removing items from the drug kits. Twelve related to receiving less kits than actual allocation in the distribution schedule; six pertained to receiving loose items instead of complete kits; and the remaining cases related to receiving a mixture of dispensary and health centre kits. Various RHFs reported receiving completely sealed containers with no drugs in them. In other instances, some containers were packed with items different from those stated in the distribution schedule.

Similar to these findings, the EDP unearthed irregularities in the distribution and use of drug kits meant for the RHFs[19] in April and December 1990. CAG reports (1983/84: xxxvi; 1986/87: 25) also report numerous cases of pilferage which include, one, alteration of drug requisition forms to show much higher figures than the actual orders or receipts; two, payments to firms for what they have not delivered through manipulation of stores' records; three, over-ordering of drugs in complete disregard of the laid down procurement procedures such as shelf life.[20] All in all, the pilferage and wastage of drugs in Kenya's EDP is not worse than the average for other countries where about 70 per cent of drugs are diverted (Foster, 1993), nonetheless they merit attention.

Fifthly, our study also revealed that *'issue of expired drugs'* caused drug shortages in Kenya's RHFs. The firms interviewed asserted that GOK's bureaucracy in processing tenders was the major cause of expired drugs by the MSCU. Seemingly, the GOK takes a minimum of six months between signing a tender and issuing a Local Purchase Order (LPO) to the manufacturers, depending on whether or not finances are available. On the other hand, once the manufacturers receive notification of the government contracts they start production immediately because of the huge orders. If for some reason the government delays in paying for the orders, such items will lie idle at the manufacturers' warehouse, more so, because the same drugs cannot be sold in the private market particularly if they are embossed with a GOK symbol. Moreover, it is expensive and laborious to unpack drug kits and offer them for sale elsewhere.

Lastly, *poor packaging* of drugs led to wastage and drug shortages. Some drug kits were either packed with loose polythene paper, or none at all thereby exposing drugs to excess moisture and pilferage. Ten RHFs complained of receiving syrup and injectables in vials which were broken because of loose packaging or poor transportation. In some instances, the contents of such drugs spilt over other drugs causing additional wastage. Four facilities complained of receiving metrifonate tabs clamped in one heap because the tablets were packed in containers whose caps were loose exposing the sugar coated tablets to excess moisture.

II   CONCLUSIONS AND POLICY RECOMMENDATIONS

Various conclusions can be reached from our discussion of the effectiveness of SAP in increasing the profitability and availability of PPs in Kenya. These are discussed under the different topics below.

Profitability of T-goods including PPs

Depreciation of the RXR did not make the production of T-goods more profitable during the period of our investigation because: i) changes in the RXR under SAP were not accompanied by appropriate macroeconomic policies as required in the orthodox package; ii) in other instances, the adverse macroeconomic conditions such as drought led to low profitability of T-goods sector; and iii) the high import intensity of locally produced PPs. In part, these factors led to low profitability in the T-goods sector including PPs, and poor performance of pharmaceutical exports.

Notwithstanding these facts, SAP had a positive impact on the performance of some indigenous firms who responded to price incentives and were large enough to tackle the export market. Unfortunately, these firms could not exploit the full benefits of SAP because of constraints such as poor administration of export incentives, unfavourable political environment, protectionist policies and foreign exchange constraints in the export markets. As can be seen, some (but not all) of these factors are likely to change with SAP. The non exporters were relatively less affected by SAP because they were either too small to export, or because, as in case of the MNCs they would not compete with associate companies or had relatively weak business connections in the export markets. These results have various implications: one, depreciation in the RXR should be co-ordinated with suitable macroeconomic policy instruments as advocated in the orthodox adjustment packages to increase the profitability of the T-goods sector.

Two, the administration of the export incentive schemes needs to be improved to expedite payment of claims, provide wider coverage, and control corrupt activities. However, this may not be an easy task if some high ranking government officials still have vested interests in the schemes.

Three, the export incentives need to be re-structured to: i) allow pharmaceutical firms to operate subsidiaries within the EPZs while retaining the domestic market; and ii) provide more incentives to relatively more sophisticated PPs that have been more successful in the export market.

Four, it appears that the changing socio-economic conditions in East and Central Africa may limit future exports to the traditional markets. Kenya's geo-political advantage since independence (Coughlin and Ikiara, 1991: 243), appears to be ending. Lifting of sanctions against South Africa, and to a lesser extent Zimbabwe imply increased competition. The end of war and political stability in Uganda, and change in the political orientation and implementation of SAP in Tanzania also imply recovery of production in these countries and subsequently less demand for PPs from Kenya. As noted by Coughlin and Ikiara (1991: 251), to promote exports in the PTA, Kenya needs to buy more from the PTA states and institutionalise policies towards promoting these imports. Other government policies should also play an important role in removing some of the constraints to pharmaceutical exports. For instance, barter trade with trading partners should be encouraged whenever possible and to the advantage of the trading partners.

Use of Local Inputs

SAP was relatively less effective in promoting the substitution from imported to local PPs. A series of non-price factors were more significant in influencing the substitution. Those factors in favour include: i) foreign exchange scarcity; ii) easy availability or reduced need to hold large stocks when inputs do not come from far away; and iii) lack of hassle at the border. Of these, only the first factor is likely to change as a result of a depreciation of the RXR. Factors against use of local inputs include: i) quality; ii) prejudice by MNCs; and iii) monopoly of supply by MNCs. Again, none of these factors is likely to change much because of SAP.

It seems that, for some time, Kenya's pharmaceutical industry will continue to rely on imported active ingredients which are heavily guarded by MNCs, and which the country does not have the capacity to produce. The firms should, however, be encouraged to use more of the local inputs where available and of acceptable quality. Negotiation with the MNCs for less restrictive technology transfer agreements should be encouraged. Again, the local manufacturers wishing to be sub-contracted by MNCs should be encouraged in order to strengthen the local technological capability. Closer co-operation with the MNCs in technology transfer may also lead to the exploitation of indigenous inputs in the future. Whilst pursuing these policies, it should be noted that there is likely to be resistance from the MNCs who safeguard their technologies, and who may regard such policies as hostile to foreign investment.

Increased Availability of Imported PPs

Depreciation of the RXR made imported PPs relatively more expensive, and this decreased the availability of imported PPs and, partly encouraged the substitution of locally produced for imported finished PPs. In addition, the existence of high protection through non-tariff barriers constrained the availability of imported PPs thereby offsetting the positive effects of trade liberalisation.

Reductions in government spending which is advocated under SAP adversely affected the availability of essential drugs in the early 1980s, and the RHFs shouldered a large portion of the cuts. In turn, this led to an increase in government and health spending in the late 1980s. Nonetheless, drug shortages still persisted in the late 1980s indicating that the recovery was not adequate. It was also found that apart from financial constraints, drug shortages in the late 1980s were caused by a series of structural problems in Kenya's health sector.

These results have various implications. Firstly, Kenya's EDP requires additional financing considering that DANIDA is scheduled to withdraw from the programme in 1994. A specific proportion of user charges recently introduced in various health institutions should be allocated towards the purchase of drugs and dressings. The money should, however, not be tied up in bureaucratic obstacles or lie idle in bank deposits as was the case with Ksh. 70 million collected from user charges between December 1989 and September 1990 (*New Africa*, 1990: 28). As noted by Abel-Smith and Rawal (1992), patients are willing to contribute towards health services including drugs so long as they are assured of getting the drugs. However, the problem with using the user fees to sustain drug supplies is that the poor who are not able to afford the fees may be crowded out of the public health institutions. Furthermore, it is difficult to develop a mechanism to exempt such people in countries like Kenya.

Secondly, there is need for an increase in expenditure allocations towards drugs and dressings for the RHFs. The RHFs serve about 80 per cent of the population but only receive 18 per cent of the drug expenditure allocations. Therefore, expenditure should be re-allocated within the health budget, so that RHFs receive a bigger share. If this is not possible, then perhaps the country could negotiate for specific programmes to sustain health care services including the purchase of essential drugs. This should however be accompanied by an improvement in the management of the drugs. In a way, this recommendation highlights the importance of 'good governance', which is now advocated as part of many SAPs in relieving institutional constraints. In line with the above recommendations, the GOK should maintain: i) central purchasing by the MSCU; ii) buying using generic names; and iii) the restricted essential drugs list which addresses the key morbidity cases in the country.

It can be argued that structural adjustment promoted the production of PPs in Kenya (though not significantly), but was relatively less effective in increasing the availability of essential drugs in Kenya's EHFs. On the whole, this chapter has demonstrated that SAP is a *necessary* but not *sufficient* condition to increase the profitability and availability of PPs in Kenya.

Notes

1. This chapter is based on the author's DPhil thesis (Owino, 1993), from which research data and findings are taken.
2. See part about price incentives and use of local inputs for a detailed explanation of input usage in Kenya's pharmaceutical industry.
3. The study used a simultaneous equilibrium econometric model similar to those used by Goldstein and Khan (1978), Riedel (1988), Muzulu (1993). See Owino (1993: 185) for the model specification.
4. Spearman's correlation coefficient was used to determine the relationship between bilateral real exchange rate changes obtained from Owino (1993) and exports by country of destination obtained from the Annual Trade Reports.
5. In most cases, other family members owning businesses within the PTA.
6. The MNCs prefer to promote their own brand formulations over which they have strong price influence.
7. Devaluation decreases the real earnings of drug suppliers in the event of delays in payments. On this understanding, the devaluation clause entitles a manufacturer to a reimbursement by the government of the full extent of devaluation, if the exchange rate is devalued by more than 5 per cent between the time of making an order and settlement of the claims.

8. About 90 per cent of pharmaceutical products marketed between 1960 and 1990 were discovered and developed in only ten industrialised countries.

9. The ERPs were estimated using Milner's (1990) model which specify:

$$ERP_m = \frac{T_m - A_{im}T_i}{1 - A_{im}} \qquad\qquad ERP_x = \frac{S_x - A_{ix}T_i}{1 - A_{ix}}$$

where T_m is the import tax on finished PP_s and S_x the subsidy on exports. A_{ix} and A_{im} are input-output coefficients for exportable and import competing products respectively under free trade conditions.

10. It is only in the production of generics that price and production availability appear to be more important sources of competition than product efficacy. The market for generics accounts for only about 8 per cent of global sales (1991) (Ballance *et al.*, 1992: 12).

11. At times, the government in MNCs countries of origin, like USA, go further to ensure that their patents are protected globally (see Owino, 1993 for a detailed explanation).

12. For instance, several insurance companies in the USA (e.g. Aetna, Metropolitan, Prudential, Blue Cross/Blue Shield) notify policy holders that they will be reimbursed the full cost of generic drugs, but only 80 per cent of the price of brand drugs (Alexander, 1984: 76).

13. Unless otherwise stated, the expenditures in US$ in this part are at current prices, and are obtained by converting the corresponding expenditures in Ksh (Table 8.1) using the yearly average nominal exchange rates obtained from IFS, 1992.

14. Shortage of Kit 2's has more severe consequences to the health care of the nation since it contains drugs required to treat the commonest diseases such as malaria, upper respiratory tract infection and ear infections (Havemann *et. al.*, 1990).

15. Our study covered five districts: Kisumu, Makuru, Tana River, Nyeri and Kajiado. From these districts, 38 RHFs were selected through a systematic sampling technique.

16. SIDA withdrew from the programme in 1991, while DANIDA, under a new contract, is scheduled to extent financial assistance for the purchase of drugs till June 1994 providing 30 per cent of procurement of kit 1's in 1991/92, 20 per cent in 1992/93, and 10 per cent in 1993/94.

17. The situation at the MSCU is much better since November 1987 when the EDP acquired a new storage facility. According to MOH and SIDA (1988a: 46), the new facility has improved security and provided more storage space.

18. The tablets had bad odour or were clamped together (especially those which were sugar coated).

19. Personal communication with the management of the MOH and MSCU depot.

20. Between 1981 and 1984 alone, GOK lost about Ksh. 40 million representing more than ten months requirements through over-ordering (CAG Report, 1983/84: xxxvii).

References

Abel-Smith, B. and Rawal, P. (1992) 'Can Poor Afford 'Free' Health Services? A Case Study of Tanzania', *Health Policy and Planning*, Vol. 7, No. 4, pp. 329–41 (Oxford University Press).

Alexander, C.P. (1984) 'Prescriptions for Cheap Drugs', *Time*, New York, September, 14.

Ballance, R., Poga'ny, J. and Forstner, H. (1992) *The World's Pharmaceutical Industries: An International Perspective on Innovation, Competition and Policy* (Aldershot: Edward Elgar).

Controller and Auditor General's Report (CAG), *Kenya: Appropriation Accounts* (various issues).

Coughlin, P. and Ikiara G.K. (eds) (1991) *Kenya's Industrialisation Dilemma* (Nairobi: Heinemann).

de Groot, A.W. (1991) 'Adjustment Policies and the Real Exchange Rate in Kenya since 1975', *World Development*, vol. 19, no. 10.

Foster, S.D. (1993) 'Economic Aspects of the Production and Use of Pharmaceuticals: Evidence and Gaps in Research', in Mills, A. and Lee, K. (eds) *Health Economics Research in Developing Countries* (Oxford: Oxford University Press).

Goldstein, M. and Khan, M. (1978) 'The Supply and Demand for Exports: A Simultaneous Approach', *Review of Economics and Statistics*.

Havemann, K. *et al.*, (1990) 'A Study of the Utilisation of Essential Drugs in Three Districts of Kenya', *Vol. I and II, Essential Drugs Programme* (Kenya: Ministry of Helath), Nairobi, Kenya, October.

International Monetary Fund (IMF) *International Financial Statistics Yearbook 1992–93* (Washington DC: *IMF*).

Julin, E. and Levin, J. (1992) 'Kenya: Macroeconomic Performance 1990 and Some Issues Related to Structural Adjustment Programmes', Department of Economics, University of Gothenburg, Report No. 30/92.

Kanji, N. *et al.* (1992) *Drugs Policy in Developing Countries* (London: Zed Books).

Kenya, Government of, *Statistical Abstracts*, Government Printer, Nairobi (various issues).

Kenya, Government of, *Annual Trade Reports*, Government Printer, Nairobi (various issues).

Kenya, Ministry of Health, '*SIDA Supported Health Programmes in Kenya: Workplan and Budgets*, Nairobi (various issues).

Killick, T. (1990) 'Exchange Rates and Structural Adaptation', Overseas Development Institute, Working Paper No. 33, London.

Laird, S. and Yeats, A. (1988) ' Trends in Nontariff Barriers of Developed Countries 1966–1986', *World Bank Working Paper*, WPS 137, December.

Milner, C. (1990) 'Policy Appraisal and the Structure of Protection in a Low-Income Developing Country: Problems of Measurement and Evaluation in Burundi', *Journal of Development Studies*, 27:1, pp. 22–42.

Ministry of Health (MOH) and SIDA (various issues) *SIDA Supported Health Programmes in Kenya: Progress Report (January–June)*, Nairobi: Ministry of Health.

MOH/SIDA/DANIDA/WHO (1984) *'Management of Drug Supplies to Rural Health Facilities in Kenya'*, EDP Evaluation Report, EDP, Nairobi.

Mosley, P. (1991) 'Kenya' in Mosley *et al.* (eds) *Aid and Power* (London: Rontledge).

Muzulu, J. (1993) 'Real Exchagne Rate Depreciation and Structural Adjustment: The Case of the Manufacturing Sector in Zimbabwe (1980–91)', D. Phil Dissertation, IDS, University of Sussex.

New Africa (1990) IC Publications Ltd; No. 278, November.

Owino, P.S.W. (1993) 'The Impact of Structural Adjustment on the Production, and Availabiity of Pharmaceutical Products in Kenya', DPhil Dissertation, IDS, University of Sussex.

Owino, P.S.W. (1985) 'The Pharmaceutical Industry in Kenya', unpublished MA Research Paper, University of Nairobi.

Riedel, J. (1988) 'The Demand for LDC Exports of Manufactures: Estimates from Hong Kong', *Economic Journal*, vol. 98, no. 389, March.

Segall, M. *et al.* (1989) *Expenditure and Financing of the Health Sector in Kenya*, Report of a Study Commissioned by the World Bank and Performed in Association with Ministry of Health (Kenya).

Velasco, A. (ed.). (1988) *Trade, Development and the World Economy: Selected Essays of Carlos Diaz-Alejandro* (Oxford: Basil Blackwell).

World Bank (1987) 'Kenya: Industrial Sector Policies for Investment and Growth', Report No. 6711-KE, Vol. I and II, Washington DC.

World Bank (1990e) 'Kenya Stabilisation and Adjustment: Towards Accelerated Growth', Report No. 9047–KE, Washington DC.

9 What Role for Stock Exchanges, Venture Capital and Leasing Companies in Developing the Private Sector in Africa?

Mike Faber

I INTRODUCTION

Outside an office on the second floor of the Kingsway Building, Kwame Nkrumah Avenue, Accra a bright sign cheerfully invites the visitor 'Buy a Company Today'. It is the office of the Ghana Stock Exchange (GSE). In fact, it is not possible to buy a company through the GSE – any more than it would be feasible to do so through most of Sub-Saharan Africa's other Emerging Market exchanges.[1] What it is possible for African investors to do is to buy shares, and therefore partial ownership, of a range of publicly quoted companies. How important a step forward is that?

For growth rates to improve in most Sub-Saharan Africa (SSA) countries, both domestic investment and domestic savings rates need to be increased. The productivity of investment also needs to be improved. That much is almost a truism. Less attention has been paid to the types of investment and, more particularly, to the types of savings required and to the problem of matching these requirements to each other. For example, it is now widely acknowledged that a larger proportion of future investment in virtually all SSA countries should be in the private sector, much of which will need to be long-term. For such investments to happen, savers and those who are entrusted with investing other peoples' savings will need to be convinced that there are opportunities that are both profitable and secure, or that the risks involved can be spread and therefore managed. Moreover if the structure of the business attracting this new investment is to be sound, a major part of their financing will need to come in the form of equity capital.

Therein resides a number of difficulties. In most SSA countries, local residents have had neither the means, nor the knowledge, nor the opportunity, nor the encouragement to invest in equities. Other potential sources of equity finance –

174

pension funds, insurance companies, mutual funds, unit trusts, immigrant communities, foreign portfolio investors – have often been prohibited or have felt inhibited from doing so. Development Finance Corporations (DFCs) provided relatively little equity capital, or in some cases none at all.

The record of DFCs in Africa has been poor.[2] At a 1994 seminar in Harare, the chief executive of one such DFC diagnosed the most frequent causes of failure as being: (i) weak management; (ii) excessive government interference, especially when government itself was a major shareholder in the DFC; (iii) too many loans to parastatals over which the DFC had very little control; (iv) inadequate capitalisation of most borrowers, i.e. shareholders' funds were too small; (v) an unfavourable economic climate and mistaken macro-policies; (vi) lack of support services which should have been provided by the DFC to the project; (vii) no initiative by the DFCs to widen the scope of its business products to meet client needs; (viii) too much loan capital provided and not enough equity; (ix) DFCs borrowed extensively in foreign currency, either imposing the risk of domestic currency devaluation on those to whom they on-lent, or taking the risk themselves without provisioning.

Later in this chapter we will look at the role that Venture Capital Companies (VCCs) and Leasing Companies are being looked upon to play in remedying some of the deficiencies identified from the disappointing performance of the DFCs. In advance of that, we examine the role of some of the Stock Exchanges (SEs), ancient and modern, which now exist in anglophone African countries. Surveying the recent proliferation of these exchanges and the expectation they have aroused, it appears almost as if they are now regarded as a magic key to successful capitalism. How realistic are these expectations?

II   STOCK EXCHANGES: OBJECTIVES AND BASIC ISSUES

The classic functions of a stock exchange are to provide a source of capital for business while also providing an outlet for saving which combines reasonable liquidity with the prospect of a positive real rate of return and participation in economic growth.

For African developing countries, a number of other purposes may also be served by the establishment of a local stock exchange. First, it can widen the ownership of domestic assets, giving a larger number of the indigenous population a stake in the creation of an economic environment in which private sector firms are enabled to operate profitably. Second, it can facilitate what has been called 'the creeping localisation of foreign-owned companies' while at the same time allowing for a sanitised form of foreign capital injection into locally-owned companies.[3] Indeed as the stock exchange matures, its existence provides a means of softening the sharp dichotomy between foreign-controlled and domestically-controlled large companies. Third, a stock market can be used in the privatisation of state-owned enterprises (SOEs). It may be rare for an SOE to be privatised in one step through the flotation of shares, but the flotation of minority interests in SOEs which are run on commercial lines can facilitate the move to majority privatisation. Fourth, the existence of a stock market can act as an encouragement to foreign direct investment (FDI) for one of the things that a direct investor will often be looking for is the eventual prospect of selling off all or a portion of the investment once it has matured. The existence of an active stock exchange (and the absence of exchange controls) improves the prospect of such future realisations or 'exits'.

Harvey (1993) mentions three other potential benefits arising from the establishment of the Botswana Share Market (BSM). Previously, cash savings had to be held in the form of deposits with financial institutions, all of which yielded less than the rate of inflation after payment of tax. The BSM and, in particular, a quoted investment trust, offers savers the prospect of doing better than the rate of inflation. The existence of the BSM has also made it easier for private sector firms to improve their equity: debt ratios. Previously this would have required either the use of retained earnings (a slow process even if affordable) or going into partnership with the government controlled Botswana Development Corporation (BDC), a form of involvement with the state which many private companies prefer to avoid. The existence of the BSM also persuaded some Batswana to invest in financial instruments rather than increase the size of their herds of cattle, the traditional outlet for saving. Since the over-grazing of communal lands has become a problem, the establishment of the BSM could be seen as one way of protecting the environment.

In the 1960s, economic nationalism in newly independent African countries usually took the form of 'African Socialism' and featured a proliferation of State Owned Enterprises – some the result of nationalisations or joint ventures, others the result of new business initiatives by the state in the context of a centrally directed economy.[4] The resulting economic performances, buffeted in many instances by unfavourable external conditions, gave rise to lowered standards of living and then, under the influence of the multilateral financial institutions (MFIs), to a widespread abandonment of this model in favour of tighter fiscal rectitude and recognition of the private sector as the main engine of growth. In this context it may be necessary to view the widespread founding of African Stock Exchanges, and recourse to other financial innovations as an attempt, while abandoning state ownership and central planning, to preserve the indigenous ownership and local control of most of the country's productive assets which nationalisation was intended to have achieved. This process has been described as a movement from direct state ownership to indirect ownership by the people.

A number of issues have to be decided in the design of a new Stock Exchange before its component parts can be put in place. We examine these issues below.

Enabling Legislation

It would be possible to have dealings in shares and something equivalent to a market dealing in stocks under the terms of an ordinary Companies Act. Indeed the

Botswana Share Market (BSM) did so operate for more than five years. It is more usual however for government to pass a special Stock Exchange Act, which will normally also give the Minister of Finance power to make additional regulations.

Corporate Form

The stock exchange is normally a body corporate or company which is owned by its members or shareholders. It is not, however, generally a profit-seeking enterprise paying dividends to its members. It is more in the nature of a club which confers certain privileges on its members, but which also has the right to regulate their behaviour and to suspend or expel members if their conduct is not satisfactory.

Membership

It can be assumed that the main membership of a stock exchange will be stock-brokers – either individuals, partnerships or firms. However there may also be associate members, with more limited rights and responsibilities, and non-broking members. In the early life of a stock exchange such non-broking members may be of considerable importance because of the financial support they can give the exchange in its early, loss-making days. Non-broking members are characteristically financial institutions such as merchant banks which have an interest in the successful development of the exchange without wishing to become dealers themselves. Stock exchanges differ as to whether stockbrokers can be individual persons or whether they have to be incorporated. They also differ as to whether stock broking has to be the exclusive occupation of the person or firm seeking full membership.

The members will elect a council from amongst themselves to act as their governing body. In the event of their being very few members initially, the Minister of Finance may be accorded the right to appoint a number of the members of the council. Membership of a stock exchange may be permanent in the sense that it endures until the member wishes to terminate it or until the member is expelled for misconduct; or it may be for a limited period and subject to renewal. One of the criticisms levelled against the membership rules of the Ghana Stock Exchange was that membership was subject to annual renewal, which could be seen as putting at risk the substantial investment needed to become a member in the first place.

Listing Requirements

By 'listing requirements' is meant the conditions which a company is required to fulfil in order to have its securities listed and the price of its shares quoted on the exchange. These will include the financial size and strength of the company, audited records of its financial results over a number of years, the names and occupations of its directors, and the proportion of the total share holding being offered to the public. A very considerable amount of additional information will have to be included in a prospectus whenever the company seeks to raise money through the exchange, and stringent disclosure requirements will govern the reporting of its results and the announcement of price-sensitive information thereafter.

Requirements differ in respect of whether a company wishing to list needs an established stockbroker or merchant bank to sponsor its application but in any event it is normal to employ one.

Trading and Settlement Rules

Before a complete set of trading rules can be drafted, a prior decision has to be made on the system of trading which is going to be used on the exchange. For small exchanges where a limited number of brokers deal in a small number of stocks, either the 'open outcry' or the 'call-over' system is most widely employed. All dealers can be accommodated in a comparatively small room, an official of the exchange presides, initial prices are shown upon a series of blackboards, and the quantities of shares bought and sold in the day's trading and the prices at which deals are struck get chalked upon the board. At the end of the session the exchange of contract notes between stockbrokers takes but a few minutes. Settlement rules lay down the manner and the time within which scrip must be delivered and cash settlement must be effected between stockbrokers, and between stockbroker and client.

Fidelity Fund

Most exchanges nowadays insist that all stock broking members take out insurance to ensure that in the event of a client suffering financially as the result of the malfeasance of a stockbroker or one of his employees, that client may be compensated against loss through making a claim on the Fidelity Fund established for that purpose. The fund itself may then pursue the claim against the defaulting stockbroker. The existence of such a fund will obviously create confidence amongst investors using the exchange who will at times be entrusting their stockbrokers with very considerable sums of money.

Code of Conduct for Staff

Staff of a Stock Exchange come into possession of information that would enable them or their associates to make assured but improper financial gains. For this reason it is necessary to have a code of conduct on insider trading.

Fiscal Environment

In a theoretically ideal world, all sources of finance would be treated equally by the tax man, in which case the financial structure of companies would not be influenced by fiscal considerations. In practice nearly all LDCs have tax systems which favour loan financing over equity financing. The prime reason for this is that interest payments are treated as a cost to the company and are generally paid without deduction of tax – although foreign interest payments may be subject to a withholding tax – while dividend payments have to be paid out of post-tax company income, and may also, if paid abroad, be subject to a further dividend withholding tax. Similarly, while the repayment of the principle of a loan is seldom subject to tax, the disposal of equity (or the distribution of the capital of a company) may well be subject to a capital gains tax, whose burden is increased if no allowance is made for inflation.

To compound these disadvantages, foreign exchange authorities throughout Africa have been notoriously less willing to allocate foreign exchange for the payment of dividends than they are for the servicing of corporate loan obligations. This bias has been responsible for the frequency with which quasi-equity has been provided by overseas parent companies in the form of shareholders' advances, subordinate to ordinary loan finance but repayable out of retained profits as if they were loans.

A number of measures have been urged to make equity financing and the listing of companies on a domestic stock exchange more fiscally attractive. One example of such measures can be given. In 1991 the Government of Botswana abolished capital gains tax on publicly quoted shares and a reduced company tax rate (35 per cent instead of the normal 40 per cent) was conceded for a period of five years to companies listed on the Botswana Share Market which had at least 25 per cent of their issued shares held by non-controlling interests. The consequence was a number of rights issues for which parent companies did not take up their rights in order to boost the proportion of shares held by the public. At the same time, no personal income tax was payable on locally derived dividend income.

Since company and personal tax rates were then similar, those steps made the fiscal system level as between local and equity finance for companies – loan interest was tax deductible for the company but taxable in the hands of the recipient, while dividend payments were not tax deductible by the company but were tax free to the local shareholder (Jefferis, 1993).

Viability of the Exchange

To be independent, a stock exchange should be self-supporting. An exchange's two main sources of income are likely to be the annual subscriptions of its dealing members and the listing fees of companies whose shares are traded on the exchange. These are likely to be fairly modest in the early years, which in turn argues for modest levels of staffing and modest premises – not always what the founders of new exchanges have in mind. Where revenues are insufficient to meet expenditures, either the government is called upon to help out or non-dealing members are called upon to keep the stock exchange company solvent.[5]

Regulation

The different issue of regulation almost merits a chapter on its own. Can Emerging Stock Markets be left to regulate themselves, despite the argument that an institution set up in the interests of its members will be unlikely to transform easily into one which protects the public against those same members? Should the job be done from within the Ministry of Finance, or by the Central Bank? Should a special Securities Exchange Commission be established for the purpose? In smaller developing countries, is it feasible to have a single body that will regulate the pensions industry, the insurance industry, and unit trusts as well as the stock exchange? What chance is there of attracting sufficiently experienced persons to perform these jobs effectively if salaries are tied to civil service levels?

Then there is the question as to whether the same body should be responsible for both promotion of the stock exchange and its regulation. At a conference on African Capital Markets held in Nairobi in August 1993, the Kenyan Minister of Finance opined 'In the emerging securities markets, the aspect of regulation must be subservient to the promotion of development so that new market players are encouraged.' Almost exactly the opposite approach has been adopted in Ghana, partly out of an apprehension that experienced players from Nigeria might come across and perpetrate some major scam that would discredit the GSE before it had found its feet. One is aware too of the judgement on the Bombay Stock Exchange at the time of its scandal – that this was an exchange that was over-regulated but under-supervised.

III   STOCK EXCHANGES: AFRICAN EXPERIENCE

To what extent have the stock exchanges in anglophone Sub-Saharan Africa fulfilled what were previously identified as the classic functions of stock exchanges?

Table 9.1 displays some of the main features of a number of SSA's emerging markets.

The discussion which follows attempts to summarise some of the lessons which can be drawn from the experience of these markets.

The main features of all SSA stock exchanges (other than South Africa's) is that they are very small, whether measured by local market capitalisation (the market value of all companies quoted on the exchange) or by average daily turnover, or by the number of listed companies or of dealing members. None of the stock exchanges discussed in this chapter have even one percent of the capitalisation of the Johannesburg Stock Exchange (JSE). At the end of 1993, the JSE was capitalised at $200 billion while the total for the rest of Africa's exchanges was just over $12 billion of which Morocco represented over a third. Excluding Nigeria for the moment, local market capitalisation varies from only

Table 9.1   Main features of some African emerging stock markets

	Botswana	Ghana	Kenya	Mauritius	Namibia	Nigeria	Swaziland	Zimbabwe
1. Name of Exchange	Botswana Share Market	Ghana Stock Exchange	Nairobi Stock Exchange	Mauritius Stock Exchange Commission	Namibia Stock Exchange	Nigeria Stock Exchange	Swaziland Stock Market	Zimbabwe Stock Exchange
2. Date Established	1989	1990	1954	late 1800s	1992	1960	1990	1896
3. Members	0	3	6	10	0	140	0	12
4. Number of Listed Securities	11	15	55	23	5	142 First Tier 21 Second Tier	3	62
5. Trading Method	Single broker as agent	Call over with limited auction	Open outcry	Open outcry	NSE computerisation	Call over	Single broker as agent	Call over
6. Is selling short allowed?	With conditions	No	No	No	No	No	No	With restrictions
7. Dividend Tax (per cent)	15	10	10	None	10 withholding	5	15	20
8. Capital Gains Tax	None	None	None	None	None	20% upon sale	None	Up to 30%
9. Foreign Ownership of Coys. allowed?	Should be less than 49%	10% individual, 74% aggregate	By application	By application	With permission	By application	By application	5% individual 25% aggregate
10. Charges	2% to 1%	1.75% to 1%	2%	1% flat	1% to 0.2%	3% + 1% SEC fee	2% to 1%	2% to 1%
11. Local Market Capitalisation ($m)	264	106	554	520	—	1200	97	600
12. Average daily Turnover ($)	35k	19k	47k	25k	25k	80k	0.8k	50k
13. Index in (1994) 100 was when?	256 6/89	59 11/90	130 12/89	159 6/89	— —	133 12/89	104 7/90	107 12/89

Notes: Based on Morgan Stanley 'Emerging Markets Investment Research' and contemporary stock market reports.

US$97 million in Swaziland to US$554 million on the Nairobi exchange and US$600 million in Zimbabwe. Average daily turnover varies from only US$800 in Swaziland to US$47 000 in Kenya and US$50 000 in Zimbabwe.

The number of listed securities varies from only three in Swaziland and five in Namibia to 55 in Kenya and 62 in Zimbabwe. The number of dealing members varies from one in Botswana and three in Ghana to six in Kenya, ten in Mauritius and 12 in Zimbabwe. There are apparently 140 licensed stockbrokers in Nigeria, but since the average daily turnover is only US$80 000 it is clear that many of them must be inactive or earning their living mainly from other activities – even though the average commission at 3 per cent is some five times as high as it would be on a mature exchange like that in Johannesburg.

The small size of the exchanges and the very limited number of players involved implies that markets are often very narrow and are easily led by one dominant player, prices tend to be volatile both for individual stocks and for market indices, stock is often in short supply and yet liquidity is low and an owner may only be able to sell stock at a substantial discount to the price of the last recorded deal. An extreme example of volatility is accorded by the conduct of the Zimbabwean exchange which went from being the best performing Emerging Market (1990) to being the worst (1992) and then back to being one of the best again (1993), all within a period of four years.[6]

Part of the explanation for this volatility stems from the domination of the market by one player, the Old Mutual, which is responsible for more than 50 per cent of the value of all transactions. When the Old Mutual stops buying, everybody else stops buying also and the market plummets because there is always a certain amount of stock coming forward for sale from deceased estates, etc. Another reason for a precipitate decline was the government decision in 1992 to hoist its Treasury bill rate to over 30 per cent (well above the inflation rate) to meet one of the conditionalities of its Structure Adjustment Programme. The combination of a deflationary monetary policy with an assured positive return from government paper caused a stampede from equities to government securities. Similarly it was government action again, this time in loosening the conditions for inward foreign investment and raising the proportion of company earnings that could be repatriated as dividends, that led to the market's recovery in 1993. Such volatility deters savers unless they are in a position to spread their risk across a number of different stock exchanges. Portfolio investors acting upon behalf of OECD country funds are in a position to do that, but that in itself causes some nervousness to LDC governments. In relation to the capitalisation of domestic markets, a simultaneous move by two or three external portfolio investors, triggered perhaps by some news agency report of a political incident, could actually accentuate market volatility and in the process do substantial damage to the host country's real economy.[7] Meanwhile domestic savers are frequently prevented from spreading risk across several stock exchanges by Exchange Control rules.

There is some limited evidence that the existence of stock exchanges in SSA has made significant amounts of money available for new investments. Flotations have been mainly of established firms, or rights issues to fund expansions or to procure more local ownership. In macroeconomic terms, the amounts are small; but then Mayer (1988) found that new equity issues provided less than 5 per cent of the net financing of private investment in OECD countries. The preferred order has long been retained profits, and, if external finance is required, loans have generally been favoured ahead of new equity subscriptions. However, more recent research suggests that firms in developing countries use external finance to a far greater extent than those in the USA and the UK, and in half of the developing countries sampled firms used more equity than debt. For example, in Zimbabwe between 1980 and 1988 43 per cent of the new financing raised was through equity subscriptions (Singh and Hamid, 1991). Moreover, as already noted, a stock exchange can provide an investment incentive even for those investors who do not use it initially, as a potential exit mechanism.

A look at the market indices of SSA Stock Markets (line 13 of Table 9.1) indicates that investors who had invested across the board three or four years ago would have done just about all right but would not have realised in US dollar terms a major capital appreciation (unlike many who had invested in East Asia and Latin America). The only market to have shown a gain greater than 60 per cent was that of Botswana, and the example may be a little misleading. Most of this gain was achieved in the first two years of its existence when for the first time local financial institutions were able to buy equity in a number of locally active companies and, in taking advantage of this opportunity to diversify their portfolios, drove up prices rapidly. Once that had occurred by the end of 1992, the market steadied and even contracted a bit in terms of the US$ value of its capitalisation (Stockbrokers Botswana, 1994).

IV IMPACT ON INVESTMENT AND SAVINGS

It would be difficult to show that the existence of SSA SEs has had a major impact on the mobilisation of funds for productive private sector investment. Even in Botswana, where deliberate measures were taken to encourage listing and to render equity financing no less tax favourable than loan financing, there is still reported to be a preference for loan financing.[8] Many of the stock exchange purchases that have occurred have served either to raise or sustain equity prices rather than to fund new investment, or have constituted a partial change of ownership between foreign parent companies (who nevertheless usually maintained their controlling interest) and domestic institutional investors. In Nairobi, stock brokers earn a major part of their commissions by managing clients' external investments and by trading in foreign exchange certificates rather than by mobilising funds for domestic private sector companies, at least until such trading ceased in August 1993.

It would be useful to know whether the existence of stock exchanges facilitated and favoured new investment in particular sectors of SSA economics. Indeed, this could be an interesting topic for future research. An impressionistic review of the names of quoted companies suggests a working hypothesis that the most favoured sectors for equity investments were, in order, (1) financial institutions; (2) property companies; (3) trading companies (including wholesaling and department stores; followed by (4) mining; (5) transport and communications (especially telecommunications); (6) hotels, tourism and leisure activities; with (7) agricultural investments (including agro-processing); and (8) manufacturing coming last.

Does the existence of stock exchanges lower the supply price of equity capital or improve the equity loan gearing and thus the financial robustness of companies? Do they have a significant impact on the location of the control of companies? Theory suggests that all three of these processes should be facilitated by the existence of stock exchanges. The author's visits to five SSA stock exchanges suggests that they can facilitate the indigenisation of control especially where, as in Nigeria, legislative action is taken to promote this objective. There must have been some impact upon the supply price of capital, especially since most initial flotation's have been under-priced, but unambiguous evidence of the effect of this upon gearing ratios is not easy to adduce. When a company's equity:loan gearing improves, for example, it may not always be easy to say whether this is because equity funds have become comparatively cheaper or whether it is because the company concerned requires a financial restructuring to avoid insolvency.

Do people in Africa save more than they otherwise would in order to build up a personal portfolio of equity shares? Almost certainly not. Despite that invitation outside the Ghana Stock Exchange Office, the appeal of becoming a personal equity investor is not yet wide or strong enough to have a significant impact on personal savings rates. However, if the Botswana experience is representative, what the existence of a share market may influence is the distribution of both personal and institutional assets which people buy with their savings. For institutions the switch, at the margin, has been out of government stock and office buildings; for individuals the switch has been out of bank savings accounts, domestic housing and cattle. Whether or not *ex post facto* this improved the yield to savers will have depended upon the timing of the switch. In Botswana it probably has done so since interest rates on savings accounts have, until recently, been negative in real terms and, although the share market has been static, the prices of both office and domestic buildings have been falling.

Business Conduct

A further reason cited for the establishment of stock exchanges is the higher standard of reporting that is required of listing companies, which in turn should give rise to more open and responsive management. Even if average management performance is not thereby improved, so the argument goes, the information revealed should allow for an improved pricing of risk and, overall, to a better distribution of investible funds between competing users. This is another hypothesis which appears logical but which it is difficult to test in the short-term. Exacting reporting requirements for companies wanting to list can, moreover, cut both ways. A number of firms in Ghana interested in seeking a Stock Exchange listing were deterred from doing so by the expense involved which involved extensive reporting requirements and, for one firm seeking to raise money, the preparation of a prospectus and fees for professional advice that would have consumed up to 10 per cent of the funds which the company was seeking to raise.

The point is valid in principle. But whether more extensive reporting does in practice lead to more open, efficient and ethical management may still depend upon whether a competent group of financial analysts and financial journalists develops around the new exchange. One of the institutions most effective in procuring the more accurate pricing of risk, namely the independent credit rating agency, is usually one of the later arrivals on the scene.

Privatisations, Indigenisation and Institutional Development

The existence of a local stock market should assist the process of privatisation. This has occurred to some extent in Ghana, Kenya and Botswana mainly in connection with financial institutions previously controlled by government; but the pace of privatisations in many SSA countries which have formally embraced this policy (Ghana, Uganda, Tanzania, Zimbabwe and Mozambique are examples) has been slower than expected. The difficulty of parastatals meeting the reporting requirements for listing has been one reason. A certain ambivalence within government and amongst public officials has been another. But the limited capacity of indigenous investors to absorb large quantities of new stock brought to the market has also been a significant factor. If substantial new issues are to be taken up by local investors and not merely sold to foreign interests then the capacity of local investors such as pension funds, insurance companies and unit trusts must be developed in parallel.

This gives rise to a more general issue, namely the extent to which the government should seek to influence the performance of the market. Some degree of government support and forbearance is essential. Pension funds etc. must be allowed to hold local equities as well as government paper; more generally, governments must not raise interest rates excessively in order to corner for itself private sector funds.

Government conduct is unavoidably so influential on the performance of new, small stock markets in SSA countries that it is perhaps better to have an informed policy towards desirable market behaviour rather than to influence performance by actions taken in ignorance. If that is accepted, a defensible government policy would be to enable the market to rise so that the anticipated average yield to investors would be just a little above the yield on government stock, but at the same time to avoid favouring one company's stock over any other's.

This discussion has drawn attention to a number of the pre-conditions that need to be met if the founding of stock exchanges in Sub-Saharan Africa is to lead to the benefits that have been widely predicted. It should also have made clear that in a number of countries where new stock exchanges are being established these pre-conditions do not yet exist.

V   ALTERNATIVE SOURCES OF EQUITY FINANCE

Another attempt to remedy the shortage of equity funding for small and medium-size enterprises (SMEs) in Africa has been through the introduction of Venture Capital Companies (VCCs) or Venture Capital Funds (VCFs). These were popularised in the USA in the late 1970s and proliferated in Britain during the 1980s (Sagari and Guidotti *et al.*, 1991). By 1991, 122 Venture Capital Companies existed in the UK with investments worth £1.4 billion in 1559 companies, which would indicate an average investment in each company of somewhat less than £1 million. The prime purpose of these VCCs was to provide equity capital to companies not listed on a stock exchange, on behalf of independent investors. The aim was to pick a sufficient proportion of potential winners, to help them with corporate strategy and management advice, and then to sell out in the short to medium-term for a substantial capital gain.

Looking back on the British experience, it is possible to identify a number of general conditions that were conducive to the success of the VCC movement. First, the private sector was expanding, partly as a result of general economic growth but assisted by deliberate Thatcherite policies. Second, there was an increasing demand for risk capital from smaller businesses wishing to expand and from entrepreneurs eager to innovate. Third, there was a strong secondary market for equities which provided the possibility of exit for the VCCs. Fourth, the government itself deliberately stimulated the venture capital movement (i) by reducing Corporation Tax for companies with a turnover of less than £0.5 million a year, (ii) by providing a powerful personal tax incentive via the Business Enterprise Scheme, and (iii) by amending the Companies Act to enable companies to repurchase their own shares – another possible form of exit for the VCCs.

It is worth describing a representative UK VCF since these in a scaled-down form were to become the model of what was to be attempted in anglophone Africa (Levitski, 1994). We shall distinguish nine characteristics:

1)   The investments would comprise a 'Closed-End' Fund with a fixed life of seven to ten years, after which the proceeds would be distributed to the VCF's own investors.

2) The equity investments in the funds would themselves be managed by a separate fund management company, which might in fact manage more than one VCF, for 2.5 per cent a year of the value of the fund plus 20 per cent of fund profits.

3) A typical fund would be about £35 million in size, spread between 25 to 50 investments with an individual value of between £0.5 million and £1.5 million.

4) A fund of this size would characteristically require about six executives, which indicates both the time that needs to be expended in selecting investments and the intensity of surveillance and support required once they have been made. For this reason, very few investments of less than £200 000 were taken on.

5) VCFs invested primarily in equities, and typically looked to acquire between 20 and 49 per cent of a company's equity.

6) In the UK, VCFs invested mainly in Buy-Outs (45 per cent by value) and expansions (40 per cent of value) and specialised in the consumer products and services sectors.

7) VCF profits were made mainly through divestment for capital gain rather than through dividends received. On average a VC investment would be realised after three and a half years.

8) In order to compensate for the inevitable failures, a target rate of return for each individual investment would be 40 per cent a year.

9) The VCF would seek to exit (i) through a trade sale to another company, (ii) through a share buy-in, when the equity would be sold back to the company, or (iii) through a public sale.

The concept of venture capital funding has spread to developing countries. The Commonwealth Development Corporation (CDC) has been involved, with mixed success, in VCCs in India, Thailand, Indonesia and Papua New Guinea. This paper however will concentrate upon Africa, and in particular on the lessons to be drawn from CDC experience in Ghana, Uganda and Tanzania. Some of the early lessons from VCC experience in Africa can be summarised thus:

1) A large proportion (over 90 per cent) of the initial applications are likely to be rejected or withdrawn.

2) Many applications will be too small (e.g. less than $100 000). The costs of investigation, selection and surveillance of such companies exceed the likely gain upon disposal.

3) The quality of financial and other relevant data that applicants are able to furnish is extremely poor.

4) Applicants are unfamiliar with the commercial requirements of venture capital funding.

5) Applicants are surprised at the intensity of investigation required.

6) Applicants resent the VCF's insistence on its full share of profit in those enterprises which are successful.

7) Most businessmen in Africa are reluctant to part with part of their equity. There are a number of reasons for this amongst which is the necessity of having to keep accounts which can be scrutinised and which display that the interests of management are treated separately from the interests of ownership.

8) It is almost inconceivable that the cash flow from its investments in the early years meet costs, especially as these include the employment of expatriates. Cost are likely to consume a substantial proportion of initial capital before any returns are realised. One solution to this dilemma has been provided by external aid agencies, particularly USAID, which has covered the early costs of the (separate) fund management company, thus protecting the capital of the fund itself.

To illustrate these lessons, the experience of the Ghana Venture Capital Fund may be cited. The decision to establish the fund was taken by the CDC Board in April 1991; it was over a year before the fund was able to make its first investment. The initial size of the Fund was to be US$2 million, which was expected to grow to US$5 million after two years. Investments were to be realised and, by implication, the company was to be liquidated after ten years. Sixty per cent of the investable funds were to be subscribed in Ghanaian cedis by local sources. The fund would be managed by a separate company whose manager was mostly financed by USAID. It was assumed that the initial US$2 million would go into five projects, i.e. into investments of an average size of US$400 000.

Of the initial 156 applications, as of July 1994, 51 were withdrawn, 95 were declined, five were approved, and five were still subject to appraisal or to due diligence procedures.

The average size of approvals has been US$225 000. It is much too early to say that the concept of venture capital funds will not work in Africa. It is not too early to say that first attempts to establish them have run into greater difficulties than were anticipated – although perhaps these difficulties would have been foreseen if anthropologists as well as financiers had been involved in the initial appraisals.

In consequence, there is at the time of writing (September 1994) a new caution evident in the launching of venture capital funds and an opinion spreading that in difficult economic environments, for example Mozambique, the prior establishment of a Leasing Company might be more appropriate.

VI LEASING COMPANIES

A recent study conducted by the author into the provision of finance for the private sector in Mozambique reached the conclusion that, in present conditions, a Leasing Company rather than a Venture Capital Company would be more appropriate. Strictly speaking, a Leasing Company does not provide equity finance; what it can do is to diminish the amount of equity financing which the proprietors of the enterprise might otherwise have to raise. The following paragraphs seek to explain how Leasing Companies work, what problems they confront, and that they may be a suitable financing vehicle for certain difficult African conditions.

A Leasing Company provides equipment to a business enterprise in exchange for an agreed sequence of monthly or quarterly rentals.[9] The Lessee is often entitled to select the source of the equipment providing the supplier is reputable, that the price is reasonable and can be checked, and the equipment can be insured. There is normally a 1 per cent documentation fee and 10 per cent of the facility payable by the lessee as a deposit; thereafter monthly or quarterly rentals over the primary lease period (usually from two to five years) can be tailored to suit cash flow.

By the end of the primary lease period, the lessor will have reckoned to have recovered the initial cost of this equipment plus interest. At that point, depending upon the contract, the lessee can continue to lease the equipment at a reduced cost; or the equipment can be returned to the lessor for sale, in return for which the lessee will get a rebate the size of which will depend upon the residual value of the equipment; or the lessee can acquire ownership of the equipment for an additional charge.

Leasing is not a cheap form of credit, as Leasing Companies will look for a margin of at least 8 per cent over their own cost of funds. For that reason, large well-established companies will often avoid leasing unless there are favourable tax breaks involved, but leasing often suits less well-established companies, especially those operating in countries with a poor credit culture.

Leasing Companies tend to be less demanding of the borrower in terms of the collateral demanded or the requirements for counterbalancing deposits. The right to repossess the asset of which it retains ownership is regarded as the main security. However this ease of access should not be exaggerated. The Ghana Leasing Company requires lessors to be registered companies with at least two years of audited accounts showing a history of profitable trading, the career profiles of all the company's senior management personnel, and a credible business plan with financial projections carried forward for at least the period of the proposed lease.

Provided those requirements can be met, leasing normally offers a quicker and more flexible form of financing than injections of venture capital or medium-term bank loans, especially for second-time or more frequent users. The Zimbabwe Leasing Company states that 85 per cent of its business is done with existing or previous customers, and that with such customers a leasing agreement can be negotiated within a day.

Initial conditions for a Leasing Company are similar to those for a venture capital company: an appropriate legal, regulatory tax and accounting framework.

Since these do not normally exist in advance of the establishment of the first Leasing Company, new legislation will be required. Of particular concern to a Leasing Company are issues regarding security of ownership and the right to repossess without the delays, the uncertainties and the costs that would accompany extended court action. In a country like Mozambique, where the courts have little experience of ordering repossessions, this could be a particular difficulty. As with Venture Capital Companies in new environments, it is often argued that some form of technical assistance from international agencies is appropriate, to compensate for heavy managerial and training costs in the early years of the company's life.

Finally there are questions of potential shareholders and sources of funding for the leasing company. The potential shareholders in different African conditions as identified by EDESA,[10] are likely to include EDFUND, the IFC, CDC and a selection of local banks or Development Finance Corporations. Of particular importance is the source of local currency so that 75 to 80 per cent of leases can be denominated in local currency to avoid having to pass on the exchange risk to the lessee. Sources of local financing may include (a) letters of credit from domestic financial institutions, (b) counterpart funds, (c) local banks. Most satisfactory of all from the leasing company's viewpoint might be permission to accept local deposits from the public, but it is recognised that it is unrealistic to expect such permission to be granted until the Leasing Company itself has established a sound trading record over a number of years.

IFC reviews of their experience with 23 venture capital and leasing companies in developing economies has shown that leasing companies tend to have better performing portfolios than institutions involved in term lending or equity investments. Perhaps because the leasing companies can readily repossess their assets, lessees tend to give priority to paying lease rentals over other debt service payments. If a lessee is approaching insolvency, lease obligations are not generally subject to a moratorium in the same way as other debt service obligations; and if the leasing company does have to repossess it can retain all the proceeds from any sale of the asset, however many lease payments have already been made.

Notes

1. Evidence in this chapter is taken mainly from the performance of stock exchanges or stock markets in Ghana, Kenya, Nigeria, Zimbabwe, Mauritius and Botswana. All of these are classified by the IFC as 'Emerging Markets' although several of them have operated for over forty years. Stock Markets are also being planned or are in the act of being established for Uganda, Tanzania, Malawi, Zambia and Swaziland.

2. See the *World Development Report*, 1989 for a compelling exposition of the failings of many LDC development finance corporations. For the mainly non-

financial reasons for DFCs choosing between equity and loan investments, see McKendry (1992).

3. The description is from Harvey (1993).
4. See Martin (1972) for an account of this process at work in Zambia.
5. An examination of the accounts of the Ghana Stock Exchange for 1991 suggested that turnover would have to increase about six-fold for the stock exchange company to be fully self-supporting.
6. See IFC, *Emerging Stock Markets Fact Book*, 1990–3.
7. Singh (1992) develops this argument.
8. Stockbrokers Botswana, interview, October 1994.
9. The brochure of the Ghana Leasing Company lists the following assets as being amongst those that can be leased: Motor Vehicles, Agricultural/Forestry Equipment, Quarrying, Mining and Construction Equipment, Manufacturing Equipment, Hospital Equipment and Office Equipment.
10. Economic Development Fund for Equatorial and Southern Africa, a Swiss-based private company with wide experience of leasing operations. In December 1993 EDESA combined with Germany's DEG, France's PROPARCO and Sweden's SWEDFUND to set up EDFUND SA, an ECU 6.1 million fund to facilitate private sector investment in SSA.

References

Harvey, C. (1993) 'The Role of Government in the Finance of Business in Botswana', *IDS Discussion Paper*, 337, December.

International Finance Corporation (1990–1994) *IFC Emerging Stock Markets Fact Book*.

Jefferis, K. (1993) 'The Botswana Share Market and its Role in Financial and Economic Development', University of Botswana, Department of Economics Seminar Paper.

Levitski, A. (1994) 'Venture Capital and Leasing', ODA Commissioned Study.

McKendry, I. (1992) 'The Use of Equity Finance by Development Finance Institutions in Malawi', DPhil Thesis, University of Sussex.

Martin, A. (1972) *Minding their Own Business: Zambia's Struggle Against Western Control*, (London: Hutchinson).

Mayer, C. (1988) 'New Issues in Corporate Finance', *European Economic Review*, June.

Sagari, S.B. and G. Guidotti (1991) 'Venture Capital: Lessons from the Developed World for the Developing Markets', *IFC Discussion Paper*, 13.

Singh, A. (1992) 'The Stock-Market and Economic Development: Should Developing Countries Encourage Stock-Markets?', *UNCTAD Discussion Paper*, 49.

Singh, A. and Hamid, J. (1991) 'Corporate Financial Structures in Developing Countries', *IFC Technical Paper*, No. 1.

Stockbrokers Botswana (1994) 'Stockbrokers and the Botswana Share Market'.

10 Economic Crisis, Adjustment and the Effectiveness of the Public Sector in Zambia

Dennis Chiwele and Christopher Colclough

I INTRODUCTION

The delivery capacity of the public sector in Zambia has been severely affected by the economic crisis that started in 1975. It is difficult to quantify the extent to which this happened; but it is generally recognised within and outside the government that the standards of the public sector have been in decline ever since the fall in copper prices. Senior officials in government admit that the amount of time taken to undertake routine jobs, such as passing memoranda between government ministries, has increased by many days. Newspaper reports further reveal a growing public dissatisfaction in the way the government provides its services. More and more complaints are being made about growing civil service corruption, absenteeism, and a general decline in the quality of the services provided.

This chapter argues that the effectiveness of the public sector declined partly as a result of the erosion of skills that had been built up with some considerable success over the first ten years of independence: the growing economic crisis made it difficult to train and attract qualified workers to the public sector. But the problem was further compounded by three factors: first, the manner in which the government sought to reduce its manning levels; second, the ways in which expenditure cuts were made, and most particularly the practice of cutting recurrent departmental charges most; third, the huge fall in earnings during the 1980s which forced workers and their families to adopt survival strategies, which were often incompatible with the maintenance of acceptable levels of efficiency and productivity in their jobs.

These developments, as elsewhere in sub-Saharan Africa, were a direct product of Zambia's economic crisis. However, by undermining the delivery capacity of the public sector, they further contributed to the creation of an environment in which it was difficult for economic adjustment itself to be implemented coherently. Measures to reduce the size of the civil service, government expenditure and

192

the public sector wage bill will continue to be an important part of the adjustment effort in sub-Saharan Africa. This chapter evaluates how such measures could deleteriously affect the effectiveness of the public sector, if their adverse consequences were not to be explicitly recognised and integrated in the design of economic adjustment.

The chapter is organised as follows. Part II documents some of the skill problems facing the public sector in Zambia and how they were affected both by the economic crisis beginning in 1975 and by the adjustment programmes undertaken in response to it. Part III analyses the main changes that have occurred in levels of wages, salaries and allowances. It serves as a background to Part IV which discusses the response of public sector workers to declines in earnings. These included a sharp rise in moonlighting and absenteeism as workers turned to the informal sector for survival. Corruption in the public sector also rose significantly as a mechanism for survival.

II SKILL SHORTAGES IN THE PUBLIC SECTOR

Shortages of skilled and educated workers have always presented a major problem for Zambia's development. During the colonial period the education of Africans was severely neglected. In spite of the comparative wealth of Northern Rhodesia, far more money was spent upon the education of European children than upon all forms of education for the remaining 97 per cent of the population. In addition, racial discrimination in both the public service and the private sector was often explicit. For example, until 1959, legislation prevented Africans from being taken on as apprentices. Thus, the training and experience necessary for advancement was often not available to the African population.

In consequence, Zambia started out with a major deficit of professional and industrial skills, which was to prove very difficult to remove. The vast majority of the 236 000 Africans employed at independence had little or no formal schooling, and less than 1 per cent of them had five years of secondary schooling or more. Over the following two decades, however, the educational expansion initiated by the new government altered this educational profile sharply. By 1983 over 20 per cent of Zambian employees had at least 'O' level (secondary, Form 5) qualifications, and about half had some secondary schooling (see Table 10.1). These were major achievements for a country which, twenty years earlier, had inherited a school system which was thoroughly inadequate in both quantitative and qualitative terms.

However, this progress fell far short of meeting the needs of the country for the full range of technical and professional skills, and a substantial number of non-citizen skilled workers had to be employed throughout the period. This was despite the implementation of rapid localisation, which was assigned high political priority soon after independence. Effective progress with localisation, however, was less

Public Sector Effectiveness in Zambia

Table 10.1 Educational qualifications held by Zambian employees, 1965 and 1983[a]

Qualification[b]	1965		1983	
	Number	%	Number	%
Less than Form II	226,681	96.0	189,514	54.4
Forms II/III	7,282	3.1	85,123	24.4
'O' Level	1,516	0.6	45,308	13.0
'A' Level/Diploma	517	0.2	17,566	5.0
Degree	150	0.1	10,759	3.1
Total	236,146	100.0	348,270	100.0

Notes:
(a) Data for 1965 refer to Africans, rather than Zambians. Those for 1983 are based upon a simple survey of employees along the line of rail, covering almost 70 per cent of total formal employment. The percentage distribution revealed by that survey has been applied to separate estimates for total Zambian employment, published by CSO.

(b) Form II is two years of secondary schooling.
'O' and 'A' Level are examinations typically taken after five years and seven years of secondary schooling, respectively.

Source: GRZ 1966, Table II.3, GRZ 1983, Table 8.0, and GRZ 1985, Table 6.

satisfactory than the aggregate figures tend to show. First, although large numbers of non-citizens left Zambia after 1975, not all of those workers were replaced by adequately qualified and experienced Zambians. Many of their jobs remained vacant. This was particularly so for those expatriates who vacated their jobs in professional and technical jobs after 1985 and who left the country primarily because they faced declining real incomes in the face of the Kwacha devaluations which occurred. By 1987, the situation in the health sector was particularly serious, with large numbers of foreign doctors having left Zambia, without replacement by either Zambian or expatriate personnel. Second, the aggregate quantitative picture of Zambianisation hid qualitative problems in the labour market which affected most sectors of the economy, particularly the public sector: localisation had not always and everywhere been efficiently handled. It is evident that key posts were sometimes filled by Zambians who had insufficient training or experience. This problem became particularly acute as regards deficiencies in management skills - often at quite senior levels of the public service.

Finally, those non-citizens who remained in employment were often concentrated in particular specialised or technical areas, requiring long periods of high-level training. Thus the process of localising the remaining jobs held by expatriates appeared more problematic than had typically been the case in the past. Equally, the premature departure of such workers would generate problems that would be commensurably more difficult to solve. Examination of the occupational composition of expatriate employment provides evidence for the incidence of relative shortages of Zambian skills. Although non-citizens were, by 1983, a comparatively small proportion of total employment – less than 5 per cent – they were nevertheless proportionately much more important in professional and technical occupations, where they comprised 12 per cent of employment, and in administrative/managerial jobs where they accounted for more than one-fifth of total reported employment (see Table 10.2). Some occupations in the professional group were still heavily dependent upon expatriate skills. The case of engineers is particularly startling, where more than 1000 expatriates were employed, comprising almost half of all such workers. Zambia also remained heavily dependent upon expatriate doctors who comprised more than three-quarters of all doctors in the country. Other occupations where at least one-quarter of all jobs were occupied by non-citizens included physical scientists, statisticians, accountants, university teachers, and managers. These data suggest, therefore, that, even by 1983 a significant training task remained in order to localise all of these professional posts.[1]

Thus, the reductions in the number and proportions of non-citizens employed by the government which occurred over 1975–85 were not so strongly indicative of an increased availability of Zambian skills as they might first appear.

Table 10.2   Sample of employees by major occupational group and nationality, 1983

Occupational group	Zambian (1)	Non-Zambian (2)	Total (3)	(2) as % of (3)
Professional, Technical and Related	37,676	5,285	42,961	12.3
Admin. & Managerial	2,563	744	3,307	22.5
Clerical	39,925	816	40,741	2.0
Sales	4,583	321	4,904	6.5
Service	35,580	752	36,332	2.1
Agric., Forestry, etc.	16,021	527	16,548	3.2
Production, Transport & Related	114,886	4,188	119,074	3.5
Not stated	900	35	935	3.7
Total	252,134	12,668	264,802	4.8
Estimated % of Total Employment	72	82	73	

Source: GRZ 1983; GRZ 1985.

Considerable numbers of expatriates left the country owing to the declining purchasing power of the Kwacha. Those who left the public sector were often not replaced – sometimes because of an inability to attract new staff, and sometimes because of a wish to focus the impact of expenditure cuts on non-citizen, rather than Zambian staff. One result was a significant increase in the number of vacancies amongst professional and technical grades in all sectors of the economy.

Even those skilled workers who remained found it difficult to carry out their functions effectively. Given the fall in mineral rents, and as part of the stand-by agreements signed with the IMF, the Zambian government was forced to cut its spending substantially. Expenditures on supporting services (such as transport and materials) were reduced to levels incompatible with efficiency. Thus Gulhati (1989: 15–16) points out that within recurrent expenditure, recurrent departmental charges (RDCs) were cut more drastically and concluded that 'the large scale curtailment of RDCs meant the undermining of government delivery systems for agricultural extension, education, and health as well as physical impairment of government capital assets'.

The skill capacity of the public sector was further adversely affected by the way in which the government tried to reduce its size. In 1984 the government, as part of the conditionality imposed by the IMF and the World Bank, agreed to introduce a freeze on recruitment to the administrative cadre of the public service. A sharp increase in the vacancy rate occurred. By 1985 approximately 10 000 of the 77 000 established posts in the civil service were vacant. This approach to reducing staffing levels in the civil service tended, however, further to undermine its effectiveness, rather than to improve its efficiency: retirement, or contract expiry, does not necessarily occur in a way which reflects staffing priorities. An unstructured approach to reducing public sector staffing via 'natural wastage' seemed therefore to compound the problems of production and service delivery.

An example can be given from the Ministry of Health, which, in 1985 undertook a review of medical manpower. High and unevenly distributed vacancy rates for nurses and technicians were causing major difficulties for the provision of health care, particularly away from the urban centres. The situation amongst doctors, however, was particularly critical. Although there had been a net reduction of 86 expatriate doctors over the previous four years, they were 'replaced' by an increase of only 41 Zambian doctors. Accordingly, the vacancy rate rose from 20 to 30 per cent over the period. Again, the intensity of the shortages varied widely in different parts of the country – with vacancies reaching almost 60 per cent at Ndola hospital on the copper belt. As it happens, these vacancies were caused by foreign doctors leaving the country owing to a deterioration in the value of their local salaries, rather than by the freeze in the number of established posts. But they are illustrative of the potentially misleading import of aggregate data on the extent of localisation 'progress' achieved. The shortage of skills remained an important rigidity in the Zambian economy – increasing the costs of economic restructuring, and reducing both its speed and potency.

Notwithstanding the shortages of particular skills reported above, and in spite of the stabilisation in the size of the establishment which took place over the 1980s, in general the government remained over-staffed. Following further pressure from the World Bank for the government to reduce budgetary commitments, 20 000 non-established workers were laid-off in May 1992. However, this again occurred in a completely unplanned way, and resulted in the paralysis in the work of some departments. By consequence, the decision was quickly revoked. A revised target became the achievement of 10 000 redundancies by the end of 1992 with a similar number to be achieved during 1993. Retrenchment amongst non-established workers was viewed to be easier to achieve than amongst those in established posts, partly because in these cases the government was not obliged to finance redundancy pay. As attention moved upwards in the hierarchy more resistance was met.

III   WAGES AND SALARIES IN THE PUBLIC SECTOR

In the early 1990s, one of the greatest personnel problems facing the government remained that of recruiting and retaining professionally qualified people due to the low pay prevailing in the public sector. Furthermore, by forcing those workers who remained to adopt strategies to supplement their incomes – strategies which often made it impossible for them to carry out their work efficiently – declines in earnings made it difficult for the public sector to perform effectively. This part, therefore, documents the movements in earnings in the public sector and provides the context for a subsequent discussion of their impact on the behaviour of public employees.

Changes in Public Sector Earnings

Figure 10.1 shows that the 1960s were characterised by rapid increases in both the nominal and real earnings of African workers: the average real wage for Africans in the public sector rose almost five-fold between 1964 and 1968–9. This partly resulted from the drive towards salary unification for African and non-African employees that occurred in the 1960s. The wage scales for African and non African workers in government (and elsewhere) had been completely different until 1961. Over the following seven years a unified non-racial pay scale emerged, which involved granting very significant increases in pay to African staff. This trend was consolidated by the recommendations of the Whelan Commission which, in 1966, unified pay scales in the public sector with an average pay rise of 22 per cent (Meesook *et al.*, 1986, Table 3.3). By the late 1960s, Zambia had become a high wage economy by LDC standards. However, some awareness of the potentially damaging effects of wage inflation for the country's prospects for economic growth began – for the first time since the early

Figure 10.1   Average government real wage

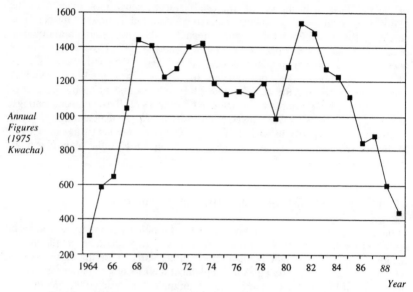

Note: 1975–77 are budgeted figures
Source: Calculated from GRZ (Ministry of Finance), *Financial Report for the Year Ended 31 December (1965 to 1992)*.

1960s – to be voiced. The Turner Report on wages and incomes policy in Zambia (ILO, 1969) argued for a policy of wage restraint, and resulted in a temporary wage freeze followed by a 5 per cent nominal increase in pay awarded in 1971 by the O'Riordon Commission. Figure 10.1 indicates that for most of the 1970s increases in salaries in the public sector were less than the rate of inflation. The real wage recovered in 1980 and 1981 but fell to less than its 1967 level by 1989, and to less than one-third of its 1981 peak.

The decline of government workers' real wages in the 1970s resulted from a combination of the implementation of this wage restraint policy and rising inflation. The wage restraint policies of 1969/70 and those which were subsequently part of the one year stand-by agreements with the IMF in 1976 and 1978, reduced the real wage in the public sector to below the levels which had been reached by 1968. Meanwhile, inflation rose from 4 per cent in 1968 to 9 per cent in 1973 and reached 17 per cent and 18 per cent in 1975 and 1976 respectively. Therefore, the average nominal increase of 20 per cent awarded to government employees in 1975 by the Mwanakatwe Commission had little effect in real terms. The rise in the real wage in 1980 and 1981 emanated from the pay awards by the Muchangwe Commission which ranged from 12 per cent to 60 per cent for high and low paid workers respectively. Inflation had also declined to an average rate of 12 per cent per annum over those two years.

A further important component of government wage policy – officially known as 'narrowing the gaps' – concerned the wish to reduce the large economic disparities between richer and poorer workers. The main operational principle of this policy was to grant greater nominal increases in earnings to the lower paid than to the richer workers – a principle which was to be applied in the public sector until the late 1980s. The consequence was to compress significantly the salary structure in the public sector. Although the real index of the starting salary of an under-secretary or a director fell from 149 in 1967 to 11 in 1990, that of the lowest paid civil servant only fell from 100 to 38 over the same years (see Table 10.3). In 1991 significant real increases in wages and salaries were granted to all employees – allowing (at least temporarily, given the high rates of inflation which were current at that time) a 50 per cent increase in the real incomes of those in

Table 10.3   Index of real wages/salaries in the civil service, 1966/7–1991/2

| Year | Real starting salaries Index (1975 = 100) | | | | | |
	S3	S7	S12	S13	S21	DCE
1966	149	151	127	125	100	–
1971	131	123	105	104	98	95
1975	100	100	100	100	100	100
1979	63	60	61	59	82	77
1980	69	62	66	68	93	89
1982	55	50	48	50	79	80
1983	47	42	41	44	83	88
1984	39	36	38	40	89	95
1986	29	27	29	31	85	92
1989	11	11	10	11	30	32
1989	12	12	12	13	40	44
1990	11	11	11	12	38	41
1991	16	17	22	24	75	83

Notes:

S3	=	Under Secretary, Director;
S7	=	Assistant Director, Deputy Chief;
S12	=	Entry Point for University Graduate;
S13	=	Entry Point for Diploma Graduate;
S21	=	Lowest Paid Civil Servant;
DCE	=	Daily Classified Employee.

First notch of each salary scale used in each case

Two salary revisions were introduced in 1989 – in July and September

Source: Calculated from GRZ (Cabinet Office), Personnel Circulars, 1975–92 and Meesook *et al.*, 1986, Table A.1.4.

senior positions. However, the proportional increases for the lowest paid were still greater – such that the differentials between the pay of these two groups were further reduced, albeit only very slightly.

These trends are shown more directly in Figure 10.2 which presents the ratio of the nominal starting salary of a director to that of the lowest paid civil servant between 1967 and 1992. The years shown are those in which salary changes were effected. The Figure shows that the decline in the ratio was greatest in the salary revisions introduced in the years 1975 and 1979. It can be seen that the trend towards narrowing differentials was arrested in 1990/91, and actually reversed the following year. Thus the policy of 'narrowing the gaps' appeared to be in suspension at that time. Perhaps the limit to which salaries could be narrowed had been reached. It certainly reflected a general belief within official circles that the reduced differentials were imposing a major constraint on recruiting, retaining and motivating skilled workers.

Many of the changes in public sector earnings described above occurred in the context of IMF and World Bank-supported economic adjustment. Pay awards in the public sector featured high on the list of IMF conditions because of their fiscal

Figure 10.2   Ratio of director's to lowest paid civil servant's starting salary

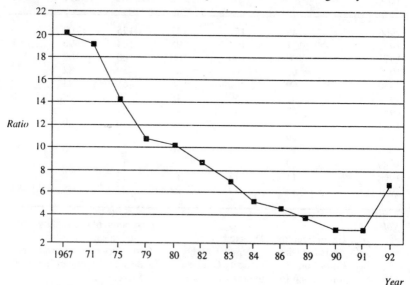

Source: GRZ (Cabinet Office), Personnel Circulars, 1975–92 and Meesook *et al.*, 1986, Table A.1.4.

implications. For example, the 1978 interim wage policy which was part of the one-year stand-by agreement froze public pay, but only placed a ceiling increase of K6.00 per month on the private sector. And in 1983, as part of another one-year stand-by agreement, there was again a total freeze on basic pay increases in the public sector while those outside government received a 10 per cent ceiling. Although it is doubtful that the policy of wage restraint was effective in the economy as a whole, it appeared to have had some fiscal success when applied to government workers.[2] As shown in Figure 10.3, there was, for example, a significant reduction in the share of personal emoluments in total budgetary expenditure, from 21 per cent in 1975 to only 16 per cent in 1992.

Allowances in the Public Sector

The drastic compression of wages presented above was lessened by trends in non-wage earnings. There is clear evidence that allowances became more important in the total earnings of government employees by 1991 than they had been in 1980. The Prices and Incomes Commission estimated that allowances in the public sector rose from 12.8 per cent of the basic salary in 1983 to as high as 99.2 per cent in 1991. The greatest part of these allowances was housing allowance, which in 1991 represented 88 per cent of the total allowances received by public sector workers (PIC, 1992). If we add housing allowance to basic salaries, the real index

Figure 10.3   Share of personal emoluments in total budgeted expenditure

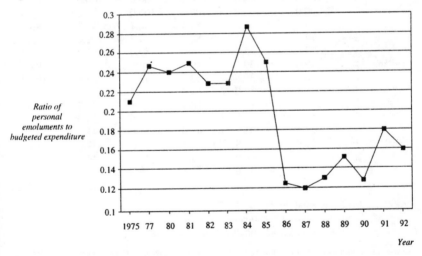

Source: GRZ (Ministry of Finance), *Budget Address*, 1975–92

for the director's earnings in 1991 would be 24.0 instead of 11.8 while that of a telephonist would be 44.7 instead of 37.6 (see Table 10.4).

Because housing allowances (in cash) now accounted for a larger share of total allowances, those without government houses, often in low grades, benefited most. There were major increases in housing allowances in 1990, leading to many cases where junior workers, on very low scales, received more cash earnings than those in government accommodation on supervisory scales, adding to the discontent felt by those in the middle grades. However, the continued access of these latter groups to subsidised government housing helped somewhat to protect their real incomes, although they nevertheless lost out relative to those unhoused in the lower grades. Table 10.4 shows that when the imputed value of housing is added to the basic salary, the index of a director's earnings rises to 30.6 instead of the 11.8 without the imputed value of housing. That of a telephonist rises to 60.8 instead of 37.6 in 1991.

Table 10.4   Index of public sector compensation: basic salary plus housing benefits

Year	Key	Permanent Secretary	Director	Engineer	Clerk	Telephonist	Unskilled Worker
1975	1	100.0	100.0	100.0	100.0	100.0	100.0
	2	100.0	100.0	100.0	100.0	100.0	100.0
	3	100.0	100.0	100.0	100.0	100.0	100.0
1980	1	73.5	68.8	80.4	80.7	96.8	86.3
	2	74.5	70.1	82.1	84.7	101.4	123.1
	3	77.9	75.2	87.5	89.0	101.2	86.3
1985	1	40.0	39.1	49.3	48.6	70.8	97.5
	2	40.5	39.8	52.8	57.7	83.8	141.3
	3	51.2	52.0	64.8	58.9	79.5	97.5
1990	1	12.1	12.5	18.5	18.8	33.5	36.0
	2	12.9	13.3	20.9	23.6	39.9	57.1
	3	29.1	31.1	43.0	33.6	41.2	36.0
1991	1	11.4	11.8	17.5	21.0	37.6	40.4
	2	23.7	24.0	33.7	33.8	44.7	64.0
	3	29.7	30.6	42.3	39.2	60.8	40.4

Key: 1 = Basic salary only;
            2 = Basic salary plus housing allowance;
            3 = Basic salary plus imputed value of a house.

Source: Calculated from GRZ (Cabinet Office), Personnel Circulars 1975–1991).
            Imputed rent for 1975 and 1980 obtained from Meesook *et al.*, 1986, p. 86.

Although the imputed value of a house was the commonest and perhaps biggest form of payment-in-kind to public workers, there were other forms which mostly benefited the people in top grades and helped to reduce the fall of their real earnings. For example, a permanent secretary and director, had access to a person-to-holder car and, prior to this being converted into a cash allowance in 1991, could draw a specified number of litres of government fuel. The government also met a specified amount of telephone, water and electricity bills and paid for house servants. These benefits provided to top civil servants were altered by the changes that took place in 1992 when the government took a decision to tax all allowances. In addition, it decided to lump together all those payments that had been kept separate from the basic salary. The effect was to widen the differential between low/middle level civil servants and those at the top, as presented in Figure 10.3. It was obvious that there had been much hidden payment, in previous years, which seemed partly to compensate for the massive decline in the basic salary of senior public sector workers. The people who lost most from the massive salary declines were those in middle grades, who were not entitled to the generous fringe benefits given to top civil servants nor were effectively protected by the policy of 'narrowing the gaps'.[3]

IV   RESPONSES TO REAL WAGE DECLINE

In response to a decline in earnings, public sector households forged a complex pattern of responses to prevent themselves from falling into destitution. They sought to diversify income sources, particularly by increasingly involving women and children in informal sector activities. Often, however, public sector workers themselves became involved in these activities, thereby leading to a sharp increase in the incidence of moonlighting and absenteeism. There was also a big rise in corruption which moved from a few top officials in the early 1980s to incorporate a larger number of middle and low ranking public sector workers by the end of that decade.

The sharp decline in the real wage shown in previous parts indicates why it was virtually inevitable that workers would resort to such adaptive strategies. But Figure 10.4 indicates even more dramatically the desperate situation facing public sector workers. The Figure plots the ratio of the cost of a basic nutritionally adequate food basket with respect to the average public sector wage plotted in Figure 10.2. The food basket adopted is one that was devised by the Prices and Incomes Commission (PIC), consisting of food items regularly consumed by Zambian households. It was based on the PIC's 1985 Pilot Household Budget Survey and was thought to yield an adequate amount of calories for an average household of six members (two adults and four children). It is important to point out that the estimates of calorific requirement for an average sized household were based on FAO/WHO estimates that became controversial in the early 1970s (Lipton, 1988:

12). But their value lies in guiding the choice of a nutritionally 'adequate' food basket whose cost could then be analysed on a time series basis. Even where the requirement is overestimated (or underestimated), a time series examination would at least yield very important information on the extent to which the ability of public sector households to meet their nutritional needs might have changed.

The adoption of such a food basket covering the period 1975 to 1989 assumes that public sector workers' consumption patterns were not significantly different from those of households in other sectors and that they remained constant throughout the period. The cost of the food basket is based on CSO's annual average urban prices. As the prices were collected from established retail outlets, they would not reflect the actual prices that most households were forced to meet, since they had largely to rely on the black-market owing to shortages, where prices were often much higher. Therefore the costs discussed here would tend to underestimate the actual costs incurred by households. This again underlines the fact that change over time is more important than the point estimates.

The Figure confirms the increasing difficulty of public sector workers in meeting their basic needs. Whereas in 1975 the cost was only 39 per cent of the average earnings in the public sector, it had risen to 159 per cent in 1989. Thus, by the end of the 1980s, public sector households were unable to finance a standard food basket from one wage income and could only survive by adopting the strategies mentioned above.

Figure 10.4   Cost of a food basket to average government earnings (1975–89)

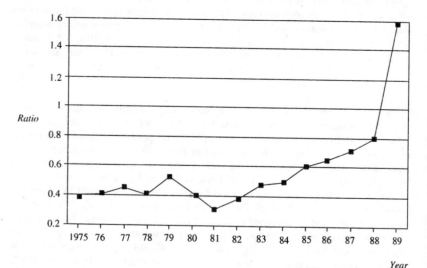

Informal Sector Activities and Moonlighting

Interviews in Lusaka in various government departments indicated that the commonest response to adversity was for other members of the household, particularly women and children, to seek work in the informal sector. This was not confined to the public sector alone but was widespread across the formal sector. It led to the increase in the number of females and children involved in the informal sector. Table 10.5 indicates that, whereas in 1980 46 per cent of the urban informal sector participants were female, the proportion rose to 57 per cent in 1986. At the same time the age profile appeared to decline. Only 0.4 per cent of the participants recorded were aged between 12 and 14 years in 1980. This figure rose to almost 5 per cent in 1986. It is possible that the involvement of children was much higher because children below 12 years of age were reportedly becoming much more active in the informal sector as the economic crisis deepened.

It was sometimes possible for public sector workers to leave informal sector activities to other household members. However, the nature of coping strategies adopted by informal sector enterprises, in response to increased competition and reduced effective demand, required a very active involvement of business

Table 10.5   Sex and age profiles of the informal sector

| Age | Dristribution by age | | | | Share of female | |
| | 1980 | | 1986 | | | |
	Male	Female	Male	Female	1980	1986
12–14	0.03	0.04	4.87	4.53	0.48	0.55
15–19	2.34	3.19	13.99	11.36	0.54	0.52
20–24	9.56	10.33	18.51	18.98	0.48	0.58
25–29	11.73	13.25	14.68	17.73	0.49	0.62
30–34	11.99	16.11	10.34	13.53	0.53	0.63
35–39	10.97	15.20	8.69	12.48	0.54	0.66
40–44	11.23	13.89	7.30	7.35	0.51	0.57
45–49	10.94	9.49	5.39	5.91	0.42	0.59
50–54	9.11	6.37	5.30	3.94	0.37	0.50
55–59	6.47	3.46	4.17	2.10	0.31	0.40
60–64	5.15	2.45	2.35	0.85	0.29	0.33
65+	6.64	2.53	3.56	1.05	0.24	0.28
NS	3.86	3.70	0.87	0.20	0.45	0.23
Total	100.0	100.0	100.0	100.0	0.46	0.57

NS = Not Stated

Source: CSO, 1985, Table 2.3 and 1989, Table 9.1.

owners, particularly in the areas of the acquisition of materials and other inputs. This was the prime cause of the increase in moonlighting. Evidence for moonlighting is always very difficult to establish. But in one study that concentrated on the adaptive strategies within the informal sector (Chiwele, 1993) it was observed that those running businesses operated by relatives or workers in the markets, while retaining their formal jobs, were involved in high levels of moonlighting. One obvious symptom of moonlighting is that absenteeism in Zambia was reported to have risen substantially over the years, with public sector workers reported absent for between one-fifth and one-half of their working time. This level of absenteeism contributed to the sharp decline in public sector standards. Some workers increasingly used the skills, for which they had been employed in the first place, in private business. This, for example, was often so for artisans. Apart from leading to moonlighting, associated problems of pilfering of government materials for use by workers in their private businesses became common. This compounded further the difficulty of the public sector maintaining high standards.

Moonlighting has also been reported to have been widespread in the private and parastatal sectors. Simutanyi (1993) in a study on Zambia Railways employees noted high levels of moonlighting. However, it appeared more problematic in the public sector, partly because earnings of senior public sector workers fell much more sharply than in the other sectors. In such circumstances there was little incentive for supervisors to enforce a strong code of discipline because they were themselves engaged in the battle for survival and in flouting the same rules. This left them little moral authority with which to impose discipline among their subordinates. Equally, supervisors who were themselves absent from their jobs could not, in any practical sense, supervise those under them. This experience was mirrored in other African countries where the real wage sharply declined. Thus, Chew (1990: 1009) reports that, in Uganda, civil service supervisors were 'reluctant to reprimand moonlighting staff who need to make financial ends meet. Their moral authority to insist that regulation hours be respected evaporates when they are themselves guilty of the same fault'. But even where this was not so, the cumbersomeness of the disciplinary procedure made it difficult to dismiss or punish perpetual offenders.

Corruption as a Survival Strategy

In order to adapt to the decline in their earnings, public sector workers resorted increasingly to corruption. The problem was perceived to be serious enough by 1980 to warrant the passing of the Anti-corruption Commission (ACC) Act of 1980. The ACC itself became operational in 1982. Since then, its operations increasingly changed from investigating cases of corruption due to greed to those caused by economic necessity.[4] The former was the most common in the early 1980s and was practised by people who were already relatively rich but utilised their privileged positions to enhance their wealth through corrupt practices. The latter was practised by people who had been impoverished by the declines in their real earnings and was used as a means to survive the crisis. According to the ACC, 'corruption of economic necessity' became particularly prominent in the wake of the 1985 auctioning of the hard currency. It was reported to become more entrenched in those parts of government which directly provided services to the public such as police officers, customs and immigration officials and workers in the government building department. The ACC further noted that the amounts required to bribe somebody seemed to have been getting smaller and smaller as corruption and bribery became more generalised and as the real wage declined.

V CONCLUSION

This chapter has identified factors that affected the delivery capacity of Zambia's public sector in the 1980s and 1990s. Two main factors have been identified: the erosion of skills and the decline in earnings. These have been mainly attributed to the economic crisis that followed the collapse in the price of copper, Zambia's largest foreign exchange earner. But the implementation of economic adjustment appeared to aggravate rather than relieve this problem. This is specifically seen in the ways in which the government tried to reduce the size of the public sector and the centrality given to public sector real wage reductions in economic reforms.

The requirement to reduce public sector earnings was certainly based on sound economic argument. Part of the necessary adjustment to the fall in copper prices was a reduction in consumption, which the Zambian government postponed for many years after 1975, with adverse economic consequences. In this context, some reduction in the real wage was necessary. But the extent to which the real wage in the public sector, as well as in the rest of the economy, subsequently declined appeared to have gone well beyond the level that was necessary to maintain a reasonable level of efficiency. Workers who needed to keep their consumption at tolerable levels adopted actions that undermined labour productivity – at least as regards primary jobs – by consequence of the sharp increase in rent seeking activities, excessive rates of absenteeism and low worker morale. The erosion of skills, moonlighting and corruption created an environment in which it was difficult for economic adjustment itself to be implemented coherently. Thus, these developments had sharply adverse implications for Zambia's long term economic recovery.

It is difficult to see how this situation could be reversed in the short term. One possible solution, long recognised both in official circles and by Zambia's donors, is the need to reduce the size of the public sector so that workers could be more reasonably paid and better motivated. Government officials and donors point out that this would allow the public sector to attract, train and maintain highly qualified personnel. Yet, although this solution has been on the agenda since as early as 1983, there have been economic and political constraints that have prevented its implementation. The government found it easier to cut the size of the government by freezing recruitment and accelerating retirement, even though this aggravated skill shortages and further undermined the effectiveness of the public sector.

The main problem has been that the government was not prepared to reduce radically the services which it provided. Instead it attempted to provide the same services at much lower cost. Given the complete lack of attention given to ways and means of securing efficiency savings, this inevitably resulted in gross inefficiency being promulgated within the public sector. Clearly, it is always difficult to attack vested interests, in the form of institutions which employ a large number of articulate people. Equally, it is always difficult for governments to withdraw services which are not only seen as being part of the apparatus of a modern state, but which also represent commitments pledged at some earlier time. Yet a serious response to Zambia's adjustment challenge would have required a fundamental reassessment of each branch of public expenditure: some services – particularly those in the human development sectors which are vital for future growth – should have continued to expand; but others would have been prime candidates for reduction or withdrawal. A serious approach to civil service reform was thus a precondition for the development of a successful adjustment strategy. Whilst not being a sufficient condition, this chapter has demonstrated its centrality for adjustment policy in Zambia – and in other countries where real resources for publicly provided services have been in sharp and sustained decline.

Notes

1. More recent data on the skill and occupational composition of the non-citizen labour force had not, by 1992/3, been published.
2. See the paper by Chiwele in this volume, which questions whether wage restraint policy reduced the real wage in the economy as a whole.
3. More detailed analyses of trends in the real value of allowances, and of their impact upon real earnings differentials in the Zambian public sector, are provided in Colclough (forthcoming).
4. As reported by Mr Paul Russell, Chairman of the ACC since its operations began, in personal interviews.

References

Central Statistical Office (1965–91) *Monthly Digest of Statistics* (Lusaka: Central Statistical Office).

Central Statistical Office (1985) *1980 Population and Housing Census of Zambia (Analytical Report Volume III): Major Findings and Conclusions* (Lusaka: CSO).

Central Statistical Office (1989) *Labour Force Survey, 1986* (Lusaka: CSO).

Chew, David C.E. (1990) 'Internal Adjustment to Falling Civil Service Salaries: Insights from Uganda', in *World Development,* 18 (7).

Chiwele, D. (1993) 'Crisis, Adjustment and Social Change in Zambia's Urban Informal Sector', UNRISD Research Report, Geneva, December (mimeo).

Colclough, Christopher (forthcoming) 'Economic Stagnation and Earnings Decline in Zambia, 1975–91', in C. Colclough (ed.), *Public Sector Pay and Adjustment: Lessons from Five Countries* (Geneva: ILO).

GRZ (1966) Manpower Report, Cabinet Office, Lusaka.

GRZ (1983) Manpower Survey of Employees (draft) mimeo, Lusaka.

GRZ (1985) Monthly Digest of Statistics, XXI (6–7), June/July, CSO, Lusaka.

Gulhati, Ravi (1989) 'Impasse in Zambia: The Economics and Politics of Reform', *Analytical Case Studies,* 2 (Washington DC: IBRD).

ILO (1969) *Report to Government of Zambia on Incomes and Prices in Zambia: Policy and Machinery* (by H.A. Turner) (Lusaka: Cabinet Office).

Lipton, Michael (1988) 'The Poor and the Poorest: Some Interim Findings', *World Bank Discussion Papers,* 25 (Washington DC: IBRD).

Meesook, O. *et al.* (1986) 'Wage Policy and the Structure of Wages and Employment in Zambia', *CPD Discussion Paper,* 1986–1 (Washington DC: World Bank).

Prices and Incomes Commission (PIC) (1991) *Household Expenditure and Income Survey, 1991: Preliminary Results* (Lusaka: PIC).

Prices and Incomes Commission (PIC) (1992) *Consumption Expenditure in Zambia by Low and High Income Groups – June 1991* (Lusaka: PIC).

Simutanyi, N.R. (1993) 'Crisis, Adjustment and Survival Strategies of Workers in Zambia: the Case Study of Railway Workers, Kabwe', UNRISD Research Report, Geneva, July (mimeo).

11 Economic Adjustment, the Mining Sector and the Real Wage in Zambia

Dennis Chiwele[1]

I INTRODUCTION

Real wage flexibility is considered essential to a successful implementation of conventional IMF and World Bank programmes. And yet the two institutions have been pessimistic concerning the flexibility of real wages in the Third World. They attribute wage rigidity to institutional factors – workers' demands for higher wages and governments' liberality in responding to these demands (e.g. IBRD, 1981: 92–93). Thus, to help sustain the decline in the real wage induced by a devaluation, wage restraint measures tend to feature prominently in IMF and World Bank programmes. But the general decline in developing countries' real wages in the 1980s, even in countries with a long tradition of 'strong' labour unions such as those in Latin America, raised questions as to whether the role of institutional factors in real wage determination had not been overstated.

This paper investigates this issue by focusing on a widely accepted hypothesis in Zambia's real wage determination – that the mining industry is the major determinant of real wages in the whole formal sector, and that unionism is the principal channel through which it produces that effect. The hypothesis influenced the recommendations of the UN/ECA mission of 1964 and the two ILO missions led by Professor H.A. Turner in 1969 and 1979, recommendations that formed an important input in Zambia's search for an incomes policy. Its wide acceptance has for a long time been the foundation for the view that institutional factors, and not underlying economic (market) factors, determined the trend in Zambia's real wage. However, although the hypothesis has been widely accepted, it has never been conclusively proved. Some serious questions have been raised concerning its validity. This paper provides an alternative explanation for real wage determination by studying the role of underlying economic (market) factors. It utilises a model which highlights the role that economic adjustment played in the decline of wages that occurred in the 1980s. The main conclusion drawn from the analysis is that the mining industry did indeed have a major impact on real wage movements in the formal sector. However, the transmission mechanism was in the way mining profitability affected relative prices and rela-

210

tive factor endowments, which in turn affected the real wage. This would suggest that even at the time that real wages were on the increase, workers may not have derived a disproportionately bigger rise in the real wage than that dictated by underlying economic factors.

II THE ECONOMY AND CHANGES IN THE REAL WAGE

Zambia, then Northern Rhodesia, attained British protectorate status in 1911. Its creation resulted from the activities of the British South African Company (BSA) which acquired land and mineral rights in Northern Rhodesia. At first the economic role of Northern Rhodesia amongst the British territories in Southern Africa was to act only as a labour reserve for Southern Rhodesia and South Africa. It became an important mining economy when copper mining was intensified on the Copperbelt in the 1920s. Various policies of the colonial government appeared to discourage the development of agriculture and manufacturing (see Klepper, 1979; Seidman, 1979). Thus the colonial legacy at independence was an economy highly dependent on copper mining, contributing 41 per cent to gross domestic product, 71 per cent to government revenue and 93 per cent to foreign earnings (Gulhati, 1989: 18). During the colonial era, there had been little development in the social sectors (health, education and housing). Although rising copper prices in the 1950s ensured that enough revenue that could have been utilised for this purpose was available, much of it was diverted to Southern Rhodesia with the advent of the Federation of Rhodesia and Nyasaland in 1953. At the same time, mining royalties and dividends were shipped abroad, further reducing the impact of mineral rents on the rest of the economy (Daniel, 1979: 11).

There was therefore a lot of optimism at independence that the economic imbalances inherited from the colonial period would be significantly altered. The dismantling of the Federation of Rhodesia and Nyasaland, the quick take-over of mineral royalties by the new government, and rising copper prices provided high mineral rents to achieve this goal. Tremendous achievements were made in building educational, health, and other social infrastructure at a rate rarely seen in Africa. Unfortunately these achievements were accompanied by a wastage of resources through over-designed projects with high unit costs. Their execution was usually delayed, further escalating the cost of implementing them. At this time, the government started spending a substantial amount on food subsidies which later became a major political constraint on economic reforms. These developments led to a rapid expansion of government expenditure which by 1970 accounted for 41 per cent of GDP (Gulhati, 1989: 14).

The major beneficiaries appeared to have been manufacturing, transport and services whose respective growth rates averaged 7.9 per cent, 6.8 per cent and 10.0 per cent between 1966 and 1974. This altered the structure of production away from mining, whose share in GDP declined from 41 per cent in 1965 to 33 per cent in 1974, to manufacturing and services whose contribution to GDP rose from 7 per cent and 14 per cent in 1965 to 13 per cent and 21 per cent in 1974 respectively. The rising share of services in GDP resulted from the massive investments made in education, health and housing. The share of agriculture in GDP fell from 14 per cent in 1965 to 11 per cent in 1974. Thus rural-urban disparities established in the colonial period remained, a factor which accounted for the urban demographic explosion once colonial restrictions on population movements were lifted.

It was inevitable that a decline in the price of copper would have severe implications for the Zambian economy. This happened after a sharp fall in the price of copper from US $0.93/pound in 1974 to US $0.56/pound in 1975 (see Figure 11.1). The current account moved from a positive balance of US $8.4 million in 1974 to a deficit of US $726.1 million in 1975. The terms of trade index with 1987 as the base year fell from 215.5 in 1974 to 126.3 in 1975. Foreign reserves were rapidly depleted from SDR 164.4 million in 1974 to SDR 92 million in 1976. The contribution of copper to government revenue substantially declined and in 1975 the budget went into a state of chronic deficit. From growth of 6.5 per cent in 1974, GDP fell in 1975 by 2.3 per cent. 1974/75 proved to be the watershed year in Zambia's economic performance, as the variables that deterio-

Figure 11.1   London metal exchange copper prices: 1962 to 1991 (US cents/pound)

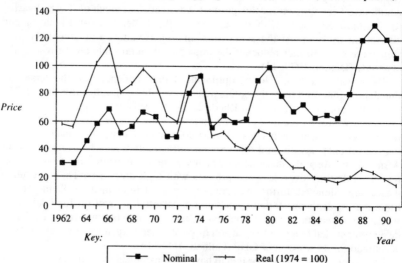

Source: IMF, *International Financial Statistics*, 1992.

rated with the fall in copper prices never fully recovered. The economic crisis continued to deepen such that the government was forced to negotiate a number of stand-by agreements with the IMF, starting in 1976, and intensified after 1982. However, general economic indicators show that Zambia failed to benefit from the economic reforms of the eighties (see Table 11.1) such that the decade of the 1990s opened with the country facing unmanageable external debt servicing difficulties, chronic shortages of foreign exchange, a treble-digit rate of inflation, and deteriorating infrastructure and social services.[2]

The mineral boom of the first ten years of independence was accompanied by a rising real wage (see Figure 11.2); it rose almost continuously until it reached its peak in 1974. Although the immediate post-independence stance of the new government appeared to favour rising real wages, it started viewing with concern these high rises by the end of the 1960s. Some experts had began expressing misgivings even earlier. The Seers Report of 1964 recommended that wages and salaries be restrained so as to 'encourage investment, economic diversification and the competitiveness of Zambia's exports; to discourage rural-urban migration, and thus to sustain agriculture and a manageable rate of urbanisation' (Quoted in Daniel, 1979: 144). The report emphasised that Zambia could either have growth in wages or employment but not both. In 1969, the government invited Professor H.A. Turner to study the case for a wage policy. His letter of invitation outlined four basic areas of concern; that the wage and salary awards of the 1960s were: i) inflationary; ii) unevenly distributed among different groups of workers; iii) fostering rural/urban migration due to the rising income disparities; and iv) restraining growth in employment (ILO (Turner Report), 1969: 1). These concerns were very similar to those expressed by the Seers Mission.

Table 11.1   Economic indicators for Zambia: period averages

	1970–74	*1975–82*	*1983–86*	*1987–90*
GFCF (% of GDP)	34.51	20.83	16.80	12.38
Employment (% Change/Yr)	3.24	–0.58	–0.41	1.12
GDP (% Change/Yr)	5.31	0.12	0.10	1.71
CPI (% Change/Yr)	6.23	12.88	32.34	83.34
GNP Per Capita (1975 Kwacha)	386.79	268.55	207.49	188.48
Total External Debt (US $ million)	772.60	2 676.98	4 488.75	6 847.95

Source: IBRD, *World Tables 1992*; CSO, *Monthly Digest of Statistics,* various issues.

Figure 11.2   Annual average real wage

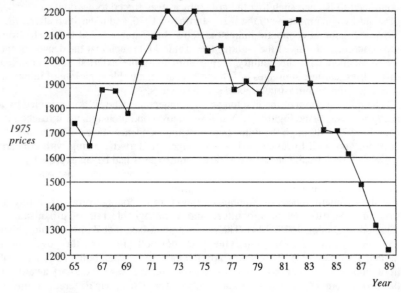

Source: CSO, *Monthly Digest of Statistics,* various issues and *National Accounts Bulletin, Nos 1 to 3.*

Following the recommendations of the Turner Report, the government imposed a 5 per cent ceiling on wage increases in 1970. But this did not deter the real wage from its upward trend as it rose by 12 per cent in 1970 and continued to rise up to 1974. Wage ceilings were again imposed in 1976/77 and 1978/79 when Zambia signed stand-by agreements with the IMF. Unlike the earlier attempt, wage ceilings were now accompanied by an increase in the real wage of only 1 per cent in 1976 and a decline of 9 per cent in 1977 while it remained almost stagnant in 1978 and 1979. When the government signed a one year stand-by agreement in 1983, a total wage freeze on public sector pay was imposed, accompanied by a ceiling of 10 per cent for other workers. This was associated with a decline in the real wage of 12 per cent in that year, the biggest annual decline between 1965 and 1989. Wage policy shifted in 1984 to free collective bargaining. This coincided with the period when the real wage went into a free fall. By 1986, formal sector workers were getting less than they had earned in 1965, and by 1989 their real earnings had declined to two thirds of their 1965 level.

Why did the policy of wage restraint fail in 1970 and only appear to succeed afterwards? It is important to note that on all occasions when the policy was associated with its desired results, it was undertaken in the context of economic reforms. This raises the possibility that the downturn in real wages seen in the 1980s could have resulted from the implementation of economic adjustment policies, particularly if one notes that the government could not have enforced the policy even more effectively with the move to free collective bargaining. There were no established criteria that determined whether the bargaining units were complying with official guidelines on wage restraint. An examination of collective agreement files containing correspondence between the Prices and Incomes Commission (PIC), the Labour Commissioner, employers and unions failed to reveal a single instance when a collective agreement could not be registered on the grounds that it failed to comply with the principle of wage restraint.[3] The nearest this happened was when the PIC questioned the huge increases awarded to government employees in 1989 and 1990 on the grounds that they were likely to be inflationary. But in both cases, political pressure appears to have been brought to bear on the PIC and the collective agreements were eventually registered. There is therefore reason to believe that the government would have found it even more difficult to implement a wage restraint policy during the period of free collective bargaining than when it simply promulgated wage ceilings. If the policy of wage restraint succeeded after 1983, it must have been achieved by means other than the direct operation of guidelines for wage negotiations.

III THE CASE FOR WAGE LEADERSHIP

The basic argument of the wage leadership hypothesis could be summarised as follows. Because labour costs form a smaller part of its value added, and the strength of the Mineworkers Union of Zambia (MUZ), the mining industry tends to pay higher wages than other industries. Wage demands of the non-mining unions in turn are based on what takes place in the mining industry (Fry, 1979: 132). The hypothesis appeared as early as 1952 in the Fallows Commission Report and was repeated in the 1960s by the Seers Report of 1962 and Turner Report of 1969. The view has been mainly based on the fact that Zambia for a long time stood among sub-Saharan African countries as a country with one of the strongest labour movements.

Historically, the formation of the Northern Rhodesia African Mineworkers Union (NRAMU) in 1948 was the catalyst that spread unionism amongst African workers. It has been suggested that the ability of NRAMU to organise work stoppages and the rising real wages of its members associated with it seemed to display the advantages of African workers organising themselves (see Bates, 1971 and Quinn, 1971). But Daniel (1979) questions whether the rise in African workers' wages on the mines in this period has not been attributed disproportionately to the influence of NRAMU. He argues that as early as the 1930s, African earnings in general, but particularly those for miners, had begun to rise as the practice of paying subsistence wages to African workers became difficult to maintain. The rationale for a subsistence wage had been that an African worker and his family remained tied to the soil. It increased the rate of turnover of African workers as they kept going back to their rural families. In the end, mining employers recognised that the practice of paying subsistence wages to African workers undermined productivity which would otherwise have been enhanced by a more stable work force. He argued that the profitability of the mines at this time was an important factor in the adoption of the stabilisation concept and the eventual rise in the African real wage.

It is argued that the mining industry exercised the role of wage leadership in the 1960s partly as a result of the government's willingness to support workers' pay claims in order to achieve political control of unions, especially in the case of mineworkers. For example, during the sittings of the Brown Commission appointed in 1966 to review miners' salaries after a wave of strikes, UNIP accused the copper mines of 'putting forward a low wage policy cloaked in the garb of a privately sponsored wages and incomes policy for the country at large' (cited in Fry, 1979: 122). However, this strategy failed and in the 1970s the ZCTU leadership was increasingly rid of leaders prepared to maintain a close alliance with the ruling party (Rakner, 1992). The relationship became more confrontational from then onwards. The landmark came in 1980 when unions strongly opposed the passing of the Local Government Act which the government did not see as falling within the unions' jurisdiction and competence. The labour movement and the government were on a constant collision course from this date onwards as the former increasingly opposed government economic policy. The government now adopted a much tougher stance than before. In March 1985 most economic activities were classified as 'essential' and strikes were outlawed (Hawkins, 1991: 846). Therefore the rise in the real wage between 1964 and 1974, following the wage leadership argument, is linked to UNIP's liberality towards workers, a stance that was reversed after the mid-1970s which helped the decline in the real wage.

The wage leadership hypothesis also appears credible when it is considered that variations in the real wage appeared to coincide with the profitability of the mining industry. It is noted from Table 11.2 that the periods when ZCCM made profits (before 1975 and between 1979 and 1981) coincided with a rise in the real wage (see Figure 11.2). It could be inferred from this that the real wage declined in the 1980s because the mining industry was hardly profitable and therefore failed to pay its workers higher wages. The wider implications for workers outside the mining industry was to scale down their demands.

Despite its general acceptance, and the apparent qualitative evidence to support it, McPherson (1978), Daniel (1979) and Kayizzi-Mugerwa (1988) have raised questions against the validity of the wage leadership hypothesis. It should be noted that these three, together with Knight (1971), are the only ones to have used simulative methods to test the mining wage leadership hypothesis. Only Knight of the four concluded that the mines were a wage leader in Zambia. But his work came under heavy criticism from McPherson,[4] Daniel and Fry. Fry himself using qualitative information concluded that the mining industry was a wage leader. He uses an impressionistic approach to detect the presence of wage leadership and states that the copper mines were the leading industry within the wage bursts that occurred around 1963, 1966/7, 1970/1 and 1974/5. But this approach has problems. Daniel (1979: 151) uses the same tabulation of events that Fry (1979, Table 5.1) used but concludes that wage leadership was only true for 1966 when salary awards by the Brown Commission led to increases in other industries. He points out that the 1964 and 1970 wage increases in the mining industry came after wage awards had been announced in other industries. It is therefore difficult to draw strong conclusions using qualitative methods as similar information could easily be interpreted differently.

IV AN ALTERNATIVE CASE: THE ROLE OF ECONOMIC FACTORS

Because of the serious questions raised against the validity of the wage leadership hypothesis, and the fact that it is doubtful that the decline in the real wage in the

Table 11.2 The financial performance of ZCCM

Year	Output (m. tonnes)	Sales ($ billion)	Net profit ($ billion)
1972	0.701	0.755	0.164
1973	0.683	0.936	0.204
1974	0.710	1.493	0.452
1975	0.648	1.161	0.141
1976	0.712	0.859	(0.006)
1977	0.659	1.028	0.029
1978	0.654	0.807	(0.026)
1979	0.584	1.116	0.113
1980	0.611	1.329	0.172
1981	0.568	1.312	0.068
1982	0.581	1.061	(0.189)
1983	0.563	0.866	(0.128)
1984	0.544	0.723	0.001
1985	0.532	0.760	0.001
1986	0.514	0.681	(0.008)
1987	0.523	0.850	(0.068)
1988	0.473	1.439	0.045

Source: Auty (1991, Table 5).

1980s could have been brought about by a wage restraint policy, it is important that we examine an alternative case that highlights the role of economic factors in setting the trend in the real wage.

The dependent economy models have been widely utilised in theoretical discussions of how real wages will behave under different economic regimes. Within these models, prediction of the movement in the real wage is made dependent on relative factor intensities in the tradables and non-tradables sectors. When a country experiences macroeconomic imbalances, there is a rise in the relative price of non-tradables (a fall in P_t/P_n) which favours the production of non-tradable goods and services. The consequence is that the non-tradables sector expands relatively to the tradables sector. The Stolper–Samuelson theory (Stolper and Samuelson, 1941) postulates that the factors of production that benefit most are those more intensively used in the expanding sector. Assuming, as Demery and Addison (1988) do, that the production of non-tradables is more labour intensive than tradables, the theory will predict that there will be a rise in the real wage following the decline in P_t/P_n. If economic adjustment succeeds in reversing the falling trend in P_t/P_n, the dependent economy models will anticipate a reversal in the long-run of the rising trend of the real wage established under a situation of macroeconomic imbalances.

In applying the dependent economy models to determine the extent to which economic factors affected the real wage in Zambia, we utilise a Stolper–Samuelson–Rybczynski (SSR) model as specified by Deepak Lal and applied to the Philippines (Lal, 1983). The conclusions drawn from his resulting general-equilibrium framework could be summarised as follows:

1) The immediate effect of a rise in the relative price of tradable goods is a fall in the real wage rate.
2) In the long-run, with the assumption of sector specific capital removed, the changes in the real wage would be '... further accentuated, and be of the same sign' (p. 18). This means that the real wage would continue to decline as the relative price of tradables rises.
3) The impact effect of raising the relative rental of traded goods caused by the rise in the relative price would be to move capital from the non-tradables to the tradables sector. This will lead to a relative increase in labour supply and a fall in the marginal product of labour, the real wage.[5]
4) The outflow of capital from non-tradables to tradables raises the rental in the former with a relative rise in the labour supply, reversing the outflow of capital from the non-tradables. The general impact would be to raise the real wage. For this reason, Lal argues that during the adjustment process, the initial decline flowing from an expansion in relative labour supply will be completely reversed.

With these conclusions, he suggests that adjustments in the real wage over time could be captured by the following model (Lal, p. 21):

$$W^*_t = a + b_1 P^*_{t-z} + b_2 K^*_{t-q} + U_t \qquad (1)$$

where:

W^* is the percentage change in the real wage.
P^* is the percentage change in the relative price of tradable to non-tradable goods.
K^* is the percentage change in the overall capital-labour endowment.
z, q are respective lengths of the lags of any exogenous change in relative commodity prices and relative factor supplies, respectively.

Following the adjustment mechanism given above, Lal expected b_1s to be negative and b_2s to be initially positive before turning negative. Since the principal strategy of economic adjustment is to raise the relative price of tradables to non-tradables, by incorporating the relative price, the SSR model becomes a useful tool to measure the responsiveness of the real wage to economic adjustment measures. The findings in the application of the model could also be taken to indicate the importance of market factors in real wage determination. By incorporating a technological variable (capital–labour ratio), the model has implications for labour demand per given level of output in the economy, which in turn should influence the real wage. It is for this reason that simulative models that test the responsiveness of the real wage to market factors such as profitability, productivity, and the share of the labour cost in value added, have often included the capital labour ratio variable (e.g. Singh, 1991).

Application of the SSR Model to Zambia

The above model was estimated for Zambia for the period 1965 to 1989. The choice of the period was dictated by data availability, as data on earnings were not available beyond 1989. We need to explain briefly the meaning and sources of the data being used. In applying the SSR model to Zambia, we follow the classifications of sectors provided in Table 11.3. Following this classification, factor intensities for Zambia are presented in Table 11.4. These have been based on the estimation done by Suckling (1985) also adopted by Kayizzi-Mugerwa (1988). Table 11.4 shows that, overall, tradables are more capital intensive than non-tradables. Due to the difficulties of estimating capital stock in the agricultural sector, Table 11.4 also shows the factor intensities of tradables without agriculture. It is seen that the capital–labour ratio for tradables was still much higher than that of non-tradables.

The application of the SSR model to Zambia relied on our being able to derive time series data on the relative price of tradables to non-tradables and the capital–labour ratio for the period 1965 to 1989. GDP deflators were adopted as indicators of prices facing each industry. Therefore P_t/P_n is the ratio of the

Table 11.3   Classification of industries by tradables and non-tradables sectors

Tradables sector	Non-tradables sector
1. Agriculture and Forestry	1. Construction
2. Manufacturing	2. Trading
3. Mining & Quarrying	3. Restaurants & Hotels
4. Electricity & Water	4. Transport & Communications
	5. Community, Social & Personal Services

Table 11.4   Capital–labour ratio by industry, 1980

Industry	K stock (K'm)	Labour (1980)	K/L (K)
Agriculture	650.0	32630	19920.32
Mining	850.0	63670	13350.09
Manufacturing	636.0	47760	13316.58
Electricity	443.3	7900	56113.92
Construction	350.0	43750	8000.00
Commerce	500.0	31350	15948.96
Transport & Com	450.0	23940	18796.99
Services	457.7	128100	3572.99
Tradables	2579.3	151960	16973.55
Non-Tradables	1757.7	227140	7738.40
T Less Agric.	1929.3	119330	16167.77

Source: Kayizzi-Mugerwa (1986);[8] CSO (1983), *Employment and Earnings, 1980*.

implicit GDP deflator for tradables to non-tradables. Figure 11.3 demonstrates that there was a continuous increase in P_t/P_n from 1983 to 1989 which had assumed a declining trend before then. The reversal in the relative price could be attributed to the adoption of economic adjustment policies. We estimated the capital stock for Zambia for the years 1965 to 1989 by using the perpetual-inventory (chronological investment) method. The selection of this method was influenced by statistical convenience rather than by its superiority in estimating capital stock.[6] We used the total capital stock estimates given in Table 11.4 for 1980 as the benchmark year to calculate the time series capital stock for 1965 to 1989. Real capital stock was obtained by using a deflator for gross fixed capital

Figure 11.3   Tradables to non-tradables relative price movements (1965–1990)

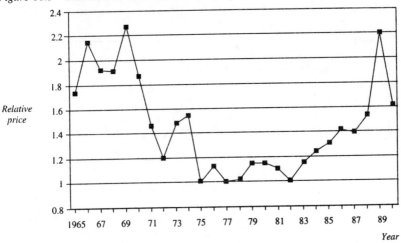

Source: Calculated from CSO, *Monthly Digest of Statistics,* various issues.

formation. The time series capital–labour ratio represented in Figure 11.4 is capital stock per each formal sector employee.[7] It shows a continuous decline in the capital–labour ratio since 1976. The rate of decline would appear improbable at first sight. However, the reasons for this decline are given in Part IV below.

Regression Results

The SSR model for Zambia was tested in log-linear form. As the nature of lags could not be determined *a priori,* and due to statistical convenience, lags were created by utilising a simplified version of the Almon Scheme Polynomial Lag (see Koutsoyiannis, 1977: 299–304). The results have been corrected for auto-correlation using the Cochrane–Orcutt method. The regression results reported in Table 11.5 indicate that the SSR model provides an adequate explanation of what happened to the real wage in Zambia's formal sector. It explains 62 per cent of the variations in the real wage without lagged variables and 70 per cent when a one-year lagged capital–labour ratio was introduced. Based on t statistics, the best results could be obtained with unlagged relative price and capital–labour ratio (see equation 1 in Table 11.5) variables. In addition, the signs were as predicted by Lal above, with coefficients for the relative price depicting a negative relation-ship and that of capital–labour ratio depicting a positive relationship. When the one-year lagged capital–labour ratio was added to the equation, the sign became

Figure 11.4   The capital–labour ratio

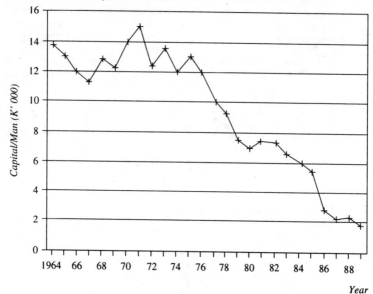

Source: Calculated from CSO, *Monthly Digest of Statistics,* various issues and *National Accounts Bulletin Nos 1 to 3.*

Table 11.5   Regression results for the SSR model

(1)	W^*_t =	7.71	–		0.17P_t	+	0.15K_t	
		$(146.86)^a$			$(-2.41)^b$		$(5.24)^a$	
	R^2 =	0.62	DW	=	1.46	SE =	0.058	

(2)	W^*_t =	7.70	–		0.14P_t	+	0.16K_t	– 0.002K_{t-1}
		$(24.56)^a$			(-1.35)		$(4.42)^a$	(-0.03)
	R^2 =	0.70	DW	=	1.51	SE =	0.056	

Notes:
a = significant at 1 per cent level of significance.
b = significant at 5 per cent level of significance.
c = significant at 10 per cent level of significance.
t statistics are given in brackets.

negative as postulated in Lal's SSR model, while the goodness of fit improved. However, in this case, the relative price and the one-year lagged capital–labour ratio failed to be significant at the 10 per cent level of significance.

Causes of Relative Price Changes

Having found that the SSR model significantly explained the variations in Zambia's real wage between 1965 and 1989, it is important that we examine factors affecting movements in the relative price ratio and the capital–labour ratio. It would appear that the variations in P_t/P_n are in line with the proposition of a variant of the dependent economy models established to explain what happens to factor prices in mineral-dependent economies (Corden and Neary, 1982; Daniel, 1985). This model seems well applicable to the Zambian economy whose economic trends have been driven by the fortunes of the copper industry. It postulates two effects under a mineral boom which results from either a discovery of the mineral or a rise in its international price. In Zambia the rise in the international price of copper in the 1960s explains the mineral boom.

The first effect postulated is the resource movement effect towards the mineral sector. This should cause the real wage (marginal product of labour) to rise in this sector, causing labour from both the non-tradables sector and the remainder of the tradables sector to move to the mineral sector until the marginal product of labour is equalised in all sectors. This will have a general upward impact on the real wage in the whole economy. Although this would seem to explain the rise in the real wage before 1975, the theoretical assumptions surrounding it are very difficult to justify in the case of Zambia. Between 1964 and 1974, employment in the mineral sector, where growth averaged 2 per cent per year, grew less fast than in the non-mining tradables (4 per cent) and non-tradables (5 per cent). Therefore even with the relaxation of the full employment assumption, admitting the existence of unemployment in the initial stages, relative growth in employment does not indicate a movement of labour to the mineral sector.

The movements in the relative price seem to be better explained by the second effect postulated under this theory – the spending effect. This states that there will be an increase in the economy's absorption as a result of a rise in the public spending of mineral revenue. 'The higher income resulting from the boom leads to extra spending on services which raises their price (i.e. causes a real appreciation) and thus leads to further adjustment' (Corden and Neary, 1982: 827). It is assumed here that the marginal propensity to consume services (non-tradables) increases with an increase in income. Increased fiscal spending arising out of mineral revenue in the first ten years of Zambia's independence was discussed in Part II. The rise of the non-tradables price relative to tradables price between 1965 and 1975 (see Figure 11.3) may therefore be explained by the rise in fiscal spending arising out of increased mineral revenue. This variant of the dependent economy models also suggests that because of the rise in both its relative price and demand, there will be an expansion of the non-tradables sector against the non-mining tradables sector, which would help to raise the real wage in the economy. Again Part II demonstrated that in the first ten years of independence, services were the fastest growing economic activity. Emphasis should be placed on relative expansion as the non-mining tradables also registered some growth in this period but expanded at a slower rate than that of non-tradables.

The process of a rising relative price of non-tradables to tradables ought to be reversed once the boom subsides. Figure 11.3 shows that although P_t/P_n's downward spiral was arrested between 1975 and 1982 in the wake of a fall in international copper prices, a complete reversal only came after 1982 when it started rising. Theoretically, this could arise from the downward rigidity in the real wage caused by non-market reactions or due to a failure to reduce government spending. We are unable to explain the behaviour of the relative price between 1975 and 1982 by real wage rigidity as in the aftermath of the end of the mineral boom the real consumption wage immediately declined and only started rising again in 1980 (see Figure 11.2). A more plausible explanation appears to be the failure by the government to reduce its spending in line with the new level of revenue. Beginning in 1975, budget deficits became entrenched in Zambia's fiscal management. The macroeconomic imbalances starting in this period could be chiefly attributed to this factor.

But this argument could be put even more simply. The decline in the profitability of the mining sector led to an increase in deficit financing. This in turn led to a rising rate of inflation which reinforced the fall in the real wage. The rise in the real wage between 1980 and 1982 could be attributed to the rise in the price of copper between 1979 and 1981 (see Figure 11.1), a factor that was beginning to bring back again the effects on the real wage of a mineral boom. A complete reversal only came after 1982 when, with the adoption of economic adjustment, P_t/P_n rose consistently and contributed to the decline in the real wage.

Explaining the Changes in Capital–Labour Ratio

The results of the SSR model show that part of the decline in the real consumption wage is accounted for by the decline in the capital–labour (K/L) ratio. What accounted for the big fall in K/L was the big decline in GFCF after 1975 (see Table 11.6). This mainly resulted from the big decline in the gross fixed capital formation that took place beginning in 1976. GFCF appeared to have reached its climax in 1975 when as a ratio of GDP (in current prices) it was 38.0 per cent. But by 1989, it had fallen to as little as 5.8 per cent, a decline of 84.7 per cent in 14 years. The real index of GFCF also fell from 191.02 in 1975 to 31.90 in 1989. The fact that the total number of workers only fell by 5.5 per cent from 1975 to 1989, and that the rate of depreciation rose from 3.45 in 1965 to 7.25 in 1975 before reaching 12 per cent in 1989, makes it clear that the substantial fall in the capital labour ratio resulted from the fall in gross investment.

Table 11.6 GFCF as a ratio of GDP and GFCF real index

Year	GFCF/GDP (%) current prices	Index 1977 prices
1965	16.93	76.28
1967	23.54	113.03
1969	19.31	114.68
1971	32.24	184.37
1973	23.95	144.45
1975	38.02	191.02
1977	24.32	100.00
1979	17.00	64.56
1981	17.69	72.96
1983	14.62	51.26
1985	10.24	41.16
1987	9.76	32.90
1989	5.80	31.90

Source: Calculated from CSO, *Monthly Digest of Statistics*, various issues.

This fall in GFCF reflected the foreign exchange scarcity that resulted from the decline in foreign earnings from copper exports, making it difficult for both the government and private investors to import the required machinery. At the same time, government cuts in capital expenditure were more than its cuts in recurrent expenditure which meant that government investment bore much of the reduction in spending (Gulhati, 1989: 15). It is possible that foreign investment could have helped to prevent some of the decline in GFCF. However, given the huge nationalisations undertaken in the late 1960s and early 1970s, and the deteriorating geopolitical environment with civil wars in Angola and Mozambique and the liberation struggle in Rhodesia, foreign investors were reluctant to invest in Zambia.

Economic Adjustment and Income Redistribution

This paper has linked the variations in both relative prices and factor endowments to the performance of the mining industry in Zambia. It is therefore reasonable to conclude that the ultimate cause of the real wage's decline in the 1980s was the end of the mineral boom. But what was the role of economic adjustment in the decline of the real wage? By raising the relative prices of tradables to that of non-tradables, economic adjustment appeared to have caused the real wage to fall at a faster rate than would otherwise have been the case. It appeared to have particularly facilitated this by redistributing income from labour to profits beginning in 1983. The share of labour costs in GDP fell from 54 per cent in 1982 to 29 per cent in 1989 (see Table 11.7). This observation appears to be in line with a cross-country study on economic reforms policies in Latin America which concluded that Fund programmes were 'most significantly and consistently associated with a reduction in labour's share of income' (Pastor, 1987: 3). Therefore a reduction in the real wage was not only caused by a fall in GDP, but was partly caused by this redistribution in income from labour to profits. The fact that such a substantial redistribution occurred proves further that underlying economic factors were able to override the ability of workers to resist a fall in the real wage.

Figure 11.5 shows what would have happened to the real wage in the absence of this redistribution, i.e. if the share of the labour cost had remained at 54 per cent.[9] It is seen that if a redistribution of income from labour to capital had not occurred after 1982, the real wage would have continued to rise until 1987 after which it would have started to fall but that up to 1989 it would have remained above its level in 1982, and far above its actual fall. Thus a fall in the real wage would not have in the end been prevented, with or without economic adjustment, although a fall in the real wage below its level in 1982 would not have occurred. Reform measures appear to have accelerated the speed at which the decline in the real wage occurred.

Table 11.7   Share of operating surplus and labour cost in GDP, 1979–89

Year	Labour cost/GDP	Surplus/GDP	Labour cost/Surplus
1979	0.45	0.33	1.37
1980	0.48	0.35	1.35
1981	0.50	0.30	1.68
1982	0.54	0.26	2.08
1983	0.47	0.27	1.72
1984	0.44	0.30	1.47
1985	0.40	0.35	1.14
1986	0.32	0.40	0.81
1987	0.30	0.41	0.73
1988	0.28	0.54	0.51
1989	0.29	0.57	0.51

Source: CSO, *Monthly Digest of Statistics*, various issues, and *National Accounts Bulletin Nos 1 to 3*.

Figure 11.5   The real wage with labour costs at constant share in value added

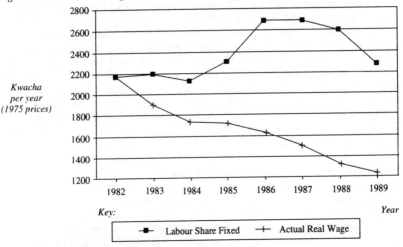

Source: Calculated from CSO, *Monthly Digest of Statistics,* various issues and *National Accounts Bulletin Nos 1 to 3.*

V   CONCLUSION

The findings arising from the application of the SSR model emphasise the import-ance of the mining industry in real wage determination in Zambia. In this aspect they are in line with the conclusions of the wage leadership hypothesis. But the results reject the view that the means by which the mining industry affected the real wage was through unionism. It is the underlying economic factors, as cap-tured by the variations in P_t/P_n and K/L, that are fundamental to real wage deter-mination. Both variables are critically linked to the profitability of copper mining.

These findings assume great importance when seen in the context of the rec-ommendations made by experts such as those in the Turner (ILO, 1969) and Seers (Daniel, 1979) reports. The rise in the real wage in the first ten years of independence was generally interpreted to arise basically from the demands of workers and wage adjustments in the public sector. The reports failed to recog-nise that unions could only be effective when there are permissive factors allow-ing increases in the real wage. The mineral boom, by leading to a fall in P_t/P_n and a rise in K/L in the first ten years of independence, was the permissive factor. This view helps to explain the apparent success of unions in winning huge salary awards in the first ten years of independence. They could not be as successful once the underlying economic factors changed.

Because of their pre-occupation with institutional factors, these reports which were highly regarded in the search for an incomes policy failed to recognise that the government's handling of the mineral boom – by leading to a sharp increase in fiscal spending – was the main factor behind the high rate of increase in the real wage. If the real wage had such detrimental effects on the social and economic development of Zambia, as stated in the Seers and Turner reports, it could be suggested with hindsight that the fall in copper prices might not have had such sustained severe ramifications on economic development if Zambia had taken steps to prudently manage her high mineral rents in the earlier period.[10]

The discussion has also shed some light on the efficacy of an incomes policy to restrain a rise in wages. It is implied that any suggestion of wage restraint, as recommended in the 1960s and applied in 1970, that did not seek at the same time to contain government spending was bound to fail to stop the real wage from rising. This is why measures to restrain a rise in wages in Zambia appear to have only been successful within the context of economic reforms. But even in this case, it is likely that their impact has been restricted to reducing real wages in the civil service causing them to fall much faster than in the rest of the economy.[11]

This conclusion also casts doubt on the orthodox pre-occupation with institutional factors as the overriding impediment to obtaining the desired adjustment in the real wage in Third World countries. In the early 1980s, the view was that wages in sub-Saharan African were too high compared to other countries at the same level of development due to governments' willingness to accede to workers' demands (e.g. IBRD, 1981: 92–3). But if this view is found invalid in Zambia, which had more developed structures for institutional factors to determine the real wage, it is unlikely to have been as generalised in sub-Saharan Africa as supposed. This should help to explain why the real wage declined even in Latin American countries with a long tradition of 'strong' labour unions. The findings add to the growing view that real wages in the Third World have been more flexible than earlier appreciated (e.g. Riveros, 1984 and Horton *et al.*, 1991).

However, these conclusions should not be taken to imply that unions had no power and that the government in its economic management was inattentive to union pressure. It was union pressure that made it politically difficult for the government to reduce food subsidies even though it appreciated the need to reduce spending on them even earlier than the 1975 fall in the copper price.[12] Therefore if unions helped the rise in the real wage in this period, it was by means of their political impact on fiscal spending. Throughout the 1980s, unions appeared to have retained the potential to disrupt the implementation of economic reforms even though they were not in a position to prevent a fall in the real wage (Hawkins, 1991). As the government took a tougher stance on work stoppages in the 1980s, unions' frustrations made them take a more political tone and they were in the forefront in calling for a return to multi-party democracy (Bratton, 1992). Thus the ruling party (UNIP) finally paid a heavy political price for ignoring workers' demands when it had to concede a multi-party election and lost it in

1991. But this political role of unionism should be differentiated from the ability of workers to directly derive a disproportionately bigger rise in the real wage than that dictated by underlying economic factors.

Notes

1. The paper summarises some sections of my DPhil. thesis submitted to the University of Sussex. I am grateful to my supervisor, Christopher Colclough, Charles Harvey and Godfrey Kanyenze for providing useful comments. I absolve them of any shortcomings of this paper for which I take full responsibility.

2. It is beyond the scope of this paper to explain why Zambia failed to benefit from the 1980s economic reforms. The issue has been the subject of numerous studies (e.g. Colclough, 1988; Callaghy, 1989; Hawkins, 1991; Loxley, 1990; Auty, 1991; Bates and Krueger, 1993).

3. From 1983 until it was dissolved in 1992, the PIC had to ratify all collective agreements before they could be effected. Unions and employers sent the collective agreement to the Labour Commissioner who would then submit it to the PIC Chairman with his comments. Within PIC, the Wages and Incomes Committee (WIC) whose members were drawn from the government, unions and employers would consider the agreement to see whether any guideline had been breached. If satisfied, the PIC Chairman would write to the bargaining units to inform them that the agreement had been approved.

4. Repeating McPherson's tests for the period 1965 to 1989 for the economy as a whole, regression results still rejected the wage leadership hypothesis.

5. Elsewhere, Lal (1984: 6) has stated that 'capital... through depreciation and new investment can be "shifted" from one of the "sectors" to the other, over time.'

6. For a detailed discussion on the definition and problems in the measurement of capital stock see Pyo (1988) and Ward (1976).

7. Ideally it is better to use total hours of work instead of the total number of workers. But information on hours of work is rarely available and the number of workers has been adopted instead.

8. Kayizzi-Mugerwa adopted the 1980 estimates of total capital stock by Suckling (1985) to estimate the sectoral distribution of capital stock. Suckling had applied a perpetual inventory method to estimate capital stock for the years 1964 to 1982. He adopted the 1964 estimates of capital stock as his benchmark. For mining, manufacturing and electricity Kayizzi-Mugerwa used values for buildings and land, transport equipment and machinery and other equipment given in the 1980 Census of Industrial Production. He assumes that between 15 per cent and 20 per cent of the total aggregate capital stock was in agriculture. The unallocated capital stock was then distributed across the other sectors using such indicators as sectoral depreciation, capital income, output and employment. It should be emphasised that the estimated value of agricultural capital stock based on a rule of thumb is very rudimentary and might have been overestimated as

shown by the high capital–labour ratio for agriculture in the table, defying the traditional low capital intensity of the sector. Our estimates of the capital–labour ratio use sectoral employment rather than man-hours as Kayizzi-Mugerwa does. His use of man-hours based on the 1980 population census also includes that of the urban and rural informal sectors, which is a mismatch given the fact that the estimates of sectoral capital stock from CSO data only cover the formal sector. We have separated K443.3 million for electricity, gas and water from the figure Kayizzi-Mugerwa gives for services as it was felt the inclusion was inappropriate. We treat this sector as a tradable sector based on the fact that of the 7300 employees in 1980 in this sector, 6000 were in electricity.

9. This assumption does not pre-judge whether the 1982 share of labour costs in the value added was the right one or not but is used here to demonstrate the impact of income redistribution from labour to profits.

10. A mineral stabilisation fund which would have helped to achieve this strategy was abandoned in 1972 (Auty, 1991: 172).

11. For example, although the attempt to restrain the rise in wages in 1970 failed to achieve its objective in the economy as a whole, it managed to arrest the rapid rise of the real wage for government workers.

12. In November 1974, the government, due to union pressure, was forced to roll back substantial price rises that had earlier been made in an attempt to scale down on subsidies.

References

Auty, Richard M. (1991) 'Mismanaged Mineral Dependence: Zambia 1970–90', *Resources Policy*, September.

Bates, Robert H. (1971) *Unions, Parties and Political Development* (New Haven and London: Yale University Press).

Bates, Robert H. and Anne O. Krueger (eds) (1993) *Political and Economic Interactions in Economic Policy Reform* (Oxford, UK, and Cambridge, Mass: Blackwell).

Bourguignon, Francois (1988) 'The Measurement of the Wage–Employment Relationship in Developed Countries: A Short Survey', in *Labour Law and Labour Relations Programme, Occasional Paper*, 2 (Geneva: ILO).

Bratton, Michael (1992) 'Zambia Starts Over', *Journal of Democracy*, April 1992.

Callaghy, Thomas (1989) 'Lost Between State and Market: The Politics of Economic Adjustment in Ghana, Zambia, and Nigeria', in Joan M. Nelson (ed.), *Economic Crisis and Policy Choice: the Politics of Adjustment in the Third World* (Princeton, New Jersey: Princeton University Press).

Central Statistical Office (1988–90) *National Accounts Bulletin Nos 1 to 3* (Lusaka: CSO).

Central Statistical Office (1965–91) *Monthly Digest of Statistics* (Lusaka: Central Statistical Office).

Chiwele, Dennis K. (1993) *Stabilisation, The Real Wage, Employment and Welfare: The Case of Zambia's Formal Sector Employees.* Unpublished DPhil Thesis, University of Sussex, Brighton.

Colclough, Christopher (1988) 'The Zambian Adjustment Strategy – With and Without the IMF', *IDS Bulletin*, 19 (1) (Brighton: Institute of Development Studies).

Colclough, Christopher (1989) 'The Labour Market and Economic Stabilisation in Zambia', *Research Working Papers*, WPS 222 (Washington DC: IBRD).

Corden, W.M. and J.P. Neary (1982) 'Booming Sector and Deindustrialisation in a Small Open Economy', *The Economic Journal*, 92 (368).

Daniel, Philip (1979) *Africanisation, Nationalisation and Inequality: Mining and the Copper Belt in Zambian Development* (Cambridge: Cambridge University Press).

Daniel, Philip (1985) 'Zambia: Structural Adjustment or Downward Spiral?', in *IDS Bulletin*, 16 (2) (Brighton: Institute of Development Studies).

Demery, Lionel and Tony Addison (1988) 'Adjustment and Income Distribution: The Role of Labour Markets', *Working Paper*, 81 (University of Warwick: Development Economics Centre).

Dholakia, Bakul H. (1976) 'Determinants of Inter-Industry Wage Structure in India', in *Indian Journal of Industrial Relations*, 11 (4).

Disney, Richard (1989) 'Testing Equilibrium Models of Employment for Singapore, 1966–87', *Studies in Economics Number 89/4*, University of Kent.

Fallon, Peter R. and Luis A. Riveros (1989) 'Adjustment and the Labour Market', *Research Working Papers*, WPS 214 (Washington DC: IBRD).

Fincham, Robin and Grace Zulu (1979) 'Labour and Participation in Zambia', in Ben Turok (ed.), *Development in Zambia* (London: Zed Press).

Fry, James (1979) *Employment and Income Distribution in the African Economy* (London: Croom Helm).

Ghani, E. (1988) 'Alternative Approaches to Devaluation', in G.T. Renshaw (ed.), *Market Liberalisation, Equity and Development* (Geneva: ILO, World Development Programme).

Gulhati, Ravi (1989) 'Impasse in Zambia: The Economics and Politics of Reform', *Analytical Case Studies*, 2 (Washington DC: IBRD).

Hawkins, Jefferey J., Jr. (1991) 'Understanding the Failure of IMF Reform: The Zambian Case', in *World Development*, 19 (7), pp. 839–49.

Horton, Susan, Ravi Kanbur, and Dipak Mazumudar (1991) 'Labour Markets in an Era of Adjustment: An Overview', *IBRD Policy Research Working Papers*, WPS 694.

IBRD (1981) *Accelerated Development in sub-Saharan Africa: An Agenda for Action* (Washington, DC: IBRD).

IBRD (1987) *Zimbabwe, A Strategy for Sustained Growth* (Washington DC: IBRD).

IBRD (1992) *World Tables 1992* (Washington DC: IBRD).

IBRD (1993) *World Debt Tables, 1992–93* (Washington DC: IBRD).

ILO (H.A. Turner) (1969) *Report to Government of Zambia on Incomes and Prices in Zambia: Policy and Machinery* (Lusaka: Cabinet Office).

ILO (1977) *Narrowing the Gaps* (Addis Ababa: Jobs and Skills Programme for Africa).

ILO (1981) *Basic Needs in an Economy Under Pressure: Zambia* (Addis Ababa: Jobs and Skills Programme for Africa).

IMF (1986) *International Financial Statistics: Supplement on Price Statistics* (Washington DC: IMF).

IMF (1987) *International Financial Statistics: Supplement on Trade Statistics* (Washington DC: IMF).

IMF (1988) *International Financial Statistics: Supplement on International Liquidity* (Washington DC: IMF).

IMF (1990) *International Financial Statistics Yearbook* (Washington DC: IMF).

IMF (1992) *International Financial Statistics Yearbook* (Washington DC: IMF).

Kanyenze, Godfrey (1993) *The Impact of Economic Stabilisation on the Wage Structure in Zimbabwe: 1980–90.* Unpublished DPhil Thesis, University of Sussex, Brighton.

Kayizzi-Mugerwa, Steve (1988) *External Shocks and Adjustment in Zambia,* Goteborg University.

Klepper, Robert (1979) 'Zambian Agricultural Structure and Performance', in Ben Turok (ed.), *Development in Zambia* (London: Zed Press).

Knight, J.B. (1971) 'Wages and Zambia's Economic Development', in Charles Elliot (ed.), *Constraints on the Economic Development of Zambia* (Nairobi: Oxford University Press).

Knight, J.B. (1976) 'Devaluation and Income Distribution in Less-Developed Economies', in *Oxford Economic Papers,* 28 (2).

Koutsoyiannis, A. (1977) *Theory of Econometrics: An Introductory Exposition of Econometric Methods* (London: Macmillian).

Lal, Deepak (1983) 'Real Wages and Exchange Rates in the Philippines, 1956–78: An Application of the Stolper–Samuelson–Rybczynski Model of Trade', *World Bank Staff Working Paper,* 604 (Washington DC: IBRD).

Lal, Deepak (1984) 'The Real Effects of Stabilisation and Structural Adjustment Policies: An Extension of the Australian Adjustment Model', *World Bank Staff Working Paper,* 636 (Washington DC: IBRD).

Lopez, Ramon E. and Luis A. Riveros (1989) 'Macroeconomic Adjustment and the Labour Market in Four Latin American Countries', *Research Working Papers,* WPS 335 (Washington DC: IBRD).

Loxley, John (1990) 'The IMF's Structural Adjustment Programmes in Zambia and Ghana: Some Issues of Theory and Policy', *Leeds Southern African Studies,* 12 (Leeds: University of Leeds).

Marinakis, Andres E. (1992) 'Public Sector Employment in Developing Countries: An Overview of Past and Present Trends', *Occasional Paper,* 3, Interdepartmental Project on Structural Adjustment (Geneva: ILO).

McPherson, Malcom (1978) 'Wage Leadership and Zambia's Mining Sector – Some Evidence', *Development Discussion Paper,* 43 (Cambridge, Massachusetts: Harvard Institute for International Development).

Meesook, Oey A., David Lindauer and Parita Suebsaeng (1986) 'Wage Policy and the Structure of Wages and Employment in Zambia', *CPD Discussion Paper,* 1 (Washington, DC: IBRD).

Pastor, Manuel, Jr. (1987) *The International Monetary Fund and Latin America: Economic Stabilisation and Class Conflict* (Boulder and London: Westview Press).

Prices and Incomes Commission (1991) *Social Economic Bulletin*, 1 (1) (Lusaka: PIC).

Pyo, Hak-Kil (1988) 'Estimates of Capital Stock and Capital/Output Coefficients by Industries for the Republic of Korea (1953–1986)', *KDI Working Paper*, 8810, Korea Development Institute.

Quinn, S.J. (1971) 'Industrial Relations in Zambia, 1935–69', in Charles Elliot (ed.), *Constraints on the Economic Development of Zambia* (Nairobi: Oxford University Press).

Rakner, Lise (1992) *Trade Unions in the Process of Democratisation: A Study of Party–Labour Relations in Zambia*, Chr. Michelsen Institute of Social Science and Development, Report 1992: 6.

Riveros, Luis A. (1984) 'Structural Reforms and Wage Settings Across Sectors: A Test of Chilean Labour Market Efficiency', *Documento Serie Investigacion*, 66 (Santiago: University of Chile).

Riveros, Luis A. and Carlo E. Sanchez (1990) 'Argentina's Labour Market in an Era of Adjustment', *Research Policy Working Papers*, WPS 386 (Washington DC: IBRD).

Seidman, Ann (1979) 'The Distorted Growth of Import Substitution: The Zambian Case', in Ben Turok (ed.), *Development in Zambia* (London: Zed Press).

Singh, Lakhwinder (1991) 'Changes in the Inter-Industry Structure of Wages: The Case of Punjab', *Indian Journal of Industrial Relations*, 27 (2), October 1991.

Stolper, W.F. and Paul A. Samuelson (1941) 'Protection and Real Wages', *Review of Economic Studies*, November 1941.

Strickland, Richard (1991) *Stabilisation Strategies of the International Monetary Fund and the Effects on the Income and Welfare: The Case of Zambia*, Unpublished D.Phil. Thesis, Institute of Development Studies and University of Sussex, Brighton.

Suckling, John (1985) 'The Impact of Energy Price Increase on an Export Dependent Economy: Zambia, 1970–82', *World Employment Programme Working Paper*, 147 (Geneva: ILO).

Sussex, Edward (1989) 'Workers and Trade Unions in a Period of Structural Change', *World Employment Programme Research Working Paper*, 25 (Geneva: ILO).

Ward, Michael (1976) 'Problems of Measuring Capital in Less Developed Countries', in *The Review of Income and Wealth, Series 22*, 3, September 1976.

Young, Roger (1988) *Zambia: Adjusting to Poverty* (Ottawa: North–South Institute).

Young, Roger and John Loxley (1990) *Zambia: An Assessment of Zambia's Structural Adjustment Experience* (Ottawa: North–South Institute).

Index

Abbott, J.C.   97
Abel-Smith, B.   169
absenteeism   206
Adams, D.W.   16
Addison, Tony   30, 105, 218
adjustment process   *see* structural
    adjustment
Agere, S.   58–9, 71
agriculture
    employment   67, 68, 109
    lending to   23–4
    Tanzania   78
    see also maize marketing
Ahmed, Z.U.   16
aid
    dependence on   133
    Indonesia   113
    as proportion of imports by
        country   133
    see also structural adjustment
Aleke-Dondo, C.   22
Alexander, C.P.   171
Amjad, R.   100
Arusha region maize marketing   76–97
Auty, Richard M.   217, 230n
Azis, I.J.   108

Ballance, R.   158, 162, 171
bad debts   5, 134, 145–8, 149
    repaid by government   81, 89, 112,
        142
banks/banking   149
    proximity of branches and
        savings   11, 12
    see also commercial banks; financial
        sector; bad debts
barter trade   41
Barya, John-Jean   137
Bates, Robert H.   215
Bernard, A.   80

Bhatt, V.V.   12, 13
Biggs, T.S.   20
Bird, G.   38
Blejer, M.I.   10
borrowing decisions
    cost of capital   17–18
    impact of real interest rates
        14–20
    influencing factors   16–20
    perceived problems   19
    transaction costs   16–17
Botswana   43
    financial sector reform   148, 179
    privatisation   185
    Share Market   176, 177
    stock exchange   181, 182, 183, 190n
Bourguignon, F.   66, 72n
Bratton, Michael   228
Bryceson, D.F.   79, 80
budget deficit   104, 132, 148
    Tanzania   77, 114
    Zambia   212, 224
    Zimbabwe   30

capital market, Kenya   21–3
capital–labour ratios   34–8, 220, 222,
    224–5
Chandavarkar, A.   10
Chavunduka Commission Report   56
Cheasty, A.   10
Chege, J.D.   22
Chew, David C.E.   206
Chhibber, A.   53, 57
Chile   5, 69, 106
    adjustment process   108–9, 111–12,
        115, 116, 125
    debt re-scheduling   112
    employment policy   123, 124
    employment and unemployment
        figures   117

Chile *continued*
  indices of real wages
    (1970–1990) 118
  Indonesia and Tanzania
    compared 107–11
  inflation 112–13, 121
  labour force 110, 111
  social dialogue 127
  wages and employment 116–18,
    121–2
Chiwele, Dennis 56, 135, 192–209,
  210–33
Cho, Y.J. 10
civil service
  absenteeism 58–9, 192, 193, 207
  allowances 136, 201–3
  moonlighting 58, 135, 137, 193,
    205–6, 207
  reform 134–8
  skill erosion 57, 192
  and success of structural
    adjustment 134
  and wage policy 58–9
  Uganda 58
  Zambia 192–208
  Zimbabwe 58–9
  see also public sector
Colclough, Christopher 56, 192–209
Colombia 68
commercial banks
  bad debts and market share by
    country 145–7
  deposit rates 11
  and financial sector reform 144–6
  number of branches 26
  real maximum lending rates 18
  and SMEs 9, 15–16, 22
Commenwealth Development
  Corporation (CDC) 187–8, 190
Confederation of Zimbabwe
  Industries 56–7
co-operatives
  credit 12, 76
  Tanzania 79, 81, 86–7, 93–6, 97
Corden, W.M. 223
Cornia, G.A. 100

corruption 193, 206–7
Coughlin, P. 168
Coulter, J. 82, 85, 93
credit
  co-operative societies 12, 76
  diversion to public sector 148
  and impact of real interest
    rates 20–3
  impact of state controls and
    intervention 23–5
  and interest rate liberalisation 7–26
  and market failure 20–1
  measures to improve 25
  non-interest determinants 20–1
  other constraints 22–3
  and parastatals 81, 140
  and redundancy 130
  restrictions 138
  subsidised 113
Crockett, A.D. 30
currency devaluation 102, 104, 105,
  107, 132, 134, 148, 175
  Chile 112, 115
  and efficiency in use of capital 44
  Indonesia 113
  Kenya 4, 152, 153, 154, 156, 166
  mis-judged 107
  Tanzania 113
  Zambia 194, 210
  Zimbabwe 2, 30, 34, 53
  see also real exchange rate

Dailami, M. 17
Daniel, Philip 211, 213, 215, 216–17,
  223, 227
Davies, R. 40
de Groot, A.W. 153
de Kadt, E. 123
debt re-scheduling 1, 112, 113
  Chile 112
  see also bad debts
debt; equity ratio 176, 183
debt service ratio 113
debt service payments 186
  Zambia 213
Demery, Lionel 30, 105, 218

deposit rates and interest rate
reforms 11
devaluation *see* currency devaluation
Development Finance
Corporations 21, 175
reasons for failure 175, 190n
Drabu, H.A. 44–5, 48n
Durevall, D. 36

Ebrill, L.P. 16, 17
economic liberalisation 102, 108, 111
125–7
economic recovery
constraints on 130–50
and stabilisation programmes 5
see also structural adjustment
EDESA 190, 191n
Edwards, S. 48n
employment
civil service 134–8
and growth 66, 68, 69–70
legislation 54, 68, 70n
and real exchange rate depreciation
32–4, 61–9; labour demand
functions by sector 67; model
65–9; tradable and non-tradable
goods sector 63–9
security of 37, 53, 54, 65, 68
structure and adjustment
process 109–11
and wages 60–9
employment policy
and development planning 101
effect of 122–5
macro-incompatible 105
and structural adjustment 100–29
equity finance
sources of 174–5, 186
and stock exchanges 184
see also leasing companies; stock
exchanges; venture capital
companies
Eriksson, G. 140
exchange rates
dual 146
expectations 2, 10, 115

fixed 153
indices, Zimbabwe 31
and interest rates 11
overvaluation 78
policy and savings 10–11
policy in Chile 111, 115
policy in Tanzania 115
policy in Zimbabwe 30–47, 53
unofficial 145
see also real exchange rate
exogenous shocks 109
Tanzanian response 77, 78
exports 29, 30
Chile 111
and devaluation 30, 40–3
direction of 43
Indonesia 113
Kenya 154–7, 168
multinational company constraints
on 161
Nigeria 133
and product quality 37, 39
Tanzania 140
Tanzanian policy 78
Zambia 213, 225
Zimbabwe 40–43
external debt, Zambia 213

Faber, Mike 174–91
Faini, R. 16, 17
Fallon, P.R. 37, 52, 68
Farruk, M. 93
Fernando, N.A. 12
financial innovations 176
financial sector 5–6, 142–8
deregulation 113–14, 116
informal 12
Kenya 21–2
fiscal policy and savings 10
see also tax; budget deficit
food subsidies 132, 211, 228
foreign exchange
liberalisation in Tanzania 113
shortages and pharmaceutical
products 157, 158
see also real exchange rate

foreign investment *see under* investment
Foster, S.D. 154, 167
Foxley, A. 108
Fry, James 215, 216–17
Fry, M.J. 10, 12

Gambia
  civil service 138
  financial sector reform 147–8
Garcia, N.E. 118
Ghana 5, 150n
  CDCs 187, 188
  civil service 137
  commercial banks 145, 146
  economic recovery 149–50
  Leasing Company 191n
  ODA as proportion of imports 133
  parastatals 139, 140, 142
  privatisation 185
  real interest rates 143, 144
  stock exchange 174, 180, 181, 182, 190n, 191n
  structural adjustment 131, 132
  tax system 132
  VCF 188
Goldstein, M. 29
government expenditure *see* budget deficit
government intervention
  Chile, Indonesia and Tanzania compared 110–11
  and financial market 185
Green, R.H. 36, 57
Greenaway, D. 125
Grosh, B. 21
growth of GDP
  and aid 149
  and employment 66, 68, 69–70
  and exports 119
  inhibiting factors 70
  in importing countries 43
  and invesment 45, 112, 149
Guidotti, G. 186
Guinea, civil service 137
Gulhati, Ravi 196, 211, 225

Hahn, F.W. 65
Hamermesh, D.S. 66
Hamid, J. 183
Harding, Peter 56
Harper, M. 19
Harvey, Charles 1–6, 23, 130–51, 176
Havemann, K. 171
Hawkins, A.M. 68
Hawkins, Jefferey J.Jr 216, 228
Hays, H.M. 93
Helleiner, G.K. 7
Horton, Susan 52, 69, 228

Ikiara, G.K. 21, 168
IMF *see* International Monetary Fund
import-intensity of production 40, 154, 167–8
imports
  and aid 133, 160
  and cost of capital 66, 70
  and drought 79
  import substitution, Kenya 158, 160
  import substitution, Tanzania 168–9
  liberalisation 43, 159–62
  licencing 78, 155
  manufacturing inputs, Tanzania 154, 157, 160
  manufacturing inputs, Zimbabwe 38–40
  restrictions 114, 153
incomes policy 54, 198, 210, 216, 228
income distribution 101–2, 225–7
India 180
  VCCs 187
indigenisation and stock exchanges 185–6
Indonesia 5
  adjustment process 108, 111, 112–13, 115, 116, 126
  Chile and Tanzania compared 107–11
  employment 109, 110; policy 123–4
  financial deregulation 113
  real wages indices 120
  unemployment (1982–90) 119

VCCs 187
wages and employment 118–20,
121–2; by sector 119
inflation
and bad debts 147
and budget deficit 132
and cash budgets 148
Chile 112–13, 121
and credit 76, 78
and exchange rate policy 30
and food subsidies 132
and government spending 153
and interest rates *see* real interest
rates
inertial 121
and parastatal losses 79, 104
and stock exchanges 176
Tanzania 76, 78, 79, 109, 114
variability of 19, 143
and wages *see* real wages
Zambia 198–9, 213, 224
informal sector
and civil service employees 135,
137, 205–6
financial, Kenya 22
labour market 106
sex and age profiles 205
and taxation 132, 143–4, 178–9
interest rate
cost of capital 66
international 101, 112
interest rate reforms
and allocative efficiency of
credit 7–26
and IMF and World Bank 7
impact on financial savings 9–12
and interest margins 13
Kenya 7–9
and lending and savings rates 7–9
objectives 8
policy 142–4, 148
and uncertainty 101, 112
see also real interest rates
International Monetary Fund 1
and aid dependence 133
and Chile 112

conditions set by 7, 210
and economic recovery 130–1
and interest rates 7
and Kenya 7
and labour market liberalisation
52–3
and Mozambique 140
and Nigeria 141
and real exchange rate
depreciation 29
and Tanzania 113
and Zambia 136, 196, 198, 200, 213,
214
and Zimbabwe 30, 48n
see also structural adjustment
investment
and banking 134
demand constraints 18–19
and economic recovery 130
foreign: and stock exchanges
175–6; Ghana 141; Tanzania
114, 169
and growth 149
impact of real interest rates 14–20
internal constraints 19
Kenyan capital market 21–3
operational constraints 18–20
private sector 174
and privatisation 141
and real exchange rate
depreciation 44–7
and real maximum lending rates 18,
19, 20
and tax incentives 20
transaction costs of borrowing
16–17, 19, 20

Jefferis, K. 179
Jenkins, Carolyn 142
job creation 124
job destruction 124
job security, *see* employment, security
of
Johnson, O.E.G. 30
Jolly, R. 100
Julin, E. 153

Kadhani, X.   36, 57
Kanji, N.   155
Kanyenze, Godfrey   37, 52–75
Kaplinsky, R.   49
Kariuki, Peninah   7–28
Kayizzi–Mugerwa, Steve   216, 219, 220, 229n–30
Kenya   2
  commercial banks   8–9
  Development Finance
      Corporation   13–14
  exports   154
  financial institutions   21–2
  growth and employment   68, 69–70
  health expenditure indicators   163
  Income Tax Act   17
  interest rate reforms   7–9
  NBFIs   8–9
  pharmaceutical products   152–71
  privatisation   185
  real interest rates (1968–90)   8
  Small Enterprise Finance
      Company   13–14
  SMEs   2, 7–26
  stock exchange   21–3, 180, 181, 182, 183, 190n
  see also commercial banks; interest
      rate reforms; pharmaceutical
      products in Kenya; savings; SMEs
Khathate, D.   10
Kilby, P.   9
Killick, T.   7, 12, 20, 107, 154
Kitchen, R.L.   7
Klepper, Robert   211
Knight, J.B.   105, 216
Kornai, J.   100–1
Koutsoyiannis, A.   221
Kunaka, C.   42

labour market   52–75, 107–8
  informal sector   106
  moonlighting   58, 135, 137, 193, 205–6, 207
  role in adjustment process   70n
  small open economy model   105–6

and structural adjustment   100–29
  women   126
  Zimbabwe   52–3, 60–9, 70n
labour relations legislation   37, 55
Ladman, J.R.   16
Laird, S.   162
Lal, Deepak   218–19, 221–3, 229n
Lall, S.   43
leasing companies   175, 188–90
  African experience   190
  conditions for   189–90
legislation, employment   54, 55, 68, 70n, 105, 111, 193
Lehman, G.I.   16
Lehman, H.P.   53
lending
  rates, Kenya   8–9
  transaction costs   13–14
Levin, J.   153
Levitski, A.   186
Lindauer, D.L.   54, 58
Lipton, Michael   203
Lirenso, A.   90
localisation   193–5
Lopez, R.   53
Lucas, R.E.B.   37, 68

McCoy, J.H.   93
McKinnon, R.I.   8
McKinnon–Shaw hypothesis   8, 9, 10, 14–15, 18, 20, 25
McPherson, Malcolm F.   148, 216
maize marketing in Tanzania   76–97
  co-operatives 79, 81, 86–7, 93–5, 96, 97
  liberalisation   81–2; analysis of
      market integration   89–93;
      barriers to trade and entry
      87–8; choice of market channel
      86, 87; classification on basis of
      date of entry   83; coercive
      tactics   88, 96, 97; and
      economic performance   88–9;
      estimates of amounts marketed
      through different channels   84;

estimates of intra- and
inter-regional trade 83;
intra-regional transfer patterns
83; marketing margins 88, 89;
milling facilities 85;
organisation of trade and maize
flow pattern 82; ownership
pattern of market facilities
84–5; prices 88–9, 93; private
traders' operations 85, 86, 87,
88, 96–7; storage facilities 85,
97; structure and competitiveness
of private marketing 82–4,
96–7; transport facilities 84–5
NAPB 78
National Milling Company 78–9,
80, 96, 97; financial performance
95–6
parallel market 78
policies 78–82
pricing policies 79–81
recommendations 97
Strategic Grain Reserve 80–1
Makings, G. 56, 71
Malawi 190n
Malinvaud, E. 65
managerial capability 19
manufacturing sector
capital–labour ratios 34–8, 48n
domestic inputs 157–9
exchange rate depreciation 29–5;
and choice of technique 34–8;
and employment 31, 32–8; and
investment 44–7; and sourcing
of inputs 38–40
exports 154–7
ICORs 44–5
price incentives in Kenya 152–4
trade liberalisation 159–62
see also exports
Martin, M. 12, 20
Mauritius, stock exchange 181, 182,
190n
Mayer, C. 183
Maynard, J.E. 21

Meesook, O. 197, 200, 202
Meller, P. 106
Mexico 127
Milner 171
minimum wage 54–5, 60–1, 67, 105,
111, 116, 118
mining sector, Zambia 210–30
moonlighting 58, 135, 137, 193,
205–6, 207
Morawetz, D. 65
Morissey, O. 125
Morocco, stock exchange 180
Mosley, P. 156
Moyana, K.J. 36
Mozambique
commercial banks 145, 146, 147
leasing companies 188–9, 190
ODA as proportion of imports 133
parastatals 140
privatisation 140, 185
venture capital funds 188
Muchangwe Commission 198
Muzulu, Joseph 29–51, 53, 61, 158
Mwanakatwe Commission 198
Mwandihi, L.A. 12
Mwega, F.M. 12

Namibia, stock exchange 181, 182
Neary, J.P. 223
Ng, F. 48n
Nigeria 150n
adjustment process 132, 133, 149
commercial banks 145–6
ODA as proportion of imports
133
parastatals 141, 142
pharmaceutical products 162
real interest rates 143, 144
stock exchange 180, 181, 182, 184,
190n
Nissanke, M. 16
non-tradable goods 30–3, 34, 38, 45,
61–4, 105–7, 115, 126, 152–5,
218–24, 225
non-traditional exports 115

OECD countries, stock exchanges 182, 183
Oi, Y. 64–5
Owino, Pius 152–73

Pack, H. 37
Papua New Guinea, VCCs 187
parastatals
    access to foreign exchange 39
    and banking reform 146–7, 149
    banks 23–5
    credit for 81, 97, 175
    losses 79, 104
    moonlighting 206
    privatisation 185
    reform of 138–42, 149
    and success of structural
        adjustment 134
    Tanzania 77–8, 114, 124
    Zimbabwe 39
Parsalaw, Willy 76–99
Pastor, Manuel Jr 226
pharmaceutical products in Kenya 4,
        152–71
    availability of imports 169–70
    DANIDA 160, 165, 169, 171
    delays in payments by
        government 156
    distribution of drug kits as percentage
        of requirements 165
    drug shortages 164–5, 169, 171
    Essential Drugs Programme 164–7
    expenditure allocations and
        availability in RHFs 162–7,
        169–70
    expensive and poor quality
        inputs 159
    export incentives 156, 168
    export markets 156–7, 168
    foreign exchange shortages 157,
        158, 168
    generics 155–6, 171
    government intervention 161–2, 168
    health expenditure indicators 163
    import substitution 160
    MNCs 155, 158, 159, 169, 170n
    non-availability of active
        ingredients 158
    and non-tariff barriers 161
    ownership and size of firms 154–6
    pilferage and wastage 166–7, 171
    political environment 156–7, 168
    poor storage and transportation 166
    prefential treatment 157
    price incentives and exports 154–7
    protection of 161–2
    recommendations 167–70
    restrictive licence agreements 159
    SIDA 160, 171
    trade liberalisation and manufacture of
        products 159–62
    use of local inputs 157–9, 168–9
policy *see* fiscal policy
Posthuma, A. 49
poverty and structural adjust-
        ment 54–5, 101–2, 105–7, 123
price controls 133
    Zimbabwe 33, 40, 42, 47, 53
    Tanzania 79, 114
prices and exchange rate depreciation
    export versus domestic 41–3, 49n
    factor 35
    relative 31, 62–3
    see also maize marketing in Tanzania;
        non-tradable goods; tradable
        goods
private sector investment 130, 134, 174
privatisation 112, 113, 138–42, 149
    and banking reform 146–7
    and stock exchanges 175–6, 185–6
public sector
    absenteeism 192, 193, 207
    corruption 193, 206–7
    employment census 136
    employment in Chile 109
    inefficiency 106
    informal sector activities 205–6
    moonlighting 135, 137, 193, 205–6,
        207
    response to real wage decline 203–7

skill shortages 193–7, 208
wage restraint 57–8, 69, 214
wages and salaries 134–8, 197–203, 227
Zambia 192–208
Zimbabwe 57–8
see also civil service; privatisation
Public Service Review
    Commission 58–9

Quinn, S.J. 215

racial discrimination in public
    sector 193
Rakner, Lise 216
Ravallion, M. 90
Rawal, P. 169
real exchange rate appreciation 30, 111, 115
real exchange rate depreciation 112, 113, 148, 152, 155
    benefits 29, 30, 52; evidence for 47–8
    bilateral 11, 43 154
    and exports 40–3
    and factor prices 35
    and inflation in Chile 111
    and investment 14, 44–7
    and leasing 189
    and manufacturing sector 29–51, 52
    and sourcing of inputs 38–40
    and structural shifts in
        employment 61–9
    see also tradable goods; non-tradable
        goods
real interest rates 8–9, 26, 142–4
    Chile 112
    (1979–1992) by country 143–4
    impact on allocative efficiency of
        credit 20–3; borrower survey
        22–3; other constraints 22–3
    impact on intermediation margins and
        lending factors 12–14
    impact on investment and borrowing
        decisions 14–20

impact on savings 9–10, 184
    Indonesia 113
    Tanzania 114
recovery *see* economic recovery
Reddaway, W.B. 44
Rees, A. 66
resource allocation and real exchange
    rate depreciation 29, 30
Riddell, R. 40
Rights Accumulation Programme 148, 150n
Riveros, L.A. 52, 53, 228
Roe, A.R. 13
Russell, Paul 208n

Sagari, S.B. 186
Saito, K.A. 13
Samuelson, Paul A. 218
savings
    and exchange rate policy 10–11
    and fiscal policy 10
    and growth 174
    influential factors 10–12
    and initial investment capital 86
    and interest rate reforms 7–9, 10–11, 144
    and proximity of bank branches 11, 12
    and stock exchanges 176, 183–4
    and type of investment 174
Schkolnik, M. 123
Seers Report 213, 215, 227, 228
Segall, M. 162, 164
Seidman, Ann 211
Sender, J. 110
Serven, L. 30
Shaw, E.S. 8
    see also McKinnon–Shaw hypothesis
shocks *see* exogenous shocks
Sierra Leone 150n
    civil service 137
    ODA as proportion of imports 133
    real interest rates 143, 144
    Rights Accumulation
        Programme 148

Simutanyi, N.R.   206
Singer, H.   68
Singh, A.   183
Singh, Lakhwinder   219
skill shortages, public sector   57, 59, 125, 193–7, 200, 207–8
skilled wages   57, 60, 135
small and medium scale enterprises *see* SMEs
SMEs
    banking relationships   24
    cost of capital   17–18
    Kenya   2, 7–26; access to credit   7; borrower survey   22–3; capital market   22–3
    number with annual increases in commercial bank credit   15–16
    self-finance   22
    transaction costs of borrowing   16–17
    and transaction costs of lending   13–14
    use of commercial bank facilities   15–16
Smith, S.   110
social dialogue   127
socialism   176
    and structural adjustment   131
Solimano, A.   30
Solow, R.M.   65
Somalia   150n
South Africa   43
    stock exchange   180
South Korea, exports   43
Sri Lanka   68
stabilisation programmes   1
    conditions for success   104
    definitions of   102
    and development policy   100
    and economic decline   5
    and labour markets   104–7
    reasons for failure   107–8
    and wage structure   52–75
    see also structural adjustment
Standing, G.   53

state controls
    impact on allocative efficiency of credit   23–5
    and real interest rates   12–14
    role of   25
    see also wages; price controls; exchange rates
Steel, W.F.   38
Stewart, F.   100, 105
Stiglitz, J.E.   25
stock exchanges
    African experience   180–3
    business conduct   184–5
    code of conduct for staff   178
    corporate form   177
    dividend payments   179
    enabling legislation   176–7
    and equity capital   184
    fidelity fund   178
    fiscal environment   178–9
    and foreign investment   175–6
    Ghana   174
    and government intervention   185
    impact on investment and savings   183–6
    indigenisation and institutional development   185–6
    Kenya   21
    listing requirements   177–8
    main features   180–1
    membership   177
    objectives   175–6
    and privatisation   175–6, 185–6
    regulation   180
    trading and settlement rules   178
    viability of   179
    volatility   182
Stockbrokers Botswana   183
Stolper, W.F.   218
Stoneman, C.   48n
structural adjustment   1
    big bang approach   102, 125, 126
    changes in 1990s   132–4
    Chile, Indonesia and Tanzania compared   107–11

constituents of 102–3
constraints and pharmaceutical
products 152–71
and employment structure 109–11
evaluation of 103–4
inter-country comparisons 114–16
and interest rate liberalisation
7–28
and labour markets 104–7; and
employment policy 100–29
and maize market
liberalisation 76–99
persistence with 130–2, 134, 148–50
and policy errors 115
problem in late 1980s 130–2
and public sector
effectiveness 192–209
and real exchange rate
depreciation 29–51
schematic representation 129
sequencing 102
social costs 100–29
social dialogue 127
success: and food subsidies 132; tax
response 132
wages and employment: choice of
policy instruments 122; effect
of wages policy 58, 69–70;
recommendations 125–7;
trends 116–22
see also employment; wages
subsidies
on credit 113
consumer goods 30
food 132, 211, 228
housing 202
labour 123
maize flour 80
and pan-territorial prices 80
and parastatal losses 8, 140, 142
petrol in Nigeria 132
Suckling, John 219, 229n
Suzuki, Y. 80
Swaziland stock market 181, 182,
190n

Tanzania 3, 5
adjustment process 108, 111,
113–14, 115–16, 126
aid dependence 133
banking 145–7
CDC 187
Chile and Indonesia com-
pared 107–11
civil service 136
commercial banks 145, 146–7
debt re-scheduling 113
economic indicators (1970–1990) 77
economic performance 76–8, 150;
factors responsible for decline
77–8
Economic Recovery
Programmes 81–2; objectives
81
employment policy 124–5
financial deregulation 113–14
growth of GDP 149
inflation 109
labour force 110
maize marketing 76–97
National Milling Corporation 3
ODA as proportion of imports
133
parastatals 124, 140–1
privatisation 146, 185
real interest rates 143, 144
socialism 109
stock market 190n
unemployment 120
wages and employment 120–1
see also maize marketing in Tanzania
Tarp, F. 103
tax
on exports 78
and financial structure of
companies 178–9, 183
Ghana 132
and interest rates 11, 17–8, 142–4
and persistence with reform 132
reforms in Chile 123
reforms in Indonesia 112–13

tax *continued*
  and savings   10
  and venture capital   186
Taylor, L.   115
Thailand   187
Thomas, V.   30
Thorbecke, E. and Associates   103, 121
Tokman, V.   53
Toye, John   100–29
tradable goods   152
  data weaknesses   126
  dependent economy model   218–24
  and income distribution   225
  and labour markets   61–4, 105–7
  and price incentives in Kenya
      152–4; contributions to GDP
      153
  and real exchange rate depreciation
      167–8; before and after
      analysis   63–4; Chile   115;
      Zimbabwe   29, 30, 31, 32–4, 45,
      52
  see also non-tradable goods
trade liberalisation   152, 154, 159–62
trade liberalisation   152
  Kenya   153–4, 159–62, 169
  Indonesia   108
  Zimbabwe   43, 53, 70
trade unions   54, 215, 227, 228,
    230n
Turkey   108
Turner, H.A./Report   198, 210, 213,
    214, 215, 227, 228

Uganda   5, 58, 150n
  CDC   187
  civil service   137, 138
  commercial banks   145, 147
  economic recovery   149, 150
  ODA as proportion of imports   133
  parastatals   139
  privatisation   185
  real interest rates   143, 144
  stock market   190n
  structural adjustment   132

unemployment   106
  Indonesia   119
  and structural adjustment   101–2
  Tanzania   120
  see also employment
UNICEF   157
United States
  pharmaceutical products   162, 171
  trade with Zimbabwe   43
USAID   188

Velasco, A.   154
venture capital companies   175
  African experience   187–8
  characteristics   186–7
Villanueva, D.P.   13

wage leadership hypothesis   215–17,
    227
  validity of   217–18
wages
  definitions   70n
  effect of economic
      stabilisation   52–72
  and employment   60–9, 70n–1,
      116–22
  indexation   113, 117
  inter-country comparisons   121–2
  and food basket, Zambia   203–4
  impact of minimum wage
      policy   60–1, 67
  legislation in Zimbabwe   54–5
  policy   54–8; Zambia 199–201,
      213–15
  public sector   57–8, 69, 197–203;
      response to decline   203–7
  real wages indices in Chile   118
  real wages indices in Indonesia   120
  restraint   57–8, 69
  and role of institutional
      forces   53–61
  SSR model   218–19; application to
      Zambia   219–21, 227;
      capital–labour ratio   220, 222,
      224–5; causes of relative price

changes 223–4; regression
results 221–3
trends in real and average
consumption, Zimbabwe 62
and Zambian mining sector 210–30;
cause of decline 225; role of
economic factors 217–26
Zimbabwe 52–72
Walton, M. 17
Webster, L.M. 38
Willowvale scandal 58
women
in informal sector 205
labour force participation 126
wages 120
World Bank 1
conditions set by 7
on employment 66, 67, 69
and interest rates 7
and real exchange rate
depreciation 29
Revised Minimum Standard
Model 102–3
on wages policy 54, 60, 210
and Zambia 197
see also structural adjustment

Yeats, A. 162

Zambia 4–5, 150n
adjustment process 149; and income
redistribution 225–7
annual average real wage
(1965–89) 214
cause of real wage decline 225
civil service 135–6, 192–3
colonial legacy 211
commercial banks 145, 147
copper prices 228; implications
212–13
economic indicators (1970–90) 213
economy and changes in real
wage 211–15
educational qualifications of
employees 194

employees by occupation and
nationality 195
expatriates 195, 196
external debt 213
financial performance of ZCCM 217
food subsidies 211, 228
GDP and government
expenditure 211
medical manpower 196
mineral boom 213, 227
mining sector 210–30
MUZ 215
ODA as proportion of imports 133
O'Riordan Commission 198
parastatals 138, 139
public sector: allowances 201–3,
208n; average government real
wage 199; changes in earnings
197–201; corruption as survival
strategy 206–7; effectiveness
192–208; index of real wages in
civil service 199; ratio of
director's to lowest paid civil
service salary 200; response to
real wage decline 203–7; wages
and salaries 197–203
real interest rates 143, 144
skill shortages 193–7, 208
stock market 190n
structural adjustment 131, 132
trade unions 215, 227, 228, 230n
Turner Report 198
UNIP 216, 228–9
wage leadership hypothesis 215–17,
227
wage policy 199–201, 213
Wages and Incomes Committee
229n
and World Bank 197
Zimbabwe 2–3
annual earnings by sector 56, 61
CZI 56–7
devaluation 30
Development Plans 72
Employment Act (1980) 54, 68

Zimbabwe *continued*
  employment and exchange rate
    depreciation   32–4
  exchange rate indices   31
  exchange rate policy   29–51, 52, 53
  exports, direction of   43
  and foreign exchange scarcity   158
  and IMF   48
  labour markets   52–3
  Labour Relations Act (1985)   55,
    70n

  manufacturing investment   44–7
  Minimum Wages Act (1980)   54
  privatisation   185
  relative prices and exchange rates   31
  Riddell Commission   54–5
  stock exchange   181, 182, 190n
  tradable goods   31, 32–4, 52
  trading partners   43
  trends in real and average
    consumption wages   62
  wage structure   52–72